A 366-DAY DEVOTIONAL BOOK BY MEMBERS AND FRIENDS

SOUTHERN ASIAN SEVENTH-DAY ADVENTIST CHURCH, SILVER SPRING, MD, USA

GOD'S GRACE IN OUR LIVES

SUBODH K. PANDIT, EDITOR

SOOSAN VARGHESE, ASSOCIATE EDITOR AND COMPILER

Copyright © 2024 Southern Asian Seventh-day Adventist Church
All rights reserved

ISBN: 9798339857228
Formatting by Gerald "Nonoy" Christo, and eBooks Crafter
Cover design by SYNESTHEZIA Agency
Cover design concept and photo by Johny and Soosan Varghese
Publicity and advertising by David Rajamonickam and Sam Suresh

The contributing authors assume full responsibility for the accuracy of all facts and quotations as cited in this book.

Scripture quotations marked **KJV** are taken from The Authorized (King James) Version. Rights in the Authorized Version in the United Kingdom are vested in the Crown. Reproduced by permission of the Crown's patentee, Cambridge University Press. Scripture marked **NKJV** is taken from the New King James Version®. Copyright © 1982 by Thomas Nelson. Used by permission. All rights reserved. Scripture quotations marked **NIV** are taken from the Holy Bible, New International Version®, NIV®. Copyright © 1973, 1978, 1984, 2011 by Biblica, Inc.™ Used by permission of Zondervan. All rights reserved worldwide. www.zondervan.comThe "NIV" and "New International Version" are trademarks registered in the United States Patent and Trademark Office by Biblica, Inc.™ Scripture quotations marked **NLT** are taken from the Holy Bible, New Living Translation, copyright ©1996, 2004, 2015 by Tyndale House Foundation. Used by permission of Tyndale House Publishers, Carol Stream, Illinois 60188. All rights reserved. Scripture quotations marked **WBT** are taken from the WEBSTER'S BIBLE TRANSLATION, containing the Old and New Testaments, in the Common Version, with Amendments of the Language by Noah Webster, LL.D., public domain, 1833. Scripture quotations marked **MSG** are taken from The Message, copyright © 1993, 2002, 2018 by Eugene H. Peterson. Used by permission of NavPress. All rights reserved. Represented by Tyndale House Publishers. Scripture quotations marked **ESV** are taken from THE HOLY BIBLE, ENGLISH STANDARD VERSION®, Copyright© 2001 by Crossway, a publishing ministry of Good News Publishers. Used by permission. Scripture quotations marked **NASB** are taken from the NEW AMERICAN STANDARD BIBLE®, Copyright© 1960, 1962, 1963, 1968, 1971, 1972, 1973, 1975, 1977, 1995 by The Lockman Foundation. Used by permission. Scripture quotations marked **CEV** are taken from the CONTEMPORARY ENGLISH VERSION, Copyright© 1995 by the American Bible Society. Used by permission. Scripture quotations marked **EASY** are from the EasyEnglish Bible Copyright © MissionAssist 2019 - Charitable Incorporated Organisation 1162807. Used by permission. All rights reserved. Scripture quotations marked **GW** are taken from GOD'S WORD® Copyright© 1995 by God's Word to the Nations. All rights reserved. Scripture quotations marked **NHEB** are from the New Heart English Bible, public domain. Scripture quotations marked **AMP** are taken from the AMPLIFIED® BIBLE, Copyright© 1954, 1958, 1962, 1964, 1965, 1987 by the Lockman Foundation Used by Permission.

FOREWORD

"Let the morning bring me word of your unfailing love, for I have put my trust in you." Psalm 143:8

God's Grace in Our Lives, the SASDAC daily devotional book, movingly narrates and illustrates God's steadfast love and providential leading in the lives of His children.

The testimonies and experiences shared on these pages are provided to offer hope and encouragement to all, especially those passing through trying times and near-hopeless circumstances. They are meant to lift our gaze to the most dependable source of strength and courage in this world, not just in word and theory, but through the down-to-earth, raw, and unvarnished stories from those who have realized the closeness, faithfulness, and power of God in their very lives.

I have found them deeply moving and inspiring. I pray that the reader also will find strength and comfort in the stories for each day.

Start the day in God's presence with an awe-inspiring story of God's amazing grace.

"My voice shalt thou hear in the morning, O Lord; in the morning will I direct my prayer unto thee, and will look up." Psalm 5:3

John K. Daniel
Lead Pastor, Southern Asian Seventh-day Adventist Church

JANUARY 1

GOD'S GUIDING HAND

Duraiswamy Paulson David

"Before I formed thee in the belly I knew thee; and before thou camest forth out of the womb I sanctified thee, and I ordained thee a prophet unto the nations."

Jeremiah 1:5, KJV

Never failing. Ever present. Always near. Forever walking beside me – guiding me.

As a preteen, I built a wall around my heart. It probably was a survival instinct following the death of my mother at the tender age of 11. Anger and bitterness marked my path in the boarding school where I was sent after her death.

Dormitory life in the 1940s was primitive and extremely difficult. The bare essentials were scarce. Getting along with others was a different challenge altogether. So I built a core group of friends, hoping to create my destiny. I quickly gained the respect and fear of others and became well-known on the campus. Now I needed others even less and felt I had control of my destiny. I had planned to join the army, but God, in mercy, changed those plans.

He led me far from the army – to become a teacher and have a family. The next moves brought us to the USA. God again helped us survive the rough hardships of settling in a foreign country. Today, my wife and I are over 90, healthy, and living a good life!

I can clearly see God's gracious hand each step of the way. He knew and ordained me for His purpose – even before I was born. Now, every morning and every night, I fall on my knees and thank God. All I am and have, I owe to His wonderful hand.

May you find God's mighty and secure hand guiding you every step of your way

January 2

Child of Mine

Pamela D'Souza-David

"Trust in the Lord with all your heart and lean not on your own understanding."

Proverbs 3:5, NKJV

The entire plane resonated with shrill cries for help. No, it wasn't an emergency! The loud, distressing wail came from a small child – my child! He did not want to be restrained by the seat belt. I tried to portray the picture of being in control, and calmly said, "I just want to help you." But no amount of reasoning was going to avail. Ultimately, I had to hold him down with the seatbelt in place until the plane took off.

How unreasonable he was! And yet, on honest reflection, that is exactly how we behave with God – refusing to follow God's directions even in the face of glaring evidence that it is His will. Moses displayed this attitude. God Himself spoke to him and then performed miracles: the rod became a snake; his hand became leprous, then well again. Yet he refused to obey.

We might be tempted to think that we would have behaved differently, but we are no different! We don't like to be pushed outside our comfort zones. So, we resist the instructions of God. Even after experiencing God's miraculous power, the moment trials appear, we complain and doubt His good intentions.

But God is gracious and understanding. He still let Moses lead His people and perform some of the most remarkable miracles in the Bible. The same grace given to cowardly Peter, doubting Thomas, and a host of others, is extended to us. He can take our faith, even though it is the size of a mustard seed and work wonders through us. Let us trust in the Lord and submit ourselves to Him.

JANUARY 3

BRINGING IN THE SHEAVES

Richard Samuel

"I will love thee O Lord, my strength…"

Psalm 18:1, KJV

The Reserve Bank colony is pretty close to where I grew up in Byculla, Bombay (presently, Mumbai.) Every evening, my mother and I would walk down to the colony, where she would socialize with her friends while I would play with my friends. Over the years, one of them, who belonged to a staunch Hindu Brahmin family, and I became best friends. He wanted to study where I was studying, and he convinced his parents and joined my school. He even began coming with me to Sabbath School. After elementary school, we both went to Pune to study at the SDA school there.

To my delight, he chose to become a Seventh-day Adventist and later married one from the same faith. This journey from Hinduism to Christianity began with my simple friendship with him. I had not preached sermons nor run any evangelistic programs. I had just made good friends.

God can use anyone to be a witness for Him. He has given everyone at least one talent –preaching, healing, serving, and singing. When we use them, the Holy Spirit treats them like a channel and touches people around us. The "parable of the talents" found in Matthew 25:14-30 illustrates that the number of talents is not as important as our use of them.

The familiar chorus, "This little light of mine; I want to let it shine. . .Hide it under a bushel? No!" is my wish for all God's people.

"He who continually goes forth. . . will doubtless come again, bringing his sheaves with him." Psalms 126:6

Pray that the Lord will use us today as witnesses for Him.

January 4

A Mother's Faith

Esther Pauline David

"She openeth her mouth with wisdom; and in her tongue is the law of kindness. She looketh well to the ways of her household and eateth not the bread of idleness."

Proverbs 31:26,27, KJV

Mothers are naturally anxious about their children. Christian mothers are also worried about the spiritual welfare of their children.

I know that feeling of fear of the unknown. When we came to the United States in April 1972, one of my biggest fears was the unknown future for my two sons who were 15 and 11. How would they fare? Where would they end up?

As soon as we landed, I remember holding them tight and wondering if I had made the right decision. Yes, it was frightening! So at every turn along the journey in this country, I prayed, holding onto them, hoping God would keep them in His care. It was not always smooth. Sometimes my faith was tested but deep in my heart, I always trusted that God would walk next to them and guide them.

Every morning before we left our home, we recited a favorite promise: Psalms 91. It served as a reminder that my Heavenly Father was in control.

It has been decades since we first landed here. Today, I confidently say that God heard my prayers and rewarded this mother's faith. He assured me of His leadership in my and my family's lives.

I still pray for faith on behalf of all the resolute Christian mothers who are anxious about their children. Our faithful God will always lead us.

Let us continue in faith, pleading with God to keep us and our families close to Him.

JANUARY 5

A VERY PRESENT HELP

J S Navarose

"God is our refuge and strength. A very present help in trouble."

Psalm 46:1, KJV

The words "A very present help" appear only once in the Bible. They mean help that is vital and always ready. No friend or family member can give you that kind of help. Only God is prepared to send help when we are in trouble.

A few months ago, we were returning home from work when at an exit, I turned the car too sharply, and it went off the road and hit a metal rod. The dashboard signaled that one of the tires was losing pressure and was soon flat. I located the spare tire but did not know how to take it out. A stranger came by and instructed me on how to do it, but I was unable to do it. So, he took it out. Then, he raised the car with the jack and told me to unscrew the nuts to remove the flat tire. I tried but could not. He then took off his shirt, bent down, removed the flat tire, and fixed the spare one in its place. He was drenched in sweat when it was over. I thanked him profusely, and my wife said, "You are like an angel sent by God!" He merely said he was happy to help and went on his way.

It may not seem much to others, but to us, it was vital help given precisely when we needed it! We believe God helped us. Yes, He is our refuge and strength. And always, "a very present help."

Today, I pray that you will find our living God to be your refuge, strength, and a very present help.

January 6

At Gunpoint

Daisy Sharlin

"Do not worry about how or what you should speak. For it will be given you in that hour what you should speak; for it is not you who speak, but the Spirit of your Father who speaks in you."

Matthew 10:19,20, NKJV

During the initial part of the Iraq-Kuwait Gulf War, the Iraqi soldiers invaded Kuwait and brought along all their weapons. Law and order were totally under the control of the Iraqi army, and they could do what they pleased because civil rights and justice did not exist.

These were the conditions on August 2, 1990, when an Iraqi soldier stopped our family car. Seeing the people inside as foreigners in Kuwait, he grew suspicious. Pointing his machine gun at my younger brother, he yelled, "Get out of the car!" in Arabic. My mother told him not to get out because there would be no guarantee regarding his safety. Thinking swiftly, my mother got out of the car and, in loud and fluent Arabic, said, "You are a young boy, the same age as my son. If you are taking him, take me too!" The soldier was taken aback! He had not expected any of the passengers to know Arabic so well. She had sounded just like any other native resident in Kuwait. He lowered his gun and let the car pass.

None of us knew how my mother got to speak Arabic in that manner – so fluently and with such confidence that the soldier was impressed!!

We realized God fulfilled the promise in the above scripture verse and kept our family safe. Such an amazing God!

Let us meditate on God's word and be confident that the Holy Spirit will speak for us always.

January 7

At The Well

Anonymous

"The Lord will watch over your coming and going. . ."

Psalm 121:8, NIV

This story was told to me by my mom. I was part of a big family, living on a large property with a deep well not far from the house. It was a blessing but also a danger, for it had no protective wall around it. The adults stayed a safe distance away from the well, and the little ones, who were not old enough to understand, were kept under the watchful eyes of the older ones.

I was about three years old but had not yet learned to walk by myself. I would still crawl around like a seven-month-old infant. On this particular day, I somehow managed to slip away from my mother's sharp and watchful eye. She suddenly noticed that I was gone, and when she looked around, oh, horror of horrors! There I was, lying at the mouth of the well, staring into the waters below. One more move, and I would have fallen in!!

She prayed and then very silently and swiftly moved towards me. Noiselessly, she crept up behind me and picked me up in her arms, heaving a sigh of relief that only a mother could feel!

She knew that if she had called out to me, I would have been startled and lunged forward, falling into the well, with no chance of rescue! And I would not be here to tell this story today! I believe that it was God's intervention that enabled my mother to do the right thing.

The words of the scripture verse above have a special meaning! He constantly watches over us. As we go in and out today, we have the assurance that He is watching over us.

January 8

Awesome God!

Bernice Samuel

"The angel of the Lord encampeth round about them that fear Him and delivereth them."

Psalm 34:7, KJV

I had been fast asleep when multiple knockings on the window awakened me. I woke up startled and looked out the window to find a little face peering through it. It was my seven-year-old son, Bernhard. I was supposed to pick him up from school for lunch but had overslept.

I had just finished a night shift in the hospital and was still asleep because the alarm had not gone off. And here he was – having walked the whole mile from school alone! I ran out and hugged him. "How did you come? Who brought you?" I asked with great anxiety. But he seemed least perturbed. "Mom, I was wondering if you were alright because I did not see you at the parking lot."

I hugged him again, tears flowing down from my eyes, and profusely apologized to him, and then immediately knelt and thanked God for protecting him. Like most mothers, my mind went racing through all the possible ways harm could have come to him. The road from our apartment to the school was narrow and usually busy with heavy traffic. What if he had been kidnapped, or had met with an accident, or had lost his way?

I quickly gave him lunch and drove him back to school. After returning home, I reflected on the many blessings God had given me and my family. They further strengthened my faith in His unfailing love and protection. I can honestly say that He is an awesome God!

May we always feel the presence and deliverance of the angel of the Lord around us.

January 9

A Child's Prayer

Kurian George

"Therefore I tell you, whatever you ask for in prayer, believe that you have received it, and it will be yours."

Mark 11:24, NIV

Growing up in Ranchi, India, we lived in a large British bungalow on the eastern side of the hospital campus. It was secluded from the rest of the campus, and frequent power outages made that area very dark at night. Large open spaces inside and outside the campus attracted wild animals, and we didn't dare go outside our house at night.

One cold winter night, my sister (5) and I (7) were fast asleep when we woke up to loud howls and laughter-like cackles. We raced to our parents' bedroom. Mom led us back to our bedroom, but we didn't want to stay there. The sounds were terrifying. Mom explained that those were jackals and hyenas outside the wall, and neither she nor Dad could stop them. But then she suggested, "Let's pray and ask Jesus to help us with this scary problem." My sister took the lead and prayed a simple line, "Dear Jesus, please stop the hyenas from making sounds at night. Amen." Hardly had she ended her one-sentence prayer when we heard a high-pitched howl followed by silence – total silence! That was the last we heard of those hyenas and jackals.

The lesson I learned that night will stay with me through life. When caught in a situation we cannot control, God is always willing to take control if we ask Him in sincerity. The answer to a five-year-old child's prayer taught me that lesson.

Let us reach out to God in prayer when faced with problems, big and small.

JANUARY 10

BLESSED ADVICE

J S Navarose

"Blessed is your advice and blessed are you because you have kept me this day from coming to bloodshed and from avenging myself with my own hands."

I Samuel 25:33, NKJV

In the above text, Abigail courageously gave crucial advice which David accepted, thus averting needless bloodshed.

Years ago, our family lived near a family of Hindus. There were five brothers in all, and we had a very friendly relationship with them. The youngest one was especially close to us. He knew that we attended SDA schools and that our family placed great importance on prayer. He decided to become a Christian.

One day, he came to my mother for advice because people from other denominations were pressing him to join them. "What shall I do?" he asked. My mother pointed out the blessings in our family and advised him to join the SDA church to keep close to God's truth. Her advice was simple and straightforward. He respected my mother, and like David, he accepted her advice and became an Adventist. That one piece of advice spread blessings across his whole family. His eldest son is now a famous orthopedic surgeon in Chennai. All the children have stayed in the faith. They are doing well in life, and he attributes that to God's blessings on those who choose the right way.

The New Living Translation says, "Timely advice is lovely like golden apples in a silver basket." Proverbs 25:11. My mother had given him timely advice, and he had taken it to heart. Just one transaction blessed many, and brought a whole generation to the knowledge of God's truth.

May God help us to give the right advice at the right time.

January 11

Deep Waters

Anonymous

"When you go through deep waters, I will be with you. . ."

Isaiah 43:2, NLT

We lived on a property with rice fields on one side that bordered a brook. There was a time when a considerable flood surrounded the area. My parents had warned us that the flood waters were dangerous and no one should go near them. We were to stay strictly indoors.

Such strict orders only increased my curiosity. So I slipped out the door and headed alone to the edge of our property. At first, I stood on high ground, where I could clearly make out the banks. Fascinated, I edged a little closer to the water and slowly dipped my toes in. It didn't seem deep, so I took another step and then another, when suddenly, I could not feel the ground under my feet anymore. Powerful currents carried me, and I did not know how to swim!! I thought that it was the end, and in desperation, I did the only thing I could think of – I cried out to God. I had no idea what to do but was impressed to push my legs downward and kick hard. I did that and suddenly bounced out of the deep waters! I got out of the water as fast as I could and didn't stop running until I reached home! I believe God had impressed me to kick hard.

Let us heed the clear warnings given to us in life. "Better safe than sorry!"

But if ever we are in trouble, remember to call on God. He promises to be with us and deliver us, even when we have disobeyed, as long as we repent and return to Him.

January 12

God's Infinite Love

Esther Pauline David

"Great is our Lord, and of great power: His understanding is infinite."

Psalm 147:5, WBT

Chaos – Mathematics – Order. Life – Faith – God's Infinite Love.

Mathematics is the abstract science of numbers – used to create order out of apparent chaos. We can study mathematics by itself – pure mathematics, or apply it to other disciplines – applied mathematics.

I have spent a lifetime studying mathematics and practically applying my knowledge to solve problems. I enjoy the definitive solutions that mathematics offers.

However, things are not as well defined in my personal and spiritual life. There are too many variables, and they are constantly changing. But if change were the only factor in our lives, everything would have collapsed long ago! There has to be an underlying foundation that is unchanging. I realized that there was such a constant: God and His love! That simple truth was foundational.

Throughout life, I have enjoyed the constants of love and family. However, variables are equally real and can cause discomfort. With prayer as a daily formula connecting me to the constant of God, I stay steady. He is the PRIME, around which all other aspects revolve. Even though my faith is minuscule, I can still connect with God – my Constant. My faith doesn't require me to abandon all I have learned in mathematics.

On the one hand, I can comprehend numbers. On the other, numbers in mathematics go on into infinity – beyond anything I can understand or even imagine. And yet they are real. Thus, mathematics teaches me that God is real and that God's love is real, changeless, and infinite!

May God's infinite and unchanging love change our hearts to love Him.

JANUARY 13

OVERCOMING WORRIES

J S Navarose

"Which of you by worrying can add one cubit to his stature?"

__Matthew 6:27, NKJV__

Another version (NIV): "Can anyone of you by worrying, add a single hour to your life?"

I have heard the story of a cow that worried that if she ate the hay in stock, the amount would dwindle to nothing. So, she stopped eating. Naturally, she grew weaker and weaker until she died.

The story may not be true, but it shows that worry can be harmful. However, we do have fears which are real. Here are three suggestions I have found helpful. They all start with the letter C.

CONNECT. Connecting with God will help us bear our burdens of anxiety. "Cast your burden on the Lord, and He shall sustain you. He shall never permit the righteous to be moved." Psalms 55:22, NKJV. What we need will be provided. ". . . and all these shall be added to you." Matthew 6:33, NKJV.

COLLABORATE. There is an interesting saying: "Two horses can pull five times the amount that only one can pull!" Hannah collaborated with God and accomplished great things through her son Samuel in Israel! Moses collaborated with God and marvelously led a million people!

CONTRIBUTE. We must be involved in the process. "Inasmuch as you did it to one of the least of these My brethren, you did it to Me." Matthew 25:40, NKJV.

God promises that the "yoke is easy" and the "burden is light." Matthew 11:30, NKJV.

If we connect, collaborate, and contribute, these activities will keep us busy and happy without the anxieties and worries of the poor cow!

January 14

The "Jericho Plan"

J S Navarose

"So the people shouted when the priests blew the trumpets. And it happened when the people heard the sound of the trumpet and the people shouted with a great shout that the wall fell down flat…"

Joshua 6:20, NKJV

God told them to just march around the city of Jericho. Joshua and his people did exactly what God had told them, and on the seventh day, the walls of that city fell.

A similar thing happened a few years ago, but the walls were different. We, at the Madurai North Adventist Higher Secondary School, began looking for land to extend the school. The process of purchasing land is very lengthy. While we waited for the transactions, we decided to witness among the villagers. However, they were staunch Hindus and would surely not listen if we went directly with the Gospel of Jesus.

So about 15 of us went around the village every Sabbath for a few weeks with drums and timbrels, singing joyful Tamil Christian songs. The children were fascinated and followed us around the village. For the first few weeks we just walked and sang songs. Later, we gathered the children under a tree and told them Bible stories. Our lady teachers would comb the children's hair, making them look beautiful! The villagers appreciated that! We soon started classes, where the children learned crafts and good living habits.

At the right time, we conducted a series of meetings. When it ended, seven people from that village accepted Jesus and were baptized.

The "Jericho Plan" worked, the barriers fell, and the message of salvation entered Moondru Mavadi. Praise the Lord!

Let us pray that the Lord will guide us to the right plans as we live and work for Him.

JANUARY 15

TIMELY HELP

Anonymous

"Therefore do not worry saying, 'What shall we eat?' or ...'What shall we wear?'. . .For your heavenly Father knows that you need all these things."

Matthew 6:31-32, NKJV

The Covid pandemic affected hundreds of millions everywhere. Like many people, our family also went through hard times. It began when my husband was furloughed, and we had no regular income. Job openings were rare, and we were unsuccessful in our applications. We had tried to build some savings earlier but soon had to dip into them for our regular expenses. Our savings lasted only for some time, and then they were all gone! We had some money in our 401K account, but that too dwindled and disappeared. Our financial walls were crumbling, and we couldn't do anything about it. Insecurity and anxiety set in, and life became extremely stressful!

When we had come to the end of our rope, suddenly, out of the blue, we received money from the church. We hadn't described our condition to those around us, but some church members began to check on us and help us.

We had been left helpless and nearly hopeless. But all that changed when we began to get help that was right on time. We believe our heavenly Father's merciful care helped to meet our needs.

Through that scary experience, we learned that what we possess is not the final answer to life's challenges. God is the ultimate provider. During this particular experience, He used the church and His people to supply our needs. But He has many other ways to help, and He always keeps His promise!

When all seems lost, remember that God's bounty is limitless, and He is always on time.

January 16

A Touch of Love

Usha Thomas

"Be still and know that I am God."

Psalm 46:10, KJV

Migraine headaches are not only painful, they can also wreck one's outlook on life, especially if they have been going on and on. Well, I was suffering from migraine headaches for 15 years!!

Of course, I had prayed about it many times, but nothing happened, so I began to lose hope that God would provide healing.

During one of those desperate times when there seemed no hope, I had an unusual dream. In the dream, a man came walking towards me. I had a distinct impression that it was Jesus. He was wearing a white robe, and as He approached, He gently touched my hair, my head. I asked, "What would You want me to do for You?" "Two things," He replied. "One, keep in mind that many startling things are going to happen around the world. And two, you must share Jesus with others." I asked again, "Does this mean you are coming soon?" He didn't answer, and the dream faded away.

I noticed something wonderful after that dream. The frequency of my headaches began to get less until they stopped altogether! Today, I feel I am healed!! God's response lasted but a few minutes – it was just a tiny touch!! I consider it a touch of love!

Whatever storm you face, rest assured that He will see you through. So, hold on even if it takes time. He is never too early nor too late, but always on time. Trust in the Lord and the power of His healing touch.

JANUARY 17

FALSE ALARMS

Lovella Fernando

"False alarms and easygoing preaching are a thing of the past in the life of Israel. I, God, am doing the speaking. What I say happens..."

Ezekiel 12:24,25, MSG

The civil war in Sri Lanka ended in 2009. During the prior years, we had gone through tense moments, and the people had been constantly on edge.

I was working at an international school in the beautiful hilly city of Kandy when the fire alarm went off. We had done fire drills before, but since we had not been informed of a drill that morning, we treated the alarm as real. The children panicked, but once order was restored, we received word that it was not a fire but a bomb threat.

The local police and bomb squad were called in to investigate, and after a thorough and meticulous search, it turned out to be a false alarm.

False alarms have consequences and can cause trouble and disruptions. And there have been many false alarms regarding the second coming of Jesus. The faith of many has been shaken, and they have altered the lives of many. Let us not raise false alarms nor be deceived by them.

Our safest guide is the Word of God. "Don't be so easily shaken or alarmed by those who say that the day of the Lord has already begun." II Thessalonians 2:2, NLT

Let us be vigilant and watchful, earnestly studying God's word so that we correctly warn the people, but, at the same time, we do not raise false alarms. God will be our guide and take us safely through these times.

Heavenly Father, please help us to be diligent students of thy Word and rightly divide the Word of truth.

January 18

Be Like A Tree

Carol Thapa

"But his delight is in the law of the LORD, and in His law he meditates day and night. He shall be like a tree planted by the rivers of water that brings forth its fruit in its season."

Psalm 1:2-3, NKJV

Muir Woods, Sequoia National Park, and Kings Canyon National Park contain redwood trees, which are the largest species of trees and the largest living things on earth. They grow up to 300 feet in height. Their massive trunks can have a diameter of close to 30 feet and a circumference of over 90 feet. One feels tiny when walking among them.

Coming from the East Coast, the only gigantic structures I had seen were man-made skyscrapers, so seeing a natural entity of such enormous size was awe-inspiring! One can only imagine the processes involved in developing such massive trunks and branches. Large amounts of nourishment have to be transported all the way to the topmost branches. The natural forces have to be extremely powerful in order to accomplish this.

I thought of David's comparison in Psalms 1, noted above. He described the secret of the process – meditation on God's law so that it pervades the whole life.

The size of the redwoods seems to say that one can grow very big and tall indeed! There is something in the law that nourishes the person and makes him grow, flourish, and bring forth abundant fruit.

When we delight in the Law of the Lord and let it permeate our whole being, we will be like a tree, bringing forth God's goodness as fruits of the Spirit that is good for ourselves and others! Let us delight in and meditate on God's law.

JANUARY 19

CHIPPED BUT PRECIOUS

Edna Venkatraj

"I will make a mortal more rare than fine gold. . .than the golden wedge of Ophir."

Isaiah 13:12, NKJV

As a young family, we loved going on road trips. My husband preferred to be the solo driver. So, all I had to do was get our two daughters ready, pack the necessities, and then relax for the entire trip. One of our favorite stops was at outlet malls, where I headed for the kitchen stores, looking for that perfect platter to add to my kitchen collection. One day, I saw it – the perfect size, pattern, and neutral colors too! It was a bit pricey, but I made the purchase.

At home, I couldn't wait to use my special platter when we had guests over, who admired it so much that it often became a conversation piece!

When cleaning after one of our dinner parties, I noticed that my special platter had a tiny chip. I felt terrible but quickly recovered when I realized it was still usable. I have used it to this day, and I give it preferential treatment because it is chipped. It is still my special platter!

How I treat my chipped platter reminds me of how God loves me. He does not discard me even when I have failed and am spiritually chipped and broken. God keeps me even closer to Him and continues to use me despite myself. He handles me with extra care because He knows that I need it! What a wonderful, caring, and understanding God we serve!

When we feel broken, let us cheer up, knowing that He cares for us even more, and let us resolve to serve Him faithfully.

JANUARY 20

GUIDING ANGEL

Neena Eapen

"...I am sending an angel ahead of you to guard you along the way..."

Exodus 23:20, NIV

Whenever my dad would leave for evangelistic travels, mom would gather all four of us children together to pray. At that time, I thought it was just a good routine. But today, I appreciate the meaning and purpose.

You see, my dad was a widely known evangelist in India. Many of his meetings were held in small rural villages, and he sometimes walked miles to reach the meetings' sites. He told us this story.

The meeting was to be held in a very remote village. The villagers there lived by trapping animals, and laid their traps out all around the village.

When nearing the village, it grew dark. Dad couldn't see the path but could hear the distant drum calling the people to the meeting. So, he kept in the direction of that sound. But how would he avoid the dangerous traps on the ground?! Just when he felt his anxiety growing, he saw someone ahead walking with a lantern in his hand. What a relief that was! Dad would follow him and avoid the traps. He quickened his pace to catch up with the person with the lantern but just couldn't. However, he soon reached the meeting site and looked around to thank him. But nobody could identify him, and Dad never saw him again!

Have you ever felt the presence of an angel in moments of your darkness? That is how God's grace works – in the form of angels, who may come in the form of humans.

Be an angel in someone's life today.

JANUARY 21

INSTRUMENTS OF GREATER WORKS

Milind Lazarus Borge

"Very truly I tell you, whoever believes in Me will do the works I have been doing, and they will do even greater things than these, because I am going to the Father."

John 14:12, NIV

My teacher taught me how to play the guitar, and once I had learned it, I would play it regularly because I thoroughly enjoyed it. It also brought joy to others. Thus, the effect of my teacher's training reached others through me.

Just before He ascended, Jesus made an astonishing promise. He included everyone in it! "Whoever" meant that every believer would do the works He did. More than that, they would do "greater works!"

I pondered over the meaning of this promise.

Before the resurrection, the Holy Spirit worked through Jesus, touching those immediately around Him. However, after the resurrection, the Holy Spirit's work of spreading the message of His finished work would not be confined to any geographical location. It would extend all over, even to earth's remotest bounds. Our acts of love, demonstrating our connection with Jesus, are to lift people around the world to a higher plane of experience. Jesus came to accomplish this in His life. But even He could not spread the message of a completed work worldwide because soon after He accomplished it, He left. He handed this task to us. We are His trained instruments, touching people anywhere and everywhere in the whole wide world! This is the "greater work" that was promised!

The effect of His work and training will transform us and touch the lives of others on earth through us. Let's be His instruments of greater works.

JANUARY 22

WAVES OF DOUBT

Francina Kolluri

"For I know the plans I have for you," declares the Lord, "plans to prosper you and not to harm you, plans to give you hope and a future."

Jeremiah 29:11, NIV

Heroes of faith grip our attention, and we focus on them. But those who doubted God seem more down-to-earth. One such example was "doubting Thomas." I seemed to be like him.

I doubted and became unsure of the future at every step of my academic life. This led me down a path of increasing stress until I came to an emotional standstill. I had an exam coming up, and I could not study because of the negative thoughts crowding my mind. I realized that I was overwhelmed, and I gave up.

I quit praying because I doubted that God would do anything for me.

The following day, I awoke dejected as I prepared to face the inevitable – a disastrous failing grade! I completed the exam and came out in despair. The days that followed didn't change my mood at all.

Then it happened! I received my score, and would you believe it?! I passed and had the highest score in the class! One part of me was elated! The other part chided me for doubting. I had doubted the God who could move mountains and tenderly understand a "doubting Thomas" like me. That day, I decided to trust a God who had already formulated "plans to prosper [me] and not harm [me], plans to give [me] hope and a future." Everything had changed for me! It was a day filled with God's grace! I will always be thankful.

When tempted to doubt God's leading, let us remember His promise to prosper us.

JANUARY 23

MUSTARD SEED FAITH-PART 1

Daisy Sharlin

So Jesus said to them "If you have faith as a mustard seed...nothing will be impossible for you.

Mathew 17:20, NKJV

In the nursing course in Chennai, where I studied, if you failed a subject, you could repeat it but could go on to the next semester. However, in the seventh semester, you had to pass all the subjects in order to go to the eighth semester.

In 1998, Pr. Doug Batchelor from the USA was conducting revival meetings in Chennai. It was also the time for my seventh-semester examination. During the last meeting, they asked us to write our prayer requests. My prayer request was that all 35 in my class pass the examination. After I had sent in the request, I felt I had made a mistake. There were 30 in my regular class and five who had failed earlier and were much less likely to succeed. But I decided to keep to the number 35 and trust God to see us through!

One day, I heard my Pentecostal friend chanting her prayers for success. I whispered to her, "You've passed." She was shocked! "Are you a fortune teller or something?" I told her I was placing my trust in God.

When the results were out, the Dean, the Principal, and faculty came to the class to make an announcement. "Congratulations!! For the first time in Tamil Nadu, all 35 students have passed!!"

My Pentecostal friend frantically looked for me. "How did you know that all 35 would pass?" I replied, "Faith, like a mustard seed!" My faith grew stronger after that. All praise and glory to God!

Let us trust God, knowing that nothing is impossible for Him.

(To be continued)

January 24

Mustard Seed Faith-Part 2

Daisy Sharlin

"He is the one you praise, he is your God, who performed for you those great and awesome wonders you saw with your own eyes."

Deuteronomy 10:21, NIV

Six years after God's clear answer to my prayer, in having all 35 classmates pass the examination, I was in Tanuku, Andhra Pradesh, India. My neighbor was Dr. Suresh (pseudonym), a Brahmin medical doctor.

One day, he stopped by. He spoke about his prayers, and I told him briefly about Jesus and how He had answered my prayers for the 35 classmates.

That evening, I saw him very sad. His goldfish had died and was floating in the fishbowl. I, too, felt sad and suggested he put it in another water bowl. He retorted, "Why not CPR to revive it?" And then, very sarcastically, "Or better still, ask your living God to come down and give it life. He miraculously made 35 students pass, didn't He?" I couldn't stand his mockery. I railed at his powerless, lifeless stone gods, made other nasty comments, and rushed out of his place.

When I got home, I knew I had not behaved like a Christian. I asked God to forgive me and help my neighbor know the true God. So, I asked God for a miracle regarding his dead fish. I had hardly finished praying when I heard a scream from his house. I ran there and found his goldfish alive and well, swimming all over the bowl! The doctor apologized and said he would follow the living God. My God had answered yet another prayer.

Let us boldly ask our living God to increase our faith and the faith of our friends in Him, and He will answer our prayers.
(Concluded)

JANUARY 25

GOD'S GRACE

Sarah Khandagle

"Call upon Me in the day of trouble; I will deliver you, and you shall glorify Me."

Psalm 50:15, NKJV

My youngest son, then 23, had returned from a trip to California when he suddenly fell ill. We consulted our family doctor, who immediately admitted him into the Intensive Care Unit. Over the next few days, we watched him get worse. His blood pressure kept going down – a bad sign! With tears in our eyes, we earnestly prayed. We wanted him to be healed so badly that it was difficult to utter the words, "If it is Thy will." But we kept praying, along with the church, our relatives, and our friends.

Then came the day when the doctors told us that he had received the maximum treatment available and nothing more could be done. We left the hospital that night with heavy hearts. We felt we would probably not see him alive the following day.

When we returned the next morning, we could see his bed from a short distance away, and it was empty! Our hearts nearly stopped. Was he really gone? But a few steps closer, and we saw him sitting on a chair beside the bed, busy reading something! Our joy knew no bounds! My son had been brought back from the jaws of death! Our prayers of petitions turned to prayers of joyous praise. We didn't know exactly what had happened and didn't need to know. What we did know was that our God had reached down and touched him, and that touch had brought dramatic healing. We give Him all praise and honor, for indeed, He hears us when we call.

Are you facing troubles today? God says to call upon Him and that He will deliver.

JANUARY 26

SEASONAL CHANGE

Carol Thapa

'There is a time for everything, and a season for every activity under the heavens."

Ecclesiastes 3:1, NIV

Spring is my favorite season. I love the cold winds of winter, the changing colors of fall, and the ever-present sunshine in the summer, but spring is still the most pleasant of all. As the weather gets warmer, we see the lovely plants begin to sprout, and the pretty flowers start to bloom.

The writer of Ecclesiastes, in chapter 3, describes the reality of our lives. There is a time for everything; there is a time to be born, a time to die, and a time to plant and reap. So even though Spring is my favorite season, I know it won't last forever. Summer will eventually come, followed by the other seasons, and we will go through the cycle again.

This is a true reflection of our lives, for change is inevitable. But because of this change, we can conclude that there is an unchanging foundation because everything is not completely falling apart! Behind the whole scenario of change lies the sturdy hand of God, who remains changeless. Everything in life, including changes, has its challenges, but we have a God who calls himself our Savior and knows each circumstance we go through. No matter what season you may find yourself in now, take comfort that God is our constant.

There is a time for everything, including seasonal changes. But there is also a constant that never changes and keeps everything together. And He does it in love. We can safely trust Him.

January 27

He Was Talking to Me?!

Elsie Joel-Morse

"...Be still and know that I am God; I will be exalted among the nations, I will be exalted in the earth."

Psalm 46:10, NIV

"Be still!" I had heard that before but was never convinced it was a message for me. I kept hearing it repeatedly in songs, sermons, and even advice from a close friend. It was good advice, but not for me! I was in the midst of one of the most significant transitions of my life, and I just couldn't be still.

So I kept going. I knocked on every door, waiting for the sea to part, and when nothing happened, I worked even harder until I was exhausted. In fact, I became proud of my weariness. I could say I was doing my best!

It took a simple but unexpected event to make me change. We had met at Pizza Hut, and the kids of the Youth Sabbath School had presents for us leaders. All eyes were on me as I tore open the wrapping and brought out my gift. It was a painting with bright yellow flowers and clear, bold words: "Be still, I am with You." I was stunned. This was no ordinary gift. My heart melted as I realized that God had been speaking quite clearly all along.

Once I became still, God's plan was able to be set in motion. That painting now hangs in my office, where I can always see it, reminding me that I need to be still to hear Him. He has everything planned. I just need to be still so I don't miss hearing Him.

January 28

Danger on The Hill

Soosan Varghese

"You shall tread upon the lion and the cobra: the young lion and the serpent you shall trample underfoot."

Psalm 91:13, NKJV

We lived as a family in a serene village surrounded by lush green hills, valleys, and brooks in Kerala, India. I stayed home with my mom while my older siblings went to school and my dad went to work. Mom doubled as my preschool teacher, so we spent much time together.

Among our properties, across from our house in the valley, was a hill, which was rich with many fruit trees. We all – siblings, cousins, friends, and I – would go up the hill regularly in summer and gather and eat the fruits from those trees.

I was five years old when, one day, my mom and I went up the hill to gather dry leaves to use in a pit fire. First, we enjoyed picking and eating my favorite jungle flame berries and ripe mangoes. Then she gathered dry leaves in a pile, and I played in it. As she picked up a handful of leaves, we noticed she had picked up a snake along with the leaves, now dangling from her hand! "Mommy, snake!" I screamed out. She immediately flung everything away from her hands – leaves, snake, and all! We did not know if that snake was poisonous or not. Thank God we did not have to find out. He saved us from a snake bite that day.

Psalm 91 contains a beautiful promise of God protecting us from the lion, the cobra, and the serpent. The dangers we face today may be of different types. May God protect you from all dangers today and always.

January 29

Ripple Effect

Neena Eapen

Let each generation tell its children of your mighty acts; Let them proclaim your power."

Psalm 145: 4, NLT

I experienced the love of God through the many Bible stories my mother shared with me when I was a little girl. These were also the stories my mother learned as a young girl herself. Among them, the stories of Daniel and Jonah were my favorite ones, maybe because of the animal characters or the bravery of men and God's faithfulness to His children.

In Daniel's story, he was thrown into a den of lions for standing courageously on God's side, and in return, God honored his faithfulness by shutting the mouth of the lions. The story of Jonah shows a different picture. He had disobeyed God and found himself in the belly of a giant fish. One can only imagine the stress these two men had to endure. They both cried out to God for deliverance, and God heard both! In Daniel's story, we learn of God honoring His faithful servant; in Jonah's story, we learn of God listening to a repentant soul.

These stories helped me establish prayer as part of my life at a very early age. My mother left us relatively early, but the effect of her example and teachings continues to strengthen me to this day. Later in life, I used the same stories with my two children to help them build strong connections with God and grow in prayer.

God has been faithful in our darkest moments, and we must relate them to our loved ones so that these stories are passed on as a ripple effect from one generation to the next, just like my mother to me and from me to my children.

January 30

Sowing a Seed

Daisy Sharlin

Still other seed fell on good soil, where it produced a crop- a hundred, sixty or thirty times what was sown.

Mathew 13:8, NIV

In Singapore, I shared a room with a nurse named Josephine (pseudonym). Although Josephine was a Catholic, she found an SDA church for me, and I found a Catholic one for her. We invited each other to our churches and went there together. We were great friends, and she was a wonderful roommate.

One day, our conversation turned to our faiths. She said she was distraught that Pope Benedict had resigned. She was shattered. I did not want her to feel worse, so I suggested we investigate why he resigned and see if other popes had also resigned. Josephine was excited to share her belief in popes with me.

Our investigation revealed that there had been really bad popes. One put his dead predecessor on trial! Some looted money, others kept mistresses, fought for power, and even murdered to become pope. Josephine was shocked beyond belief. So was I! And we decided to take a break from our research. I explained that popes were only human, capable of sinning like anyone else.

A few years later, Josephine had to leave Singapore. As she left for the airport, I grabbed her hand and said," Ultimately, Jesus alone is the true Lord and Savior." She gave me a big hug and said she believed. I did not hear from her until last month when she contacted me.

God wants us to sow the seeds. He will take care of the rest. In our busy lives, let us pray for God's help to sow seeds of truth wherever He places us.

January 31

Delight in the Lord

Carol Thapa

"Delight yourself also in the Lord, and He shall give you the desires of your heart."

Psalm 37:4, NKJV

I was given a poster with these exact words on it. I had hung it up in my room and left it on the wall, not thinking much about it. However, there were numerous times when I felt alone, unnerved, and in severe conflicts. During those times, I was drawn to the words on that poster. I read and re-read the verse and felt encouraged.

The more I thought about the message, the more I was moved to do two things: figure out how to delight myself in Jesus and bring my desires to Him.

Here's what I learned.

Delighting myself in the Lord meant that I would spend time with Him. I didn't always have to set aside time for this. I would do this by praying while working and even as simple a thing as listening to Christian music. Once I got into the swing, they made me enjoy my time with Jesus.

Bringing my desires to Him meant just that: telling Him whatever was on my heart! Once I started pouring out my heart to God, I felt my burdens being lifted and started seeing prayers being answered.

Today, this verse has become a standalone plea in many of my earnest prayers. It is a strong reminder and assurance that He is ever present and ready to fulfill my desires. May this be your experience too!

"May the Lord answer you in the day of trouble…and strengthen you out of Zion…and fulfill all your petitions." Psalms 20: 1,2,5.

FEBRUARY 1

ALMIGHTY BUT COMPASSIONATE GOD

Beula Selvadurai

But I am poor and needy; Yet the Lord thinks upon me…"

Psalm 40:17, KJV

My favorite vacation spot is the beach. The powerful waves and the ocean's gigantic expanse are witnesses of God's majestic power.

One day, I stood on the shores of the Atlantic Ocean, looking at the mighty waves crashing onto the beach. The beach was crowded, but in the midst of that crowd, I was feeling lonely, small, and empty, and I wondered if this Most High God would care for me.

Just at that moment, a little boy came by, looking very happy because he had found a beautiful shell. It was a rare purple color, but I noticed that it was only one-half of a shell. Somehow, I felt just like that half-shell – lonely! I said, "Lord If I can find the other half of that shell, I will be happy like that boy, and also know that You are with me." I waited for some time, and when nothing happened, I was ready to return from the beach when a big wave came in. When it receded, I noticed something sticking out from the sand. I went to see what it was. Unbelievably, it was the other half of that shell!!

Imagine how I felt! Light as a feather and precious in His sight! He had answered my tiny prayer!!

"Fear not for I am with you; Be not dismayed, for I am your God." Isaiah 41:10.

"Though the Lord is on high, Yet He regards the lowly." Psalm 138:5,6.

When you feel lonely, empty, and unimportant, remember that you are precious in the eyes of the Almighty God.

FEBRUARY 2

FIRST ADVENTIST FAMILY TO LEAVE KUWAIT

Daisy Sharlin

Let me hear what the Lord will speak, for he will speak peace to his people…

Psalm 85:8, ESV.

My parents and two younger siblings were in Kuwait when the Iraq-Kuwait War began. As the invading army drove in, anarchy prevailed everywhere, looting and sabotaging. Fearing the worst, my father immediately planned to leave Kuwait. My mom made the necessary food preparations for the journey, and despite many church members' advice, my dad persisted in his plans.

The journey began with a drive across the desert into Iraq then at the border, they took a bus to Jordan. While there, my dad offered his services to the Red Cross in helping refugees fleeing Iraq and Kuwait. Soon after, the Indian government made arrangements to evacuate Indians from the war zone, and my parents reached Chennai, and we were all reunited as a family.

Sometime later, we heard that all the borders were closed, and those who were stranded away from their homes were classed as refugees and placed in tents until their turn came to leave those "refugee camps."

Thinking back, it became clear that my dad had made his decision to leave right on time. They were the first family to leave Kuwait. They escaped the conditions in the camps and made it safely home. We praise God with deep gratitude! He had urged my dad to make that quick decision to leave immediately.

We have a caring and faithful Heavenly Father who we can confidently trust. Let us trust Him, listen to His promptings, and follow His instructions always. If we follow Him, He will be with us through all dangers.

February 3

Constant Watch Care

Cinthya Daniel

"He will not allow your foot to be moved; He who keeps you will not slumber."

Psalm 121:3, NKJV

We were thoroughly enjoying our family vacation in the Dominican Republic, marveling at the beauty of God's nature. That particular day, we were to visit a beautiful island some distance away. We were to travel by a large boat and then get into two smaller ones to reach the island. When we were to get into the smaller boats, we suddenly noticed that our five-year-old son was missing. We looked around, and there he was – in the first boat, sailing away! We panicked and shouted out, but they had gone too far to be heard.

My husband then got a brilliant idea. He took out his camera, which had a powerful zoom lens, and focused it onto the boat, and there we could clearly see our son. A lady had befriended him, and when the boat had docked, she walked with him to the beach.

It was a full 30 minutes before we also docked on the island – 30 minutes that seem like 30 years! We ran over to him, utterly relieved that he was safe. We thanked the lady, for one never knows what might happen in a foreign country!

My husband watched our son constantly through the camera zoom lens and never lost sight of him for even a moment. Every one of his movements was carefully observed. So also, we have a heavenly Father who watches over us 24/7 and never lets us out of His sight. His care is constant and always done in love.

"He who keeps you will not slumber."

FEBRUARY 4

FLASHLIGHTS OF GOD

Johny Varghese

"For he will order his angels to protect you wherever you go. They will hold you up with their hands so you won't even hurt your foot on a stone."

Psalm 91:11-12, NLT

I was passionate about sports in my early adult years. I played at the district level, which meant long hours of practice and play. Many times, it would be much after dark before I got home. At night, the area was quite dangerous, with all kinds of creatures, including snakes, lurking in the grass. There were no streetlights in those days, and I did not carry a flashlight.

To reach our house, I had to walk about a mile and a half in the dark, with jagged rocks and ditches along the way. Paddy fields lined one side with waterways of varying depths next to the path. I could hear frogs croaking nearby and dogs barking in the distance.

Many times, as I reached the dark portion of the path, fireflies would begin flitting all over the place. The swarm would light up the whole area, and I avoided the ditches, the jagged edges of the rocks, and the water. I could even see the critters scurrying away as my steps approached them. The light from those fireflies kept me safe, and I never came to harm.

I thought of those fireflies as God's light troops sent to guide my physical path in the dark of night. "For You will light my lamp: The Lord my God will enlighten my darkness." Psalm 18:28, NKJV

God has a thousand ways to provide for our needs. May we realize God's promise of protection on us today and always.

FEBRUARY 5

GOD MAKES A WAY

George Abraham

"I will make a way in the wilderness and rivers in the desert."

Isaiah 43:19 KJV

I look back over more than 50 years and marvel at how God led me.

I graduated from Dental College, Bombay (now Mumbai) in 1965 and was keen to start my career outside India. But I did not know where to go and how to begin the process.

By then, my oldest brother, Dr. C.A. Ninan had gone to America for a training program in Urology. Through a series of events, he became acquainted with a Doctor from Kentucky, a very influential dentist. He created a two-year program tailored just for me and arranged for all the documents, certifications, and other formal papers required by the US Government.

By 1968, I headed to Lexington, Kentucky. My wife, Lizzie, and our two-year-old daughter, Sandra, joined me six months later. The following two years passed by smoothly with the support and encouragement of the doctor. When those two years were over, the way opened for me to go to the Loma Linda School of Dentistry.

Four years later, after completing my master's program, the University of Maryland in Baltimore hired me for a teaching position through a clearly providential encounter. It was a fruitful move – I taught and opened two successful dental practices in the area, and our third child, Georgina, came along! It was a great place to live and raise our family among fellow believers.

God had made a way at every step, and I am truly thankful.

"Before they call, I will answer." Isaiah 65:24 , NIV

FEBRUARY 6

GRACE IN SILENCE

Sonali Gupta Prates

"And God is able to make all grace abound to you, so that in all things at all times, having all that you need, you will abound in every good work."

II Corinthians 9:8, ESV

Most days, we do not realize how God's grace operates through us. But there are times when we are reminded of it.

As a nurse, I am constantly on the go, and at the end of a shift, there's nothing I want more than to get home, relax, and rest. That day, I had just finished my shift and was going down the elevator when I noticed a visitor who looked distressed. I just couldn't bring myself to turn away, so I asked her if she was okay. She broke down crying.

Outside the elevator, she told me her story. She had come to the hospital to visit her younger brother, who was terminally ill. She had flown in the day before and had nothing to eat or drink because she just could not bear to see him in that state.

Sitting on a bench beside her, I couldn't think of anything to say, so I got her some fruit and a bottle of water. Then, I just sat there with her in silence. About thirty minutes later, she looked at me and said, "Thank you!" She sounded grateful, and I knew she had been comforted, if only for a few minutes, by my silent presence.

I had merely kept her company, and that too in silence. But God's gentle grace had touched her through my presence. It was a privilege to share God's grace even through my silence!

Let us allow God to use us to comfort a hurting person.

FEBRUARY 7

HANGRY

(Composed of two words – "hungry" and "angry.")

Soosan Varghese

"People with understanding control their anger; a hot temper shows great folly."

Proverbs 14:29, NLT

My friend and I stood in line at the Five Guys Burgers and Fries at the food court in the Columbia Mall in Maryland. We had done some shopping but wanted to shop more after a quick bite for lunch. So, we got in line.

It was late afternoon, and the lines were long at all the fast-food restaurants. The people were impatiently waiting in line for their turn, and many were "hangry!" They would not tolerate anyone slipping in ahead of them.

We then noticed two women who seemed to be in a hurry – without getting in line, they walked up to the attendant at the counter. Nobody liked that, and an audible murmur arose.

The attendant quickly filled a cup of coke and gave it to one of the women. It seemed as if the attendant too, was not being fair! The woman immediately sipped the coke, then came and stood at the back of the line. She looked around somewhat embarrassed that she hadn't waited her turn like the others, and then explained herself. She had diabetes, was on medications, and had felt the symptoms of low blood sugar. She needed something with sugar immediately, so cutting the line, she went straight to the counter.

Now, the people in line were embarrassed. How quickly some had judged her.

We may not know the underlying circumstances for the behavior of others. Let us remember to be patient and understanding rather than "hangry!" May God help us to foster calm and patience.

FEBRUARY 8

LOST AND FOUND

Lovella Fernando

"For the Son of Man came to seek and to save the lost."

Luke 19:10, NIV

Several years ago, we passed through the crowded London Heathrow Airport. I was holding the hand of my daughter Michelle (5) and carrying our younger daughter (2) with my other hand. We stopped briefly at one of the monitor screens to confirm our departure gate and when we turned to go, I realized that Michelle was no longer with us! We were panic-stricken!!

We made plans instantly. My husband stayed at that spot just in case she returned, and I frantically looked for her. I returned without her. This time, my husband decided to try going ahead where we had stopped. I earnestly prayed that Michelle would be found. After a few minutes of intense waiting, he returned with Michelle in tow! What relief and joy!!

When we had stopped, I had let go of her hand briefly, but she had kept walking. When she realized we were not with her, we were out of sight, and she just broke down crying. That's when my husband spotted her. We all boarded that flight.

We like to venture out on our own, but God comes looking for us with an intensity greater than that of any earthly parent. We would never have left Heathrow that day if Michelle had not been found!!

Jesus came to this overcrowded "terminal" called planet Earth, looking for us. He kept at it until He said, "It is finished!"

Thank You, dear Jesus, for your grace. Keep me close to you today.

If ever we stray away from God, let us return to Him. He is reaching out to us.

FEBRUARY 9

PRACTICE BRINGS UNDERSTANDING

Steve John

"Keep this Book of the Law always on your lips; meditate on it day and night, so that you may be careful to do everything written in it. Then you will be prosperous and successful."

Joshua 1:8, NIV

Motorsports was in my blood from my early youth. I would keenly watch the Spicer College racing team prepare their formula car for the annual Bombay Grand Prix and dream of being involved. I vigorously pursued this dream even after coming to the USA. My team also sponsored me for an extensive driver development program because the theory had to be mastered.

The learning curve was steep. Fluid dynamics, mechanical grip, etc., were a real challenge. I had to forget what was portrayed in action movies and video games. My team would say, "That's entertainment; this is real science!" Only after the third season was I able to visualize the theoretical concepts and apply them to actual practice. When I did that, I grasped things much more quickly. It seemed like a light had come on.

It is much the same way in our spiritual lives. Whatever Jesus has done for us and offers us will be a distant, hazy idea unless we study the theory and then actually keep practicing it. It might appear complicated initially, but things will become more apparent with time and continued practice. Instead of being stressed out by the obstacles in front of us, we will look forward with anticipation and joy to what life will bring. The light will come on if we keep studying and practicing the gospel! God's grace promises us success!

May God help us to understand what we read in the Bible and put those teachings into practice.

FEBRUARY 10

SPECTACLE OF GRACE

SEC

"Thou therefore, my son, be strong in the grace that is in Christ Jesus."

II Timothy 2:1, KJV

I like athletics and love watching the champions exhibit their strength, speed, and stamina. I was watching the Rio Olympics. The next event was the 10,000-meter distance race, and there was an air of expectancy because Mo Farah of England was in it. He had already won the 5,000-meter race and was tipped to win this. If he did, he would be only the second person in history to win both events.

One of my favorite features is listening to the interesting background information regarding the athletes. The gun had gone off, and Mo was among the leaders in the race. The commentators said that he was a Somalian refugee who had suffered severe setbacks and yet made it to the prestigious Olympics. They described his grueling training regime, with everything focused on this moment.

Alas, on the seventh lap, he tripped and fell. Would this be the shattering of his dreams? Undeterred, he picked himself up and ran with such speed and determination that he beat all the competitors to win the gold medal! What an outstanding performance!

The apostle Paul compared the Christian to an athlete – the purpose, the discipline, the training, etc. Ultimately, his boast was in God's grace, enabling him to finish the race despite the setbacks.

We may fall, as some athletes do, but we are not counted out! Olympians run, not knowing whether they will win, but we are guaranteed victory. Therefore, Let us run confidently, placing our entire trust in Him.

FEBRUARY 11

GRACE EXEMPLIFIED

Sherlyn (Sweety) Injety

"For by grace you have been saved through faith. And. . .it is the gift of God."

Ephesians 2:8, ESV

What does the word "grace" portray? To many, grace is seen as a great action that impresses the public. But after January 17, 2008, I realized that it can be manifest even in small acts. That was the day Bindi Cooper, our lovely little pet puppy, came home to stay with us. She was adorable, with large floppy ears, a round button nose, and a white flame-shaped streak between her big brown eyes. My boys were ecstatic! They played with her, took her for walks, and taught her tricks. Whenever we returned home and unlocked the front door, Bindi was there, yelping excitedly and wagging her tail uncontrollably! That was her expression of love for us. And it never changed, no matter what we did. We accidentally locked her outside one stormy night. We left her in the dark one evening. Sometimes, we ignored her. Yet her love never waned.

Then came tragedy. Despite our best efforts to treat her SARDS condition, Bindi lost her vision, and her world went completely dark. Yet, her expressions of love never changed.

Even today, she tries to rush to the door when she hears the key turn in the lock. Bumping into furniture and tripping over rugs, she greets us, tail-wagging uncontrollably and yelping excitedly. It was as if nothing that we did could ever change her love for us.

Little Bindi Cooper taught me God's grace.

Our behavior proves us totally unworthy, but His grace is free, and the gift of Salvation comes with it. How wonderful! How humbling!

All we have to do is accept the Grace offered to us.

FEBRUARY 12

INVISIBLE RESCUER

Anonymous

"For He shall give His angels charge over thee to keep thee in all thy ways."

Psalm 91:11, KJV

I used to walk two and a half miles to school daily. Since nobody else went that way, I always walked alone.

One day, when I was in third grade, a man approached me and wanted to know where I was going. Although he was a total stranger to me, I told him where I was going. He told me that he could show me a shortcut. That sounded welcome to me, so I went with him. I trusted that he was helping me.

On reaching a secluded spot, he made me sit on his lap. Just then, we heard the sound of footsteps. Someone was close by and walking towards us. At the sound of the footsteps, he jumped up and ran away. Why did he run away in such a hurry? I had no idea then.

He did not return, and although I was expecting to see the one whose footsteps we heard, he also never appeared.

It was only in later life that I came to understand the danger I was in. I was totally at his mercy and far from any possible help - a situation perfect for committing horrifying crimes. If it had not been for the sound of the footsteps, I would have been a sad, sad victim.

I am convinced that a loving God had sent an angel whose footsteps sounded so close that it frightened the man away. Although my rescuer was invisible, my rescue was real!

May we go about our duties today, confident that God will send His angels to protect us.

FEBRUARY 13

HELP AT THE WATER TANK

Daisy Sharlin

"In the day of my trouble I will call upon You, for You will answer me."

Psalm 86:7 NKJV

In our garden in Chennai, India, there was a deep water tank about ten to fifteen feet deep where we stored water. The lid, which was a large slab, did not cover the top completely and left a wide gap.

One day, my two sisters-in-law came to visit. One had a newborn, and the other was almost full-term pregnant. I was busy inside the house when my three-year-old son rushed in, repeating the name of my pregnant sister-in-law and pointing outside. I looked outside. She had fallen into the water tank and was holding on tightly to the slab. I screamed and ran to the tank. My other sister-in-law left her newborn infant and came running.

I shouted for any neighbor to come and help, but none came. I feared we would lose our sister-in-law and her unborn baby if we did not act quickly. With a prayer in our hearts, we gave a big heave and pulled her out. She was bruised and bleeding a bit from the scratches on her arms and began to shiver and have chills. We immediately wrapped her in a blanket and rushed her to the Emergency Room to have her and the baby evaluated. Eventually, it turned out that both mother and baby were well, thank God!

God used my son to alert us just in time and granted us sufficient strength to pull her out. I praise God for keeping us safe.

"The Lord is your keeper. . ." Psalms 121:5, NKJV. May we each feel the presence and protection of our God continually.

FEBRUARY 14

RIPPLES OF KINDNESS

Subhashini Mesipam

"Gracious words are a honeycomb, sweet to the soul and healing to the bones."

Proverbs 16:24, NIV

Music and laughter mingled in the cool summer air outside the Columbia Mall. Everyone seemed to be having a good time. I was upbeat, too, because this was my first outing after my arthroscopic knee surgery.

I was waiting for my husband to pick me up when a group of lively, happy youngsters passed by. One of them stopped, turned around, looked at me, and complimented me – out of the blue! And then they walked on. It was so spontaneous and genuine that it got to me. It made me smile and encouraged me to compliment others in the same way.

It was the simplest of acts. I'm sure my face beamed with appreciation, which made the other person happy too. Two perfect strangers on a chance encounter, each lifted the mood of the other. I feel the warmth and connection of those few seconds to this day.

Kind words of encouragement and affirmation stay with the individual for a long time. They have power – on others, on ourselves, and through us, on yet others. No wonder the Bible has much to say about being kind in word and deed. The proverb quoted above likens gracious words to honey. No one dislikes honey because it is sweet and soothing.

And best of all, our words of appreciation are contagious. Kind words have a ripple effect that keeps going on and on long after they are uttered.

Dear God, help us to speak kind and encouraging words to uplift the people we encounter today.

February 15

Standardized Academic Test (SAT)

Kevin Daniel

"Ask and it will be given you; seek and you will find; knock and the door will be opened to you. For everyone who asks receives. The one who seeks finds; and to the one who knocks, the door will be opened."

Matthew 7:7, 8, NIV

The SAT is a huge stressor for many teens and is treated as the focal make-or-break point that decides future success or failure.

I felt this way too, and so I focused my whole attention on it. I studied hard and disciplined myself in preparation. I received a decent enough score but knew I could do better. So, I decided to repeat it. I had been through it once and felt confident. But alas! The score was worse!! I just could not fathom what had gone wrong. However, there was a tiny ray of hope – just enough time for one more chance at it before the college application deadlines.

But what more could I do? I then realized I was leaning on my own capabilities. There was something more I could do – ask God for His help. So, I prayed earnestly, asking God for His help. This time, when I took the test, there wasn't any of the earlier anxiety and stress. I felt comfortable and at peace! When I looked at my score, it was the best one yet!

The above verse from Matthew may appear too elementary, but the key is to really take it to heart.

When we go this way, we will realize that God is eager to help. All we have to do is ask, trusting that He is listening to us.

Remember to ask God to help us with all our plans, decisions, and actions.

February 16

God's Got You!

Achsha Hembrom

"For the Lord your God is the one who goes with you to fight for you against your enemies to give you victory."

Deuteronomy 20:4 NIV

I do not like to admit it, but I am truly afraid of the future. It seems like a blank, frightening page! I often wonder whether I will succeed in my career, be really happy with what I become, and be able to draw close to God. Such questions keep nagging me, even when discussing positive things like my hopes and dreams.

One of the things that often crosses my mind is where and how God will use me. Will He move me to a different country like He did Jonah? Or will He make me face my insecurities like He did Moses? However, I find comfort and assurance when I go through their stories and hear others share their experiences of God guiding them. Why should we get stressed out if God is really in control? He knows all about our limitations. He knows what we cannot handle and has promised to always care for us.

When I feel anxious and nervous about the future, it strengthens me to say aloud, "God has got me. He knows what's best for me and will keep me in His hands!"

No, I don't know the future; no one does! But we can know this: "See, I have inscribed you on the palm of my hands." Isaiah 49:16 NKJV. God has got us in His hands, and that is the safest place to be.

If the uncertainty of the future worries you today, remember that the Lord our God is with you to give you victory.

FEBRUARY 17

MY REFUGE AND FORTRESS

Joseph Kelly Pedapudi

"I will say of the Lord, 'He is my refuge and my fortress; My God, in Him I will trust.'"

Psalm 91:2 NKJV

One of my friends, who works as a nurse in a hospital, described this incident to me.

The patient brought to the ward that day was a 14-year-old girl needing the placement of a catheter in her arm. She was all alone, terrified, and shaking with fear. She said she didn't want anything done until her father came. No amount of reassurance from anyone there was able to calm her down. She was sure he would come, and until then, she was not going to let anyone touch her.

Finally, her father came to the ward, and the whole picture changed as soon as she saw him. The terror on her face instantly vanished. The change was amazing – almost magical! Now, with her dad by her side, she was willing to undergo the frightening procedure. What made the difference? Just one thing – the presence of her father!

The psalmist David faced the threat from a giant and defeated him. What was his secret? He tells us: "He is my refuge and my fortress; My God, in Him I will trust."

God wants us to be like the young girl who calmed down instantly when her father arrived. We have a heavenly Father who always stands faithfully by our side. When we recognize that, we will feel His presence, and in that presence, we will find assurance, comfort, and peace. "You will keep him in perfect peace, whose mind is stayed on You." Isaiah 26:3 NKJV

February 18

Little Things As Well

Jasmine Morse

"Indeed the very hairs of your head are all numbered. Don't be afraid; you are worth more than many sparrows."

Luke 12:7, NIV.

The number of times I've lost them is insane! I've panicked over these very insignificant objects countless times because they always seem to disappear. Some call them sunglasses. I call them shades.

When I was younger, my favorite pair of shades would go inconveniently missing whenever I needed them. One time, after a good 30 minutes of desperate searching, I had to admit defeat. But just at that point, a thought came to mind. What if I prayed about this?

But would God pay attention to my little prayer about my insignificant problem? Surely, He has bigger things to do! Why would He care about my shades?

But to my surprise, when I returned to my room, my neon shades were on my bed, right where I had left them! And just like that, my insignificant pair of shades turned my mind towards my very significant God.

God – THE GOD Almighty, who knows how many galaxies form the universe and how many grains of sand make up the beach – also knows how many hairs are on our head and even where our lost pair of shades are! He answered my tiny plea and showed me that He pays attention to the most minor details. Not only does He want to be there for the big moments, but He is equally interested in our tiniest prayers. Yes, even about where my favorite pair of shades can be found!

That means He really cares for me. How wonderful is that!

Don't worry about your prayers being unimportant to God. He loves to hear them all. Pray on.

February 19

Hang in There

Cinthya Daniel

"So we can confidently say, 'The Lord is my keeper; I will not fear what man can do to me."

Hebrews 13:6, ESV

It was my first pregnancy and I was absolutely thrilled with the thought of soon becoming a mother! At six weeks, the ultrasound test showed that I had had a miscarriage. I had a D&C and went home crushed and disheartened. I took my distress to God.

I then had to undergo a blood test. It showed an infection as the likely cause, and the doctors started me on high-potency medications for the next several months. That was not welcome news at all, and I felt even more distraught! I tried to find an explanation for my troubles but got nowhere. I just kept going to God in prayer.

A few months later, I was pregnant again. My spirits soared, but my gynecologist was cautious. I was on powerful medications that could cause abnormal growth of the baby, and she might have to recommend abortion. She said she would consult a specialist and get back to me. It took only two days, but to me, it seemed forever! I kept trusting in God's guidance.

Finally, I got a call from my doctor. The medications would not be harmful; I could carry on with the pregnancy. soon, we were blessed with a healthy baby boy who brought joy and happiness to our home. Four years later, we were blessed with another awesome baby boy.

Are you troubled and worried? Hang in there! Our heavenly Father is in complete control and will surely see you through.

February 20

God Hears Our Cries

Cinthya Daniel

"...I cried out to God with my voice – To God with my voice; and He gave ear to me."

Psalm 77:1, NKJV

February 11, 2016, was a significant day for me. I was about to pursue my lifelong dream of completing my master's program in nursing. It was thrilling to be back in school again!

One day, I felt a little dizzy. I consulted an eye doctor and was prescribed glasses. However, it began to get worse – especially when in large buildings with high ceilings. After some time, I realized it had started interfering with my daily activities. I saw several doctors, but they could not identify the cause. I had to take extended breaks from school. Sometimes, I would have to leave a concert, a graduation ceremony, or other events in which my son was participating and exit the venue in tears, feeling completely helpless. And how would I complete my master's program!? Numerous times, in my helplessness, I cried out loudly to God, pleading for some relief.

One day, I was impressed to check my symptoms on the internet. They seemed to fit a condition called Binocular Visual Dysfunction. I consulted a specialist in New York, who prescribed special glasses with prismatic lenses. What a difference that made – no more dizziness, no more frustration, anxiety, and nervousness! I graduated from my master's program in 2018, and now I am almost back to normal.

I had cried to God in my helplessness, and I believe He answered and prompted me to do the right thing. Yes, He hears: "...His ears are open to their cry." Psalm 34:15, NKJV.

If you are in a dire situation, cry out to God, for His ears are open to your cries.

FEBRUARY 21

Quiet Help

Samuel Benjamin

"I will lift up my eyes to the hills – from whence comes my help? My help comes from the LORD, Who made heaven and earth."

Psalm 121:1, NKJV

I was in the fifth grade. My friends and I were enjoying our free time together, playing on the school grounds. At one point, I was running my fastest and didn't notice that the monkey bars were right in front of me. Bang! I hit my head against them at full speed, and I stood there dazed and dizzy. When blood ran down my face, I was rushed to the nurse's office. There was a large gash across the forehead, and my parents were immediately notified. We went to the Emergency Room. The main concern was whether any injuries had occurred inside the brain.

We had to wait for five hours before being seen by the doctor. During those hours, we did not speak much but were silently praying in our minds. Yes, we were thankful that we weren't in a worse situation, but the uppermost thought was regarding internal injury, and we prayed that there was no brain damage.

During that time of quiet meditation, I learned that we can be in direct contact with God. He will hear us and calm our troubled minds.

When it was over in the Emergency Room, the evaluations showed that the bones and brain were intact. I needed just a few stitches and would soon be back to normal. Thank God!

The scar of the stitches is still on my forehead, reminding me of His presence that calms the soul. May His presence be with us today.

FEBRUARY 22

SILENCE OF GRACE-PART 1

SEC

"...there is a friend that sticketh closer than a brother."

Proverbs 18:24, KJV

I am thankful for many things, but if you asked me what I was deeply thankful for, I would say – pain. It is all-encompassing, gripping, and unrelenting. Everything gets focused on it because pain amplifies itself above everything else. No, I do not wish it for anyone. But I am thankful for pain because it was at just such a moment of excruciating pain in my life that I was granted one of the best gifts I have ever received: the gift of silence from a close friend.

Knowing my pain, my best friend would come to me every evening, and we would go for a walk. We would find a place to sit from where we could watch the sunset and silently keep company, sometimes for over an hour! Then we would get up and walk home in total silence, and it was the most meaningful experience of silence I have ever had! The support and strength I received from those times of silence were far greater than any words could have conveyed to me.

In that silence, I came face to face with the reality of life – nobody can escape pain – not me, not anyone else. And with that realization came a mental submission that brought peace to my heart – in the form of God's all-encompassing, gentle, forgiving grace!

Just as the silent presence of my friend comforted me in the hour of my intense need, so the grace of God silently surrounds us as He faithfully sits with us through all our experiences.

May you feel surrounded by the grace of God today.

FEBRUARY 23

SILENCE OF GRACE - PART 2

SEC

"And the Lord passed by before him, and proclaimed, the Lord, the Lord God, merciful and gracious, longsuffering and abundant in goodness and truth."

Exodus 34:6, KJV.

Growing up, I confess that I was a very naughty child. As a result, I learned that actions have real consequences. But in my teens, I was given a lesson through silence from my family that I will never forget.

I had broken the rules, and everyone knew I deserved punishment for my bad behavior. But instead, nobody spoke about my misbehavior at all. No one yelled at me, and no punishment was handed down. We had worship together, and at dinner, I was still asked how my day was. I had clearly hurt my parents, and yet they were treating me with love. My remorse was keen because of the complete and unconditional forgiveness given to me who had not asked for it nor deserved it.

It was an experience of parental grace! Thousands of years earlier, Moses was so angry with the Israelites that He threw down and literally broke the slabs of stone on which God's own finger had written the law. But God did the writing all over again and taught Moses and us that while the law was to be honored and kept, they were never to forget that His mercy and grace were available to all who would ask. He would keep silent and not pronounce judgment on them. He would be good to them and thus prompt deep repentance.

"…the goodness of God leads you to repentance…" Romans 2:4, NKJV

This is a picture of the grace of God.

FEBRUARY 24

RUN THE RACE

Duraiswamy Paulson David

Run in such a way that you may obtain it…everyone who competes is temperate in all things…I run thus: not with uncertainty…not as one who beats the air. But I discipline my body and bring it into subjection."

I Corinthians 9:24-27, NKJV

I was the head of the Physical Education Department at Spicer Memorial College, India, for many years. I was fortunate to have seen some fantastic athletes during the sports events. Not only did I arrange all the events, I also trained some of the competitors. Some had a natural ability, performed well, and garnered all the praise. However, I was most impressed with those who did not seem to have it naturally in them but, with dedication and hard work, developed their strength and endurance to compete and even win!

None of the athletes simply landed at the starting line. No! They had trained and practiced for months. Each had studied the event to develop the right strategy and master the details. On the other hand, team sports require that the members work together; some had to give up things for the good of the team, but the end result was well worth the sacrifice!

Sometimes, I took teams outside the college campus to compete in the bigger arenas. Here, they were challenged to compete well and be an excellent example in temperament and sportsmanship. These experiences provided life-shaping lessons.

This sports scene is a good picture of the spiritual aspects of our lives. These athletes won temporary prizes. Ours is an eternal one. May we all run the race with certainty, bringing our minds and bodies into subjection to our God and attain the eternal prize!

February 25

His Miracle Time

Vidhya Melvin

"And he said, 'The things that are impossible with men are possible with God."

Luke 18:2, KJV

We were first-time parents and excitedly prepared to receive our precious blessing! We kept to the schedule and went regularly to the doctor's office.

At the start of the third trimester, the doctor ordered immediate admission into the hospital because things were not going well. He would attempt treatment for 24 hours, and if there were no improvements, we would likely have a premature baby. This was totally unexpected. We were shocked and devastated beyond words!

In the hospital room, we saw a cross hanging on the wall in front of us. It reminded us that He is right there - the only person who truly understands our fears and deep longings. We spent those 24 hours in constant prayer. We claimed God's promises and earnestly prayed, "God, please provide a miracle and bring our baby into the world on the due date - not a day early or a day late!"

During the last few hours of the allotted time, no improvement was seen. The doctor walked in and told us that the condition was not getting any better and the only way to save the baby was surgery. He scheduled it for the next day.

Then, for no apparent reason, the condition began to improve, and surgery was not needed the next day. Things got better and better, and our baby stayed in the womb until the due date, and we were blessed with a healthy baby. Now, we were happy beyond words!

We believe God heard our prayers. He will listen to yours, too.

FEBRUARY 26

GRACE ALONG THE WAY

SEC

O taste and see that the Lord is good: blessed is the man that trusteth in him

. Psalm 34:8, KJV

It was a beautiful Indian summer's day. I had traveled across town to spend the day with one of my relatives. On the way back, I decided to save and take the less expensive route – by bus. At the bus stop, reality hit me – the heat, the jostling crowds, and the unpleasant smells were most unwelcome! But the frugal Indian in me decided to stick it out until an empty bus came by.

As we waited, I told my sister, "An air-conditioned car would be most welcome right now." A few minutes later, a car pulled up. They wanted directions. I might have asked them for a ride because they were headed toward my destination, But I didn't.

The heat was getting unbearable, and I joked to my sister, "I'd settle for a rickshaw right now." Just then, a rickshaw pulled up, and the driver pointed in the direction I wanted to go and was willing for half the rate. And yet, I refused!

When the sweltering heat had drenched us in sweat, an empty bus came by; as I was boarding it, my sister said, "You do realize that every wish you made today came to you."

I had a long, thoughtful ride back. Had I been stubborn? Had I missed something?

We ask, and God in mercy, sends us little moments of grace, but we often reject them and miss out on the much larger joys of Christian life! Even then, His grace flows out unending. Grace is experiential; may we experience it.

February 27

Miracle Amid War

Rathna Pushparaj Samuel

In my distress I called upon the Lord, and cried unto my God: He heard my voice out of his temple, and my cry came before him, even into his ears

. Psalm 18:6, KJV

We were living comfortably in Kuwait until 1990 when Iraq invaded the country. We were unsuccessful in trying to get out by car and were sent back to the Iraqi border. Then we heard the welcome news that the Indian government had been granted permission to repatriate Indian citizens.

I packed our luggage and put our money, important documents, and other valuables inside the luggage. I did not want to keep anything in our purses because the soldiers at the checkpoints were notorious for looting. Our valuables would be outside their reach in the luggage.

When we boarded the plane, our luggage was not loaded in order to accommodate as many people as possible. As the aircraft took off, I could see our baggage on the tarmac, and suddenly, I panicked! I had not taken out the documents and money from the luggage! I had nothing in my hands! No cash, no documents, no valuables! There was no telling when the luggage would arrive and whether the contents would be safe. How would we even enter India without them?! All I could do was cry out to God and ask for a miracle.

I could hardly believe my ears when, a short time later, the pilot announced that he was turning the plane around and we were returning to the airport because of a mechanical problem. Another plane was arranged the next day, in which there was enough space for all the passengers and our luggage.

What an incredible miracle from our awesome God!

Let's cry out to God when in distress. He will answer.

FEBRUARY 28

GUARDIAN ANGELS

Gladwin Matthews

He shall give His angels charge over thee, to keep thee in all thy ways. They shall bear thee up in their hands, lest thou dash thy foot against a stone.

Psalm 91: 11,12, KJV

In 1991, I moved, along with my wife Surekha and Marvin (6 months old), from Rohru Hills, Shimla, Himachal Pradesh, to Spicer Memorial College. Soon after moving, we discovered that Marvin had a condition that required a surgical procedure. On the day of the procedure, I took my wife and son on my Suzuki motorbike and headed for the appointment. At one of the traffic lights, which had just turned green, I started out but then noticed that a huge, speeding truck was coming at me. I swerved to the left, but it kept coming at me. I went further left to the curb until there was no more room, and still, the truck kept coming. An accident was now inevitable, and I braced myself for the impact. Instead, I suddenly felt as if we were being lifted up and moved, just far enough so that the tire of the truck barely brushed my right foot as it sped by. I stopped on the side of the road, my heart racing, and realized that we had got through unscathed.

But how could that have happened? The size of the truck, the speed, the angle, and the direction in which it was moving didn't leave enough room for us to pass. Did God send His guardian angel to "bear us up" so we would not be hurt?

I believe God had a purpose for me and my family. And we had experienced God's grace that day.

God's angels will bear us up and protect us always.

FEBRUARY 29

GOD'S EYES ARE ON YOU

Gloria Moses

"I will instruct you and teach you in the way you should go. I will counsel you with my eye upon you."

Psalm 32:8, ESV

My sister and I loved playing after school when we were children in Sri Lanka. We joined a group of girls who played basketball and had a lot of fun. After playing, we would go to the store and buy popcorn and other snacks or go to the market to purchase supplies that our mom wanted. We were tired by the time we boarded the bus for home.

Girls from other schools were also on the bus. Most of them spoke Sinhala, and since my sister and I spoke Tamil, they sat in different rows, leaving our row to ourselves. I was tired at the end of the day, so I would often stretch out and sleep on the empty seats while my sister would sit at the window and watch the beautiful scenery passing by.

One day, when it was time to get off the bus, my sister got out, thinking I was behind her, but I was still sleeping. She called out to me, but it was too late; the bus had taken off! However, I was now awake and got off at the next stop.

It was some distance away from home, and the place was unfamiliar. But God helped me find my way, and I walked safely home that day.

God provided me with a loving sister who looked out for me, and He helped me get home safely.

Let us live with the assurance that God's loving eyes are always upon us. He will instruct, teach, counsel, and guide us.

MARCH 1

THE JEWEL IN THE HIMALAYAS

Biju Thomas

I will lift up mine eyes unto the hills - from whence cometh my help? My help cometh from the Lord, which made heaven and earth.

Psalm 121:1,2, NKJV.

In 1990, I visited my brother, who worked at the Scheer Memorial Adventist Hospital in Banepa, a small village 18 miles east of Nepal's capital, Kathmandu. It lies near the Himalayan Mountains in a fertile valley at nearly 5,000 feet elevation. The Himalayas are the most extensive mountain range on our planet. These mountains also help to regulate our planet's climate.

Located 120 miles from the capital, Kathmandu, is Nepal's prettiest city, Pokhara. This city is on the shore of Phewa Lake and sits at an elevation of approximately 2700 ft. Pokhara's tranquil beauty has been the subject of inspiration for many. Its pristine air, spectacular backdrop of snow-capped mountain peaks, blue lakes, and surrounding greenery make it "the jewel in the Himalayas."

I had the privilege of visiting Pokhara and taking a boat ride on the ice-cold waters of the lake. The experience of traveling by boat at such an elevation and viewing the snow-capped mountains surrounding the lakes is surreal.

I was reminded of the beautiful words of Psalm 121 as I viewed the surrounding majestic mountains and peaks. We look "unto the hills" because we long for solitude, to escape life's endless hustle & bustle. "Looking unto God" is the first step in approaching Him. There is something about looking to God that saves us. God says, "Look unto me and be saved..." Isaiah 45:22: KJV.

May we always remember to look unto our God, from whom our help comes. He is waiting for us to call on Him.

MARCH 2

BLESSINGS IN DISAPPOINTMENTS

Julinda Massey

"We went through fire and through water, but You brought us out to rich fulfillment.

Psalm 66:12, NKJV

When I experience setbacks in my life, I often get disappointed, and I begin to wonder if I will ever reach my goals. However, could there have been a blessing that I was missing? I have found that the delays, the wrongs, the could-have-been moments, while disappointing, have a blessing wrapped in them – they have often led me closer to God, and I have experienced His special grace and protection in my life precisely at those moments.

After experiencing disappointments, I review them, finally arriving at this question: "Is this what God wanted for me? Is this all He intended for me, or was there more?" In asking these questions and honestly looking for answers, I have received direction for my life and gained understanding through those disappointments.

I have learned to wait on God and read His Word to appreciate His perspectives. I have been led to pray more often to reveal His purpose for my life. I have learned to include God in every aspect of my life and consult Him on every matter. Most importantly, I have learned that setbacks and disappointments are opportunities for God to work and for me to see His power clearly.

These lessons are priceless! I am reassured that nothing I go through, no matter how disappointing, will come to me without a benefit because God has arranged it. I share these thoughts because I am convinced that there are wonderful blessings to be experienced, even when things seemingly go wrong in life.

If you are going through disappointments, remember God can turn them into blessings.

MARCH 3

WAILING INTO DANCING

Cinthya Daniel

"You have turned my mourning into joyful dancing. You have taken away my clothes of mourning and clothed me with joy."

Psalm 30:11, NLT

December 4, 2004, was my first day in the USA! After two years of going through all the protocols required for my visa, I was granted approval to travel to the USA. I left my husband and three-year-old son back in India to wait until I had cleared the nursing licensure exam (NCLEX). On my arrival, I was taken to a rental apartment.

It was cold, and I was tired and hungry. Sitting alone in that apartment, in new and unfamiliar surroundings, a wave of loneliness swept over me as I thought of home and my family, and I found myself sobbing uncontrollably.

Then I heard a knock on the door. I quickly wiped my tears and answered the door. It was a nurse who lived downstairs. She brought me some food and informed me that a gentleman was coming to take her shopping and invited me to join them. I got ready and waited for the gentleman to come.

When he arrived, my whole world was transformed in a moment! The gentleman was Mr. Samuel, a very good friend of my parents!! He recognized me and said how excited he was to see me. My spirits went soaring high, and I was dancing in my heart. From that day on, his family cared for me as their own.

That was fifteen years ago, and I still get goosebumps thinking about how God changed my misery to joy in just one moment. Yes, our heavenly Father did that!

God promises to turn our mourning into dancing. Let's wait on Him and rejoice in Him.

March 4

Anxiety Versus Calmness

Jeremiah Joel

"Be strong and courageous, and do the work. Do not be afraid or discouraged, for the LORD God, my God is with you."

I Chronicles 28:20, NIV

My mother told me about how she, as a student, had won a spelling bee contest. I noticed that all the winners in our school had been girls. So, I decided to try to become the first boy in the school to win it.

For the qualifying round, I studied for an hour the night before and then woke up at 4:30 am to study again. I knew I was not prepared and was tense and anxious throughout. However, the words asked were those I had just reviewed. So, I qualified for the finals.

The final round was three weeks later. This time, I wanted to take no chances, so I studied every day. On the day of the competition, I was ready!

Round after round, it went, for two hours. I reached the top five and was the only boy left. I knew the next word, but in my excitement, I lost concentration and stated the wrong letter. I lost, but amazingly, I had been free of tension and anxiety during the whole competition.

In the qualifier, I was successful but anxious and tense the whole time. Whereas in the finals, although I was not successful, I experienced calmness and confidence. What made the difference? It was the preparation! And although I had not won, I was happy that I had done quite well!

I learned an important lesson: God wants us to do our earnest best, and the rest is up to Him. So, in everything, let us always do our best.

March 5

Lockdown Problems Solved!

Ellen G. Morgan

"My help cometh from the Lord, which made heaven and earth."

Psalm 121:2, KJV

"I'm trying to get my flight moved to tomorrow morning," texted our daughter Melody on Monday. She had been in Italy for two and a half weeks and had already cut her visit short. Why was she moving it a day earlier?

When I asked my husband, he said it was because the Italian Prime Minister had announced a strict lockdown starting Tuesday morning. My heart nearly stopped! What if she could not make it out in time?! I couldn't think of that, so I turned to God, "Oh Lord, please don't let that happen!"

Another problem loomed. She would have to be quarantined on arrival in the USA. We hadn't made concrete plans yet, and she was coming a day earlier! It was crunch time. I turned to God again, and He worked it all out. A family at church had an empty house and would allow Melody to stay there the entire period.

My thoughts then turned to her flight. Would she make it out safely? "Boarding now!" was her reply. It was early Tuesday morning. We had only a few hours to get her house ready, but we got everything done by afternoon and then headed to the Washington Dulles Airport to meet her. As we arrived at the airport, I strained my eyes to catch a glimpse of her – and there she was! Our daughter was safely back home! All the hurdles had been crossed. Praise God!

"I sought the LORD, and He heard me and delivered me from all my fears." Psalm 34:4 NKJV

MARCH 6

MOUNTAIN TOP EXPERIENCE

Saroja Moses

"Now therefore, give me this mountain of which the Lord spoke in that day."

Joshua 14:12, NKJV

The night before traveling with our son to Pacific Union College in Angwin, California, I wrote him a letter to reflect on a mountaintop experience. I described the climb - the hardships, challenges, and even discouragements. But God would guide him if he sought Him with all his heart.

We live on the East Coast, and the thought that our son would study on the West Coast was harder on me than on my son. Throughout the journey, I wondered what the future held for him. On our approach to Angwin, I noticed that the road went higher and higher, and I realized that Pacific Union College (PUC) was situated on a mountain!! Tears came to my eyes as I thought of the letter I had just written regarding a mountaintop experience. That was the moment I knew that this was according to God's plan. I felt deeply assured!

God was the Provider and Protector for the next four years of his college life. He provided good friends, mentors, and teachers. God protected him, too. I had noticed that the road to Angwin had some sharp turns, and I had heard of students from PUC who had lost their lives there. Our son graduated from PUC with a mountaintop experience!

Caleb was 85 years old when he took up the challenge of conquering the mountain. It was no ordinary mountain! The cities were fortified, and a tribe of giants lived there, but he was victorious!!

Today, let us be assured that God will be our constant Provider and Protector.

March 7

I Was Changed

Govardhan Bekkam

"Now then, we are ambassadors for Christ, as though God were pleading through us: we implore you on Christ's behalf, be reconciled to God."

II Corinthians 5:20, NKJV

I was born into a Hindu family. We worshiped many deities represented by many idols. I attended the local government school until the 4th grade, when I had to drop out of school to help my father cultivate the farm.

Sometime later, a couple encouraged my dad to send me back to school. They even offered to give me a place in their home. My father agreed, and I went there. I noticed a little red Bible on their windowsill. I wanted to read it but remembered that the Bible was for those in the lower castes. So, I threw it down and kicked it.

I had been studying in Telugu schools so far. I then met an uncle who was studying in an SDA English medium school in Nuzvidu, and he invited me to join him there. My father agreed. He packed some idols, instructed me to do puja regularly, and tied a thread around my left wrist.

At the school, a senior introduced himself and began talking about Jesus. I was fascinated. When I made my decision to follow Jesus, I was given a small red Bible, just like the one I had kicked. I read it, put away the idols, removed the thread from my wrist, and prayed earnestly to this God.

Since that time, I have felt blessed. I thank God for leading me to Jesus. I hope to be a witness for Him just like the others who brought me to Him.

May God help us to lead others to him.

MARCH 8

THE IRAZU VOLCANO

Biju Thomas

"He looks at the earth, and it trembles; He touches the mountains, and they smoke."

Psalm 104:32, NASB

Amazon has its offices in some of the most exotic locations around the globe, and Costa Rica is one of those beautiful locations. In 2016, I traveled to San Jose, Costa Rica, to train a batch of employees at Amazon's office there.

I went sightseeing too. One of the tourist attractions in Costa Rica is the scenic mountains and the volcanos. The Irazu volcano is one of the most visited volcanoes and is a fascinating sight. The central crater is almost circular, has very inclined walls, and measures 3,440 ft. in diameter and 980 ft. in depth.

As we went up from San Jose, I felt the clouds pass through my fingers for the first time in my life. The craters are way above the clouds, and the landscape and views are breathtaking!

The word "Irazu" means "thunder and earthquake mountain." It has erupted frequently – at least 23 times since its first historically recorded eruption in 1723. The most recent eruption was in 1994. So, it should be classed as an active volcano.

In our verse for today, the Psalmist describes the power and authority of God – with just a look, He can cause earthquakes; with a mere touch of His hand, He can set mountains on fire and cause volcanoes to erupt with thunder and earthquakes! At the same time, God keeps watch over His children amid all the upheavals and violence on this earth.

Remember, we depend entirely on God's power and authority to protect and care for us.

March 9

The Lord Will Provide

Bimal Nowrangi

"And Abraham called the name of the place The-LORD-Will-Provide. . ."

Genesis 22:14, NKJV

This promise is not only for the big problems we face but for the seemingly smaller ones as well.

In December of 2019, when I was on my way to Spicer Memorial College (now Spicer Adventist University,) my flight from Frankfurt, Germany, to New Delhi, India, was delayed due to inclement weather. That meant I would miss my morning connecting flight to Pune. After reaching Delhi, I tried to book another flight to Pune but could not. I spent the whole day there, waiting to catch the last flight.

I needed to inform my cousin, who was to pick me up, about the change. But when I looked at my cell phone, the battery was dead. The power outlet was 220-volt, and I didn't have an adapter. People came hurrying to recharge their phones and rushed away to catch their flights. Nobody had time to help me, so I sat down to think.

Soon, a young man came and sat down beside me. We got talking, and he said he had been a student at Spicer! He quickly lent me his 220-volt charger for just a few minutes before he had to go to catch his flight. Those few minutes were sufficient to charge my phone just enough for me to get in touch with my cousin and tell him about the change in travel plans. I told him the correct time I would arrive in Pune, and that helped avoid a lot of confusion and anxiety.

Whatever our needs, whether big or small, God is our provider and willingly fulfills them.

March 10

Mom's Miracle Watch

Daisy Sharlin

"Before they call, I will answer; and while they are still speaking, I will hear."

Isaiah 65:24, NIV

My mom has a Swiss watch that is precious to her because it holds many memories. I was in Tanuku, Andhra Pradesh, India, when she came to be with me and brought her favorite watch with her.

She usually takes the watch off her wrist and places it on the kitchen shelf when working in the kitchen. But I warned her that our helper might be tempted to steal it. One day, she left it on the shelf, and when she returned later, it was gone. It was such a loss to my mom! Seeing her that sad, I wished something could be done.

I took her to the "Mangalvar Market" that day. It is a unique market day when the vendors bring their wares out onto the sides of the streets. We went to the vendor who sold plastic containers. My mom picked up one container and suddenly began yelling, "My watch! My watch!" Was she losing her mind over her watch? I grabbed her and asked her to stop, but she kept holding her wrist and saying, "My watch!" I looked at her wrist, and there it was - her treasured watch, perfectly strapped in place.

She explained that she had been filled with sadness and earnestly wished for it when suddenly she felt her wrist being grasped. When she looked down, her watch was on her wrist!

"For there is not a word on my tongue, but behold, O Lord, You know it altogether." Psalm 139:4, NKJV. He understands even our unspoken desires.

Yes, the Lord our God knows all our needs and provides them.

MARCH 11

IN GOD I WILL TRUST

Jeanette Muppiri

"I will say of the Lord, He is my refuge and my fortress; My God, in Him I will trust." "He shall call upon Me, and I will answer him..."

Psalm 91:2 &15, NKJV

During the Second World War, when the fighting reached Rangoon (Yangon), Burma (Myanmar,) we planned to flee to India. Only women and children were allowed to travel. So, my dad had to stay back.

Three ships were due to leave on the day we were to travel. We boarded the third ship. The direct route usually took two days. The first two ships took that route but were torpedoed. Our captain took a circuitous ten-day route, but we landed safely in India.

My dad could not communicate with us, so he had no idea whether or not we had made it safely across. However, in faith, he started out on foot, and after two months of walking through the jungles that border India and Burma, we were reunited.

We moved to the United States in 1986 and made our way past many challenges. I became a widow at the age of 51, and God helped me bear the loss of my husband, Noble. He led me with His mighty hand in a way only He could.

When I turned 73, my kidneys failed, and I have had to be on dialysis ever since. God saw me through every challenge.

I am over 80 now. Yes, there are struggles, but I keep repeating Psalm 103:1-5: "Bless the Lord O my soul."

He has been faithful to me, and I am now ready to go home when He calls.

Let us trust the Lord, who has promised to be our refuge and fortress.

MARCH 12

GOD REIGNS ETERNAL

Anonymous

"The Lord on high is mightier than the noise of many waters, Than the mighty waves of the sea."

Psalm 93:4, NKJV

Matthew 24 describes the condition of the world in the end times. The events are truly frightening – wars, famines, earthquakes, cruelty, grief, and pain. And all this is just the beginning! If this is just the beginning, how will anyone make it through?

As I was thinking about this, I realized that amidst all these trials, the one thing that remains the same is God's promises to us. The words in Psalms 93 give me inner comfort. The "noise of many waters" and "mighty waves of the sea" are expressions in the Bible that describe unrest, violence, and grave troubles among the people. Yes, the world will be in chaos and the people will be greatly distressed.

But verse 4 says that the Lord on high is mightier. He still reigns and has all things in control. He is still the absolute Ruler! Even though it may seem that the swollen waters are about to engulf us, we will be protected. He is "mightier than the mighty waves of the sea!" (verse 4) Our mighty God, whose "testimonies are very sure" (verse 5,) will make a way through the waves of the sea!

The events predicted in Matthew 24 are now occurring around us, and they are only the beginning. They will increase in intensity and will threaten our very existence. But we serve a God who is "mightier than the noise of many waters." He will keep us safe amidst the mighty waves of the sea – through the most troublesome times.

MARCH 13

EYES ON THE PRIZE

Nina Palivela

"Therefore, since we are surrounded by so great a cloud of witnesses, let us also lay aside every weight, and sin which clings so closely, and let us run with endurance the race that is set before us, looking to Jesus, the founder and perfecter of our faith. . ."

Hebrews 12:1,2, ESV

School was out, and we were going to the beach as a family. I was excited and anxious to get there as soon as possible. When we arrived, my little brother and I dashed into the cool blue waves but stayed close to the shore.

After a while, I heard, "Chelli! Chelli!" (my name) I looked around and saw my dad, some distance in the ocean, with a huge shell in his hand. The shell was beautiful, and it really tempted me. So I started out, ensuring that I kept him and the shell fixed in sight.

Then, suddenly, I saw an enormous wave coming. I turned to run back to the shoreline, but that monstrous wave overtook me and sent me spinning under the water. I felt it was the end for me!

Just then, a man nearby pulled me out of the water. "Thank you!" I gasped. I was safe and out of danger.

If that huge wave had not frightened me, and if I had just kept my eyes fixed on my dad, I would've reached him and got that shell.

The frightening things of this world may distract us. But if we look to "Jesus, the founder and perfecter of our faith," God will take care of us no matter what comes our way.

March 14

Personal Time With My Creator

Vidhya Melvin

"I can do all things through Christ who strengthens me."

Philippians 4:13, NKJV

One of the main challenges after I became a mother was to find time for personal spiritual growth. I seemed too busy. I knew this was not how it was supposed to be, and my guilt grew in me. I felt disconnected from the Holy Spirit and was convinced that I could not resolve the problem on my own.

But the thirst for a healthy spiritual experience was compelling. So, I kept praying about it. I really desired to spend the early morning hours in God's presence.

Then, suddenly, I started waking up from sleep every morning around three, without an alarm clock! It was truly refreshing to be in the presence of the Holy Spirit and realize that He was making my desire come true! I had a peaceful time reading the Bible and meditating undisturbed for about two hours.

Sometimes, my day would extend until midnight. Would the Holy Spirit wake me up at three again? To my surprise, I would wake up at about five in the morning on those days. It was as if the Holy Spirit knew exactly what I needed. Of course, He knew! God created us and knows all about the needs of our bodies.

He guided me as my Creator. He knew me better than me!!

Today, with three little children, God continues to help me with a healthy spiritual life. I feel blessed! May we all find the true joys of communion with God.

"When I awake, I am still with You." Psalms 139:18 NKJV

MARCH 15

MIRACLE HEALING

Atul Nowrangi

"And the prayer of faith shall save the sick, and the Lord shall raise him up; and if he have committed sins, they shall be forgiven him."

James 5:15, KJV

I was undergoing a surgical procedure when I went into cardiac arrest. I was revived but remained in a critical condition. My condition required care at a higher level, and I was transferred to a specialty hospital.

When I regained consciousness, my wife, who had been praying constantly, said, "Everyone is praying for you, and you will be alright." It was like a balm to my soul, and I left everything in God's hands with a sense of trust and confidence.

However, a few days later, came real bad news. My liver and my kidneys had shut down. In order to survive, I would need transplants, and we would have to wait for the organs to become available. The next sixty days were complex and full of challenges.

Then the unbelievable happened! My liver started to function again, and a few days later, my kidneys also regained their function!! I did not need any organ transplants at all! The chief physician treating me said, "When you first arrived here, I didn't think you would make it!"

On arriving back home from the hospital, I called for the SASDAC pastors to anoint me. It was a time of resounding praise to God.

My family and the members and pastors of SASDAC kept faith and did not give up. So, I can testify that miracles happen even today. This experience has greatly strengthened our faith in a prayer-answering and miracle-working God! Let us stay true to Him!

MARCH 16

HE WILL NOT LET YOU DROWN

Paul Suresh

"So do not fear, for I am with you; do not be dismayed, for I am your God. I will strengthen you and help you; I will uphold you with my righteous right hand."

Isaiah 41:10, NIV

It was a hot summer day at the Kutladampatti waterfall in Tamil Nadu. I was five years old and standing on a tall rock overlooking the waterfall and a small pool. My dad tightened one end of a saree around my waist as I stood ready to jump in.

"All right, jump!" he said, and I jumped in while my dad held the other end of the saree. I had the most exhilarating two minutes of my life until I saw the other end of the saree (the end that my dad was supposed to be holding) fall in front of me. Suddenly I was on my own and knew I could not swim! I opened my mouth to yell for help, but water rushed in and silenced me. I pushed my hand up and wildly waved for help. Just then, a hand grabbed my fingers and pulled me up. Instantly, I was back to safety, held up by my dad's strong hands.

Sometimes, we get submerged in trials and difficulties that seem to have no end. But God reminds us that He is right there and will never let us down. He will never let us drown in the problems of life. "So do not fear," because He has promised to get us through any crisis – big or small.

"When you pass…through the rivers they shall not overflow you." Isaiah 43:2, KJV.

Do not be dismayed if you are going through the rivers now; God will uphold you.

MARCH 17

NOT MEDICAL MATERIAL

Vijayan Charles

"But as it is written: 'Eye has not seen, nor ear heard, nor have entered into the heart of man, the things which God has prepared for those who love Him. But God has revealed them to us through His Spirit. For the Spirit searches all things, yes, the deep things of God.'"

I Corinthians 2:9,10, NKJV

Discouraged, I boarded the train at 11 pm. I was 19, and had just been turned down for medical sponsorship by the Southern Asia Division Selection Committee. I was not fit to be a doctor - "not medical material!" they said.

The train was crowded, and so, I sat at the doorway of the coach, grabbing the handrails on either side. It would be a long journey, with plenty of time to think. I thought of my mother, who would be devastated. All my life, she had proudly introduced me as, "my doctor son!"

Suddenly, I was awakened as the train braked hard and lurched as it approached a station. My heart was pounding, as I realized that I had fallen asleep! My arms were still gripping the metal bars on either side of the door. I could have easily fallen off the running train at any time!

At home, I recounted the experience to my mother. Her response was quick and confident: "You were not holding those bars, my son. God's angels held your hands. God has a grand plan for your life. One you cannot even imagine. Cheer up!"

One year later, I attended India's most prestigious medical school, "The All India Institute of Medical Sciences." God had His hand on me.

Are you experiencing a setback in life? Cheer up. God has grand plans for you.

March 18

Breathing By Faith

Mark David

". . . for assuredly I say to you, if you have faith as a mustard seed, you will say to this mountain, 'Move from here to there,' and it will move; and nothing will be impossible to you."

Matthew 17:20 NKJV.

I am 13 years old as I write this story.

My parents told me that I was born five and a half weeks earlier than expected. Being a premature baby, I could not breathe on my own as my lungs were not fully developed.

The doctors at Washington Adventist Hospital had to insert a breathing tube down my throat (called an endotracheal or ET tube) and administer a medication that was supposed to help open the air sacs in my lungs so I could breathe. My mom tells me that it is called artificial surfactant. The ET tube was then connected to a CPAP machine, which pushed air into my lungs to help me breathe. The doctors informed my parents that if the treatment did not work, I would have to be flown by emergency helicopter to a higher-level hospital for further management.

My parents prayed and cried to God the whole time. They put their faith in God, and He heard their earnest cries and had mercy on them and me. I started getting better within a couple of hours, and after two days, I could breathe independently. Without God's intervention, I would not have survived. I believe that God gave me a chance to live.

Whatever problems you may face today, trust God; He will see you through.

MARCH 19

TRUE FRIENDSHIP

Bimal Nowrangi

"Greater love has no one than this, that a person will lay down his life for his friends."

John 15:13, NASB

I have a very special project – trying to contact as many friends as possible from bygone days. It is thrilling to connect with them, especially old classmates. I was excited to talk with one of them after a gap of fifty-three years! We shared so many memories, but one incident from our boarding school days stood out.

Six of us students were called to help the cafeteria manager purchase and bring back the groceries from town. We climbed onto the tractor, which was hitched to a trailer. Once we loaded the groceries, there was no place for us in the trailer. So, we all sat crowded, rather uncomfortably on the tractor. The only spot my friend found was the drawbar that connected the trailer to the tractor, and he sat there in a precarious position, holding on for dear life! The fact was, he was not well and looked weak and tired. It would be dangerous for him to ride there. Seeing that, I offered to switch places with him.

Soon after, while negotiating the bends on the uneven dirt road, the tractor shook so violently that I was thrown off the bar onto the road. Fortunately, I sustained only minor injuries. How much more severe would have been the injuries if my sick, weak friend had been in my place!!

God, our dearest and best friend, looks out for us similarly! We owe our lives to Him. Let us learn to appreciate the true worth of His friendship!

MARCH 20

I WAS HEALED

Sheetal Nowrangi

"Heal me, Lord, and I will be healed; save me and I will be saved, for you are the one I praise."

Jeremiah 17:14, NIV

On our return flight from India, I started experiencing some flu-like symptoms. By the time we landed in Germany, the symptoms worsened. They had become so severe that we seriously considered breaking our journey to get treated. My husband and I prayed about it and decided to continue our trip to Washington DC.

The transatlantic flight was almost unbearable. By the time we reached Dulles Airport, I was so exhausted and weak that I nearly collapsed to the floor. All we could do at that point was pray.

We proceeded straight to the emergency room from the airport. The lab results showed that I had developed a very serious condition called septicemia (the bloodstream had become infected). Unless treated immediately and very vigorously, it quickly overwhelms the body's systems. The statistics regarding this condition are frightening. It is the third leading cause of death in the USA. One life is lost to this condition every two minutes in the USA!

During my hospital stay, I prayed every day for God's healing touch and requested anointing. I knew that healing would finally have to come from God. Over the next few days, I gradually recovered, and today, I am fully well again! I did not become a mere number in the statistics regarding this condition!

I believe that God intervened, and I will always be grateful to Him. He answered the prayers, and I give Him all the praise and thanksgiving!

When you need healing, call upon our God, and He will heal and save.

MARCH 21

MY PRAYER FOR A PATIENT

Sheetal Nowrangi

"Therefore I tell you, whatever you ask for in prayer, believe that you have received it, and it will be yours."

Mark 11:24, NIV

After graduating from nursing school, my first posting was at the SDA Hospital in Shimla, India. During a night shift, I was assigned to take care of a five-year-old girl, who had started to bleed from her nose and mouth. Our treatments didn't seem to stop the bleeding, which was getting worse. The child's parents (who were of the Sikh faith) sensed that things were not going well. They became alarmed and began to cry.

I had noticed the desperation on their faces, so after my shift was over, I returned to the child's room. I tried to speak comforting and consoling words to the parents and then offered to pray. "If it is okay with you, I would like to pray for your child." The parents immediately and gratefully accepted the offer. "Please!" they said, "Please pray!" I prayed in Hindi, the language the parents could understand, and asked for healing for the girl and comfort for the parents, and then went home.

Three days later, I was told that the patient's condition had improved dramatically after my visit and prayer, and she had been discharged home to her parents. The following week, the parents came to the hospital church and gave an offering of thanks. They appreciated the prayer offered for their child and the fact that God had answered.

I have continued this practice of praying with my patients whenever permitted, because I know that we have a prayer-hearing God who cares.

Let us pray for ourselves and others. He is the one who heals the sick.

March 22

Fear Not

Anonymous

"Fear not, for I am with you; Be not dismayed, for I am your God. I will strengthen you, Yes, I will help you, I will uphold you with my righteous right hand."

Isaiah 41:10, NKJV

I was traveling by train from Bangalore (Bengaluru) to Surat for my first job. I had about four hundred rupees in hand to pay for transport and other expenses. Just prior to boarding, we realized that the gender printed on my ticket was wrong, and there was nothing we could do about it!

The first ticket examiner came by and inspected my ticket but didn't notice the gender. I felt relieved. However, a second examiner came by after a few hours and wanted to check our tickets. He noticed the problem, looked at the ticket and then at me, several times before saying that since I was not a man, it would amount to an illegal way to travel – on false identity. No amount of explanation by me, or all the other passengers around me, moved him. "You have to leave the train now, or pay a fine of Rs. 400!"

I took out all the money I had and gave it to him. I turned towards the window and put my hands over my face to hide my tears. Overwhelmed with fear, all I could do was close my eyes, silently pray, and take my problem to God. When I opened my eyes, there was a person in front of me, smiling and extending a wad of bills that amounted to Rs. 600! The passengers had taken up a collection for me!

"Fear not," is mentioned 365 times in the Bible – once for each day of the year! God stands by His word each day!

March 23

Our Incredible Journey

Energy James

"For He shall give His angels charge over you, to keep you in all your ways."

Psalm 91:11, NKJV

At the start of our life journey together, my husband, Daniel James, and I made plans to come to the USA. Daniel came first, and then one year later, our older son, Raja and I left India to join him in Takoma Park, Maryland. We were supposed to land at the Dulles International Airport in Virginia, and I don't know how, but we found ourselves at the Dallas International Airport in Texas!! I did not have the faintest clue that Dulles was different from Dallas! I felt utterly lost, frightened, and helpless in an unknown, strange, foreign place. I had no idea how to get to the correct airport! I remember closing my eyes and praying for help. But how would the help come?

Soon, two ladies, complete strangers, approached me and began to help me. They helped with rebooking our tickets, food, transportation, and a room to stay overnight. They helped with all the details to finally get us to Dulles. I would have never made it on my own. Even now, half a century later, I think of that experience as a nightmare! But I also remember that God answered my cry and sent me those "angels" to provide help.

The verses that comforted me during that scary and perplexing time were: "My help comes from the Lord who made heaven and earth." Psalm 121:2. "God is our refuge and strength, A very present help in trouble." Psalm 46:1 NKJV.

My heart is filled with gratitude for the unknown "angels."

You are never alone!

MARCH 24

GOD'S GRACE IS LIMITLESS

Merlin Ponraj

"...My grace is sufficient for you, for My power is made perfect in weakness."

II Corinthians 12:9, NIV

A routine mammogram in 2018 revealed a suspicious growth, and I reluctantly agreed to a needle biopsy. The report came back as cancer! I was distressed and began to cry initially, but then I went to the Bible for comfort and strength and placed my crisis before Him. I prayed, "I want to be close to you and not falter. Please give me a good attitude to go through the treatment."

The surgeon proposed surgery followed by radiation, but I didn't want the radiation. So, I prayed about it, and God answered my request. Yes, I had to undergo multiple surgeries (including a mastectomy, during which complications developed, causing significant loss of blood). Still, I didn't need radiation, recovered quickly and was healed. Strength came back in sufficient measure so that I could care for my two granddaughters.

I was encouraged and strengthened by our SASDAC pastors, who came home, prayed, and read God's promises from the Bible. Others visited and supported me, including my sister from California. All of them were like angels of comfort and mercy.

The promises in the Bible provide me with so much confidence:

"The Lord will sustain him on his sickbed and restore him from his bed of illness." Psalm 41:3.

"Have mercy on me, O God, have mercy on me, for in you my soul takes refuge." Psalm 57:1. "

"See, I have refined you though not as silver; I have tested you in the furnace of affliction." Isaiah 48:10.

MARCH 25

GOD'S PLAN NEVER FAILS

Sahasramsu Prabhakar

"Why art thou cast down, O my soul? And why art thou disquieted in me? Hope thou in God: for I shall yet praise him for the help of his countenance."

Psalm 42:5, KJV

This verse helped me cope during my college years. I would study hard, do all-nighters, and sacrifice sleep to get good grades. Then, the report card would show a grade far below expectations. It is a terrible feeling, making it so easy to get discouraged, give up, and let yourself go into all forbidden paths. But this is Satan's way to get us to cut our relationship with God.

I was going along this path when I came across a group of Seventh-day Adventist students on our college campus. We were similar in age and understood the demands of college life and the difficulties in holding faith on a secular campus. Meeting with this group really helped. I felt supported by those who shared my faith and ideals and was able to resist the temptation to go out all on my own.

One of the members confessed that if he had not found this group, he would have become a party animal and gone down a dark path away from God. I realized that I, too, would have slipped into those ways, if I had not kept meeting with the group. God, in His mercy, had made plans for me so that I would not lose faith, and I began to trust wholly in Him.

Now, when I get sad or disheartened, I remember this verse: "Hope thou in God." Psalm 42:5, KJV.

MARCH 26

I WILL GLORIFY GOD

Sybil Paul

"Call upon me in the day of trouble; I will deliver you, and you shall glorify Me."

Psalm 50:15, NKJV

My husband had health issues when in India and had to be hospitalized more than once. Then, in 2011, I got a call from Jaipur saying that he was in a critical condition and might not survive. He needed to be hospitalized immediately; however, protocols delayed the ambulance because I was not there to sign certain documents. The doctors and others urged me to get to Jaipur immediately, but my work supervisor would not grant me leave. My daughter went in place of me. Naturally, I felt greatly distressed, saddened, and very helpless.

All I could do was pray for my husband and pray that I get leave to go. I wanted to be there by his side. When my leave was finally approved, my supervisor warned me that the work position might not be available for me when I returned. That created another heavy burden, but I went anyway, praying that God would take care of this problem too.

I reached Jaipur to find out that my husband had a severe respiratory problem, which could be life-threatening. But, with good treatment and nursing care, things began to improve, and soon, he was out of danger. He got well enough to travel and came back home in 2012.

Things didn't go well at first when I got back to work, but that problem was solved, and everything turned out fine!

I know God answered all my prayers at a critical time, and I am genuinely thankful to Him.

Call upon God in the day of trouble, and He will deliver. Let us call upon Him in good times, too.

MARCH 27

JUST LOOK UP

Reina Morse

"Lift up your eyes and look to the heavens: who created all these? He who brings out the starry host one by one and calls each of them by name. Because of His great power and mighty strength, not one of them is missing."

Isaiah 40:26, NIV.

There are days when I feel really small. I wake up in that mood, and seeing those around me living their best and becoming successful, makes me feel unimportant and insignificant. I feel lonely and isolate myself, which makes me feel even lonelier.

It was hard to get out of that valley of despair until I found a way to feel comforted. I hope it helps you.

Whenever I begin to feel alone, I go outside and appreciate the world around me – the cool fresh air, the trees gently swaying in the breeze, and the glow of the evening sky with its remarkable shades of purple, pink, and orange. But the real show starts when the sun has finally disappeared, and the stars emerge.

I'm amazed at how the stars come in so many different sizes and degrees of brightness. What a stunning display of the beauty of the universe!

If God purposefully placed them there, and Isaiah 40:26 says that not one is missing, then I can be sure He has placed me where I am for a purpose. I am not an accident or a mistake, but was intended and planned. What a reassuring message!

So, when you go through a valley, look up and know that you are loved and planned. You are the apple of His eye! (Deuteronomy 32:10. Zechariah 2:8)

March 28

The Journey

Richard T Christian

"I will…teach you in the way you should go; I will guide you with my eye."

Psalm 32:8, NKJV

During the summer of 2019, I attended an international camporee held in Oshkosh, Wisconsin. Leading up to the trip, I had become anxious because I had never been that far away from home and had never stayed away for so long. However, my fears became less as I reflected on my past experiences.

In 2014, I attended a Christian summer camp at Mt. Aetna, only about an hour away. There, we were encouraged to be active in learning. Recreational activities, including flag football, swimming, soccer, and hiking, made the experience so enjoyable that I did not miss home. However, it was the spiritual emphasis that made the camp truly memorable. Learning Bible verses with my counselor in those peaceful surroundings helped me to connect with God in a fresh new way.

Remembering such a wonderful experience took away some of my anxiety, and I looked forward to the trip to Oshkosh, although I knew that the camp's enormous size of over 50,000 pathfinders would provide a very different experience.

The bus journey was long, and when we reached our destination, with its wide open spaces and fresh air, I wondered whether Oshkosh would have the same impact as Mt. Aetna. But once we started, the events prepared for the campers offered me a spiritual experience and a closeness to God even more incredible than those I had felt at Mt. Aetna!

My physical journey from Mt. Aetna to Oshkosh was like my spiritual journey from one level to the next.

MARCH 29

REPEATED RENEWAL

Shifali Mathews

"Therefore, if anyone is in Christ, he is a new creation; old things have passed away; behold, all things have become new."

II Corinthians 5:17, NKJV

One of the most difficult challenges I experienced was undergoing surgery to remove a mass from my liver. However, when I recovered, I felt like a new person! When I described this to a mentor, she told me how she, too, felt the same way after a similar procedure – like a new person!

The liver is one of the most fascinating organs in the human body. Before our birth, it produces blood, and it continues to filter our blood throughout our lives at 1.5 liters per minute. It is the most versatile organ and has over 200 functions involving every physiological process in the body. But to me, the most remarkable feature is its ability to grow again. It is the only organ that can completely regenerate to nearly its original size and function, even when as little as 25% is left!

These fantastic abilities illustrate God's multiple and diverse roles in our lives. He is our Comforter, Redeemer, Friend, Helper, Guide, Counselor, Father, and much more! And He knows what to provide each one, in the right amount, at the right time!

When the liver grows back, it does so in three perfectly timed phases: communication, proliferation, and termination. That is the picture of my God! He has a constant communication open to us, abundantly blesses us, and does not stop restoring us until our time on earth is done.

If we let Him, God will continually recreate us until everything is made new! Trust Him!

March 30

Our Great Wall

Shikha Mathews

"I will say of the LORD, He is my refuge and my fortress: my God; in Him will I trust."

Psalm 91:2, KJV

One of the things I love to do is travel and see places. My travels took me to China recently, and I had the privilege of seeing and climbing the Great Wall of China! Its beginning can be traced back to the fifth century BC. It is over 13,000 miles long, 16 to 26 feet tall, 15 to 30 feet wide at the base, and 9 to 12 feet at the top. It is the only man-made structure that can be identified from space. It was primarily constructed by soldiers and convicts who were serving prison sentences of hard labor. Over 400,000 people died during the construction, and many workers were buried into the wall itself!

It is not just a plain wall but has guard towers, beacon towers, stairways, bridges, and battlements. It served as an almost impassable barrier and protected the Chinese Empire against invaders who tried to overrun it repeatedly. The Chinese dynasties felt safe because of their wall.

We generally rely on physical protection, but the real protection we need is from the living God. "As the mountains surround Jerusalem, So, the LORD surrounds His people." Psalm 125:2. No, we don't need a vast wall visible from space. Instead, God is our great wall, who has promised to watch over us and protect us like a mighty fortress. "I will say of the LORD, He is my refuge and my fortress: my God; in Him will I trust."

MARCH 31

JUST BE HELD

Nischitha Pedapudi

"Thus says the Lord, the God of David your father: I have heard your prayer, I have seen your tears; surely I will heal you."

II Kings 20:5, NKJV

I am honored to have been the first grandchild in my family. My grandparents helped raise me. So, we were close and had a very special bond!

Then, suddenly, I lost my grandfather. I was shocked and devastated! I had wanted him to witness so many things in my life – my graduation, baptism, and so much more. I felt there was now a giant black hole in my heart. He had been my mentor, who had the type of relationship with God that I aspired to have.

In my grief, I became angry and blamed God. I tried to disregard my pain, pick myself up, and move on without God. However, I couldn't because my pain and anger wouldn't let me go.

During this dark experience, I remembered my grandfather's words: "Everything God does is for a reason." I realized that God didn't take him away to hurt us. Rather, in His infinite wisdom, God had taken him away for a greater purpose than I could understand. The realization that there could be a purpose higher than mine started building my trust in Him, and it became stronger than ever!

When hurting and despairing, the answer is not to blame God, but to turn to Him. No matter how strongly we feel that we can fix ourselves, the truth is only He can pick up our broken pieces. As the popular Casting Crown song states, our job is to "Just Be Held."

APRIL 1

FRIENDS TO FRIENDSHIP WITH JESUS

Sheetal Nowrangi

"The fruit of the righteous is a tree of life and he who wins souls is wise."

Proverbs 11:30 NKJV

In 2003, I worked alongside several other nurses for the Ministry of Defense in Muscat, Oman. It was a Muslim community, and the employer provided accommodation for most female employees in a gated compound. We were from different countries and also of varying faiths.

Some of us, including those of the Catholic faith, decided to meet together regularly to discuss Bible texts, and sing songs. I taught them many of the choruses I had learned while growing up in Adventist schools.

During one of the meetings, I introduced the book, The Great Controversy, to the group. Many felt uncomfortable with the subject and avoided reading it. However, one of my friends started to show interest and ask questions. As we began studying earnestly, I introduced her to my father, Pr. P. N. Bazroy (a retired preacher at that time, who was well known in Ranchi, India.) She began to attend the Muscat SDA church regularly and continued studying the Scriptures. However, she wanted to explore them deeper and went to Ranchi, to study the Bible with my father. After thoroughly going through the teachings, she joined the SDA church and was baptized by my father.

She remains an active member of the Muscat Adventist church today. She recently visited me in the USA with her brother, a Catholic priest. We continue to pray that she will be a shining light to those with whom she comes into contact.

May our friendships with people help them to blossom into friendship with Jesus.

April 2

God Wants Me

Hallie Rozario

"Come, let us return to the Lord. He has torn us to pieces but He will heal us; He has injured us but He will bind up our wounds."

Hosea 6:1, NIV

For as long as I could remember, I had prayed before going to bed. I never imagined this habit would stop, but in the summer of 2018, it did, when I had to undergo surgery to correct my bow legs.

Firstly, it took a very long time to schedule it. Secondly, it was not just one, but a series of 3 surgeries over a period of 7 months. Then, I had to go for regular painful physiotherapy sessions. I sat up countless nights, frustrated and angry: "God, why is this happening to me? When will this nightmare end? What did I do to deserve this?"

I thought God needed me more than I needed Him. So, to get back at Him for my hard times, I decided to stop praying and reading the Bible. It got to the point that I felt I was too far gone, and I stubbornly refused to turn back! Walking and talking with God was just not on my cards!

Then, one day, my pastor said words that touched me deeply. "God does not need us; He simply wants us because He loves us." Really?! That changed everything for me. I saw that I was the one angry for no reason!

I then prayed, "God, it is so wonderful to realize that You want me." And when I returned to Him, there He was with loving and open arms!

"Come let us return to the Lord. . ."

April 3

Walk and Talk With The Lord

Kavitha E Joseph

"I say then: Walk in the Spirit, and you shall not fulfill the lust of the flesh."

Galatians 5:16, NKJV

There is a quarter-mile race track on the school grounds near our house. It is well-maintained and used by community members for walking and jogging. I prefer walking in company so that I can talk while I walk. So, I asked my family to join me, but I was walking at a different pace and soon found myself alone. Now, walking alone was not only boring, but my mind quickly slipped into negative topics and memories when alone. So to keep myself occupied, I decided to talk with God. I planned to walk for one hour, covering ten laps at about 6 minutes a lap. I decided to pray for one particular topic during each lap.

As I did this, I realized that the walks were not boring; the time seemed to fly by. My mind was occupied with things I needed to share with God and the requests I wanted to place before Him. It was easier doing it here undisturbed than at work during the day.

People walk for various reasons – for health benefits (exercise, relaxation, weight loss) or a specific cause. My experience became so enjoyable that I now had a new purpose for walking – to spend quality time with my God, and I began to look forward to the times on the school grounds.

Walking is no longer just exercise but a wonderful time of communion with the Lord, bringing joy, comfort, and peace. Join me in walking with a purpose!

April 4

Angels By The Road?

Amod Hansdak

"For he shall give his angels charge over thee, to keep thee in all thy ways."

Psalm 91:11, KJV

"I'm going with Grandpa," I told my mom. At seven, I found words of admonition at home an unpleasant experience. So, when my grandpa had come to visit and described life in the village, I wanted to go there. I would avoid the limits placed upon me at home and be free.

Permission was granted, and we started in the morning by bus. After a couple of hours, the bus stopped for a restroom break. Grandpa got down, but I stayed on the bus. When the bus started to move again, I frantically looked for my grandpa. I hadn't seen him board the bus. What should I do? What would I do at the journey's end? I was greatly alarmed.

Just when the bus was about to pick up speed, the driver suddenly stopped it. The passengers looked around, wondering why it had stopped. And then, to my great relief, I saw Grandpa board the bus.

He had run after it, trying to catch up, but the bus was gathering speed, and he could never make it. Just then, some people dressed in white, some distance ahead of the bus, signaled to the driver to stop. When he did, Grandpa caught up.

Forty years later, I passed by that spot. It was out in a very lonely place. Who were those men who stopped the bus? Could they have been angels since they wore white?! If there is a video of this in heaven, I'd love to sit down and watch it!

God will use even angels to help us if needed. What a mighty God we worship!

APRIL 5

WHY WORRY?

Serena K Thummalapalli

"Therefore, I tell you, do not worry about your life..."

Matthew 6:25, NIV

Junior never seems to worry. He can hardly be called independent or self-sufficient. He relies totally on me and my husband for everything. We feed him and make sure he is looked after; and he is sure we will supply all his needs. So, he enjoys a care-free life!

Junior is our pet dog. He is always happy, playful, friendly and lives in the moment. I've never seen him get stressed about his future, or what other dogs think of him, or anxious about growing older.

On the other hand, we humans live in a world of constant worry and stress. We worry about our jobs, our finances, our health, our status etc., in a never-ending list of challenges. I often wish I were more like our dog, Junior – free of stress!

But, thinking again: Just like Junior has us to take care of all his needs, we have a wonderful heavenly Father who is all-powerful and lovingly takes care of us in an even more understanding way! Jesus said, "Look at the birds of the air; they do not sow or reap or store away in barns, and yet your heavenly Father feeds them. Are you not much more valuable than they?" Matthew 6: 26, NIV.

Junior encourages me daily with his positive attitude and reminds me of God's promises of grace, love, and protection. "Cast all your anxiety on him because he cares for you." I Peter 5:7, NIV. What a reassuring promise! Why worry!

Let us live worry-free lives, knowing that our Heavenly Father cares for us.

April 6

Rivers of Babylon

Merlyn Fernando

"Beside the rivers of Babylon, we thought about Jerusalem, and we sat down and cried. We hung our small harps on the willow trees. . .our enemies shouted, 'Sing about Zion.'"

Psalm 137:1-3, CEV

The song "By the Rivers of Babylon" was written by Boney M and sung by a Jamaican reggae group in 1970. It gained international recognition in 1972, following the movie "The Harder They Come." The words are from Psalm 137, to which are added the words from Psalm 19, "Let the words of my mouth and the meditation of my heart. . ."

Years ago, we lived near an expensive tourist hotel in Kandy, Sri Lanka. Every night, the live band at the hotel played and sang this song as the final piece of their performance. The band – led by Catholic youth, seemed to answer the question, "How can we sing the Lord's song in a strange land?" There they were, in a predominantly non-Christian country, among tourists belonging to many creeds or no creed at all!! They made the words, "Yeah, we wept," a benediction to everyone every night. It was sung to all in the hotel, for they too, were counted among God's children.

Similarly, Daniel "sang" about his hero, God, on the banks of the river Euphrates, in the region where his God had once planted paradise, even though it had now become the strange and unbelieving empire of Babylon.

Our hospital staff befriended the singers, and twenty years later, they performed at one of our events. Singing in a strange land fosters harmony and depicts God's grace.

Let us sing the Lord's songs no matter where we are.

April 7

God Knows Best

Bimal Nowrangi

"Whether you turn to the right or to the left, your ears will hear a voice behind you saying, 'This is the way, walk in it.'"

Isaiah 30:21, NIV

While a student at Spicer Memorial College in India, a friend asked two of us to join him on an extended cycling tour from Pune to Hyderabad, more than 350 miles away. We readily agreed and made the necessary preparations.

We rented brand-new bicycles, gathered enough provisions of bread, peanut butter, and jelly to last the entire trip, and got ready. Early one morning, the three of us started on the highway heading south. We were barely on the road for two hours when one of us changed his mind and turned around to return to the college without any explanation.

The two of us decided to carry on. We consulted our road maps and noted that Aurangabad's world-famous Ajanta and Ellora Caves (carved on the mountainside by Buddhist monks between 200 BC and 650 AD) were close to our route. We also visited another tourist site, a mausoleum bearing a striking resemblance to another world-famous edifice, the Taj Mahal in Agra. Overall, it was an enjoyable and memorable ride covering 400 miles!

When we returned, feeling tired but fulfilled, we learned that the friend who had returned had fallen very ill. We then realized that our trip would have been curtailed if not stopped altogether, and he would have fared much worse if he had been on the road with us when struck with sickness.

God is in charge. We should be willing to trust His leadership in all aspects of our lives.

APRIL 8

REMEMBER THE WONDERS OF OLD

Anonymous

"But I will remember the years of the right hand of the Most High..."

Psalm 77:10, NKJV

It is beautiful to share God's marvelous works in the world, but even more wonderful to share the changes that God works within us.

COVID brought significant changes to my life, both physically and mentally. My general health was worsening when my physician said that there was a problem that could be diagnosed only by surgery. That sounded truly scary! It struck terror in my heart. Then came the unavoidable question: "Why, Lord? Is it my past sins?" My faith wavered, and my fears grew stronger.

During this time of anguish and turmoil, I turned to the Bible to look for comfort to my troubled mind. When I opened it, my eyes fell on Psalm 77, and I was amazed. The words accurately depicted my very own feelings and questions. "Will God reject forever? Will He never show favor again? Has He, in anger, forgotten to be compassionate?" Tears rolled down my cheeks as I read, because God also showed me the answer. Verse 10 reads, "Remember the years of the right hand of the Most High." Those words spoke directly to me as if to say, "His arm, which has led you thus far, will see you through."

I went through the surgery. It went well, and the diagnosis was not what we had feared.

The Almighty God who rules the heavens also knows about the sparrow that falls to the ground. The chapter that asked the questions also provided the answers. He sees each tear that drops and hears us when we call.

April 9

A Nest Among The Stars

Biju Thomas

"Except the LORD build the house, they labor in vain that build it: except the LORD keep the city, the watchman waketh but in vain."

Psalm 127:1, KJV

In the late 70s, we woke up one morning to the shocking news of the impending danger from a spacecraft that would fall over the city of Bangalore (Bengaluru), where we lived. We were young and wide-eyed and spoke in hushed tones about the "Skylab" that would crash to earth and end all our dreams.

The Skylab was the first space station operated by the United States, and now, after six years, its gradually reducing orbit would cause it to re-enter Earth's atmosphere and crash into the Earth. The descent began on July 11, 1979. Before its re-entry, the ground controllers at NASA adjusted the re-entry point to minimize the risk of debris falling over populated areas. The debris scattered over the Indian Ocean and unpopulated regions of Australia.

The grand purpose of the space program was to ensure the survival of the human race in case of a planetary disaster. If humans colonized space, they would be safe from all the calamities on Earth.

But we now know that the solar system and the galaxy are so structured that an escape would be impossible. We could not build a nest among the stars to keep us safe. However, we have a God who controls all things on earth and in space, and if we entrust our all to Him, He will provide safety against any celestial disaster that threatens us.

Let us trust our loving God to lead us into the future.

April 10

An Ever-Present Help

Bimal Nowrangi

"...God is our refuge and strength, an ever-present help in trouble."

Psalm 46:1, NIV

During our trip to India in 2007, four of us did some sightseeing around Falakata in West Bengal. We went in a small Maruti car to a safari park nearby to see wild animals in their natural habitat. From a tall watchtower, we enjoyed the scenes of large herds of deer, bison and elephants grazing peacefully in the valley below.

It was beginning to get dark when we decided to head back home. The driver started the car, but it wouldn't move because its tiny wheels were stuck in the slimy forest soil. We were unable to push it out either. As the darkness deepened, we could hear the eerie hooting of owls and the howling of jackals nearby, which increased the thought of our dangerous situation in the wild. How would we get back?

We decided to pray. The driver started the car and, to our great relief, it came out of the muddy puddle! We could see the outlines of very large animals and several pairs of glowing eyes through the foggy glare of the car headlights. Those animals were the heavily built bison, just 30 feet away!

They may appear to be harmless at a distance but are known to be more ferocious and dangerous than bears or wolves, and have caused more injuries and loss of life compared to them.

We had gone there with benign intentions but found ourselves in deep trouble. God graciously kept us safe. So also, when surrounded with dangers lurking all around, He will be our present help in trouble.

April 11

God Heard My Heart's Prayer

Daisy Sharlin

"Delight yourself also in the Lord, and He shall give you the desires of your heart."

Psalm 37:4, NKJV

In December 2014, my church in Singapore hosted a year-end Thanksgiving prayer meeting and dinner, after which the pastor asked us to write down our wishes for the coming year, 2015, on a card.

Working in Singapore while my son was in India filled me with great loneliness. I longed to have my family complete and be with him. So, I took the card and wrote down my heart's deepest wish – to be back with my son and have the togetherness of a real family. I turned the card in, and the pastor took all our cards and prayed over them.

Whenever I missed the church service in Singapore, I would tune in to the online SASDAC church service. In early 2015, when listening to the SASDAC service, I felt truly blessed with the song, "Alpha and Omega" sung by the group "His Voice." I expressed my thanks to the group. That moment of inspiration started a flow of events through which God clearly worked.

Amazingly, things turned out just right, and I was granted the togetherness of a wonderful family and the reuniting with my son – all in 2015 – precisely according to my heart's deep wishes!!

Today, when I look at my family, my loving husband, and my son living right here with me, my heart is lifted up with joy, and I cannot but give thanks to the One who hears our prayers and, in mercy, grants us our heart's desires. "Bless the Lord, O my soul!" Psalm 103:1, KJV.

Let us delight in the Lord.

April 12

Beans and Eggs

Bimal Nowrangi

"Test me in this," says the Lord Almighty, "and see if I will not throw open the floodgates of heaven and pour out so much blessings that there will not be enough room to store it."

Malachi 3:10, NIV

During the early years of our married life, my wife and I lived on the campus of Spicer Memorial College (Spicer Adventist University,) where I served as a teacher. All the family expenses had to be met from my salary, since my wife was not employed. Making ends meet was difficult, but our faith in God's provisions was strong.

Some staff members resorted to novel means to supplement their income, like growing a kitchen garden or keeping a small poultry farm.

One day, a fellow staff member gave us two bean seeds. We planted them in the tiny plot of ground in front of our house. Both bean plants grew profusely and bore an abundance of beans throughout the year! We ate them daily, but we had so much that we began sharing them with others.

Another day, a young man came with five hens in a basket, asked for a loan of twenty rupees, and left the hens with us. But he never returned, and we had five hens for a mere twenty rupees. The hens laid more eggs than we needed. We had beans and eggs every day and still had a surplus to share with others!

Two small blessings made abundant to the point of overflowing revealed to us God's amazing power to provide in times of need!

When in need, turn to God and remember Malachi 3:10

April 13

LEGACY OF KINDNESS

Anita Samuel

"...Let us not love in word, neither in tongue; but in deed and in truth."

I John 3:18, KJV

I grew up in Bangalore (Bengaluru), the Garden City of India. I found it awesome and trendy back in the 80s – a city vibrant with music and rich with cultural values and religious diversity. In 1979, an American missionary, Dorothy Watts, came to live there. She decided to take poor orphans under her wings because she understood the painful journey that they had gone through and wanted to make their lives worth living in the coming years.

Her humility, love, and kindness for those disadvantaged children in Bengaluru and the neighboring states in South India resulted in the birth and development of Sunshine Home. She was a light to those who grew up there and was an instrument in God's hands to show the love of Jesus to many children through teachings and music. Gospel music is still an integral part of Sunshine Home.

She was a mother and comforter to the children and a source of inspiration to many women across the globe. Her work and influence spread, and in 40 years, the Sunshine SDA Church, Sunshine SDA School, and Sunshine School of Music grew out of those small beginnings.

The warmth of her kindness still radiates at Sunshine Home, and unknown to her, the legacy of her love has continued for generations. I know all this firsthand because I am a child raised at Sunshine Home, and I am proud to say that!

God's love takes its course if we let Jesus be our focus.

April 14

An Answered Prayer

Shantha Thummalapalli

"Blessed are the pure in heart: for they shall see God."

Matthew 5:8, KJV

This verse became real and meaningful to me in December 2016.

During the previous 11 months, I had watched my husband go downhill. Once a strong husband and father of four, he was now so frail that he could not walk and, at times, did not even recognize us. He then developed fever, abdominal pain, nausea, and vomiting and was hospitalized, but it got worse, and he became unresponsive. After two weeks in the ICU, the doctors gave up hope: "There's nothing more we can do."

That evening, I sat alone at his bedside and, with unbearable sadness, recounted our 40 years together. I put my head on his chest and pleaded with God to hear my cry and wake him up. It was 11 pm, and I fell into a deep sleep. Suddenly, I heard someone talking. I glanced around and then looked at my husband. His eyes were fixed on the ceiling. The words he said, with one arm stretched out and the other tapping his chest, will stay with me for the rest of my life: "How fortunate I am to see God!" I shook him gently. He looked at me and said simply, "I am hungry!"

I ran to the nursing station, "He is awake and talking!" The nurses and doctors could not believe it and ran into the room to see for themselves.

That night, I saw my husband smile again after a long time! God had woken him up!

Sometimes, God will show Himself face to face, and we will never be the same.

April 15

God of Possibilities

Rajam Edison

"But He said, 'The things that are impossible with men are possible with God.'"

Luke 18:27, NKJV

I have had many experiences in which God has shown me His love and understanding.

Before I came to the USA, I had to go to the embassy in India to complete some urgent paperwork. I went along with my uncle, the late Mr. N.T.N. David. When we arrived at the embassy, many people were already in line, waiting to get in. I knew we would have to wait a long time to get in and finish our work.

While we waited in that crowd, an embassy car arrived and a young gentleman got out and walked towards the building. But just before he entered, he looked around and saw my uncle. He waved his hand, gesturing for us to see him. Suddenly, we found ourselves in front of that whole line and the first to enter.

We went into his office, and he asked the purpose of our visit. When we explained it to him, he said he could do it for us and that we needn't wait in line. He told us to return in the evening, and everything would be ready for us! When we returned, they had our documents ready.

Amid that crowd, God allowed the young gentleman to spot my uncle and call him in. Truly amazing!

All we need to do is remember to be still and know that we worship a God who makes ways for His children who trust Him. He is the God of possibilities. He makes possible the things that are impossible with men.

April 16

Second Chance

Soosan Varghese

"You have allowed me to suffer much hardship, but will restore me to life again."

Psalm 71:20 NLT

My husband and I go for a long walk near our home on Sunday mornings. We get onto the hiking/mountain biking dirt trail that runs across bridges over streams and enjoy the beauty of nature.

Since our children grew up and left home, I have made it a point to send them a daily morning greeting with a Scripture verse in a beautiful picture. Sometimes, the picture is from an interesting sight on our walk. One day, I was looking for a good subject for a photograph when I noticed a tree stump on the side of the trail. The Park and Recreation maintenance team had probably cut the tree to clear the path for the hikers and bikers. It was about 4 inches in diameter and barely 2 inches in height – a young tree felled so early in its life. A sad thought when compared to human life!

But on looking closely, I noticed a new shoot sprouting from the side. I had found my subject. I focused my camera and took a photograph of this regeneration.

It was a wonderful reminder of how God gives us second chances when we mess up in life. The God of the Bible is a God of Grace who offers second chances and more!

Let's find courage when facing defeat, knowing that God never gives up on us. He is ready to regenerate us even after our worst days. What a loving God! If we forget Him and stumble, He lifts us and allows us to walk again.

April 17

Crafty Little Foxes

Bimal Nowrangi

"Catch for us the foxes, the little foxes that ruin the vineyards, our vineyards that are in bloom."

Song of Solomon 2:15, NIV

When we lived in Maharashtra, India, we lived right across a few vineyards. We often saw cute-looking foxes roaming around. Our young children used to take pride in spotting them and counting them.

Foxes are found throughout North America, Europe, Asia, Australia, and Africa. The smallest foxes grow to be 14 to 16 inches long and weigh 7 to 12 pounds. They are omnivorous and are known to eat prickly fruit like the red and purple knobs on cacti, wild grapes, as well as large insects and small prey.

Their slanted eyes make them look sly, and they are always alert, moving swiftly and stealthily in search of food. Though they look small and cute, they are a menace to vineyards because they damage the tender vines loaded with grapes. The owners often use pet dogs and decoys like scarecrows and firecrackers to drive them away.

Like the small foxes who damage the tender vines loaded with luscious fruit, being careless on minor points and in little things can also damage our lives. Things of great value often get destroyed when we overlook little things.

Our precious crop – our lives – need to be protected and saved. We must guard against the tiny influences that slip in like little foxes and wreak havoc.

"Above all else, guard your heart, for everything you do flows from it." Proverbs 4:23, NIV. If we ask God, He will give us the grace and wisdom to guard against the crafty little foxes that destroy lives.

April 18

Living in Awe

Helina Somervell

"Therefore, since we are receiving a kingdom that cannot be shaken, let us be thankful, and so worship God acceptably with reverence and awe."

Hebrews 12:28, NIV

It was January of 2005, a very special moment for us. We had waited for this a long time – 10 years to be exact! As we held our newborn son, we were overcome with a flood of emotions. It was wonderful beyond words!

Maybe you've felt it watching a spectacular sunset or recollecting how carefully God has led you all these years. What sweeps over you at those moments is awe.

Even today, after all these years, there is a unique moving and stirring in my heart when I see my son – a lovely reminder of hopelessness restored to hope by God's mercy and grace. I am frequently reminded of this and am simply in awe of His goodness!

Were Mary Magdalene and the other Mary in awe when an angel delivered the most important and consequential news in history – one of universal hope, joy, and purpose? Did they live daily in awe of Jesus' resurrection?

The central event in human history – the life, death, and resurrection of Jesus – provided each of us with complete and free redemption – a priceless gift. The early Christian church lived in constant awe. They devoted themselves to the apostles' teachings, and God performed many signs and wonders among them. They shared their meals, possessions, prayers, and commitment to the community. Can this be our purpose as a church today?

May God give us a sense of awe regarding Jesus and the courage to build relationships that lead to love, harmony, and purpose.

April 19

A Way Out

Bimal Nowrangi

"Behold, I will do a new thing; now it shall spring forth; Shall ye not know it? I will even make a way in the wilderness, and rivers in the desert."

Isaiah 43:19, KJV

We had served on the faculty of Spicer Memorial College, India, for some years when the college president called my wife and me to his office and informed us that we had been sponsored for advanced studies in the Philippines. Our three young children were to accompany us, and we should prepare to leave immediately. This was great news!

We got our passports, obtained the visas, and booked our tickets with Qantas Airlines. This was our first experience flying to a foreign country, and we were excited!

It was an 8-hour flight to Manila, the capital of the Philippines, and we were anxious to step into a new country. But then a hurdle came up, which dampened all our excitement. Our four-year-old daughter did not have a passport of her own. Her name was endorsed on her mother's passport, so she did not have her own visa, and the immigration officer was firm. He would not let her pass. We felt helpless and stuck, with no way out, and could not think of any solution.

All we could do was silently pray, asking God to intervene.

The immigration officer then passed the problem on to the higher officers, and after some deliberations, permission was granted. We were to be together as a family again! We thanked God, and our level of excitement came right back! He had opened the way for us when there seemed to be no way.

APRIL 20

HIS WORD IS THE LIGHT

Usha Thomas

"He leads me in the paths of righteousness, for His name's sake."

Psalm 23:3, NKJV

One Sunday, a visiting pastor shared his testimony about how his life had changed from being a very naughty boy to a good and well-behaved boy. He described how it had happened. One night, he saw an unusually bright light in his room, which he sensed was from God. The experience was so moving that it changed him completely.

I, too, wanted to change for the better. So I also prayed that God would show me His light. I thought it would be easy if we could change for good in just one day. That night, in my sleep, I saw this verse from the Bible clear before my eyes: "He leads me in the paths of righteousness for His name's sake." The words "He" and "His" jumped out at me. I woke from sleep and said, "God, I asked You to show me the light. Is this it?" And immediately, the response came to my heart: "My Word is the light!"

It was so clear that I understood the message without any doubt. He is the One who leads us in the paths of righteousness, and it is for His name's sake. He does it with His wisdom and His power. All praise, honor, and glory in our lives belong to Him.

Another verse goes along with this: "Thy Word is a lamp unto my feet and a light unto my path." Psalm 119:105. KJV. His Word is the light.

Let His Word be your light as you begin and end the day.

April 21

Omnipotent and Omnipresent

Bimal Nowrangi

"Where can I go from your Spirit? Where can I go from your presence? If I go up to the heavens, you are there; if I make my bed in the depths, you are there."

Psalm 139:7,8, NIV.

During my brief lifetime, traveling in various regions of the world, I have had the privilege to see a tiny portion of God's vast creation. I have seen God's signature and footprints on everything everywhere. Despite claims to the contrary, the world still has many beautiful things and places.

I have gazed into a portion of the earth's core in the Taal volcano in the Philippines, described as the world's smallest active volcano and as "a lake within a volcano within a lake!" I have driven across the vast Tundra lands of Alaska and have flown in an 8-seater tourist plane in a thrilling, unforgettable experience of landing on the top of a gleaming glacier. The Alaskan starry nights were spectacular and phenomenal. I have driven through parts of the famous rugged Badlands of South Dakota and stood before the towering 60-foot-high carvings of the four US Presidents on Mount Rushmore. Feeling engulfed in the mystifying and surreal Swedish Lapland Northern Lights, was impressive beyond words!

Every experience has lifted my thoughts heavenward and given me a clearer glimpse of His greatness, wisdom, and eternal presence.

As I continue the remaining part of my earthly journey, I pray that I will always feel His powerful presence near me and know that I can never ever flee from Him.

God is Omnipotent and Omnipresent.

May we live in reverence of the all-powerful God we serve.

April 22

Surrounded By Grace

Amber Solomonraj

"My grace is sufficient for you. . ."

II Corinthians 12:9, NKJV

"Grow in grace and in the knowledge of our Lord Jesus Christ."

II Peter 3:18. NKJV

I grew up in a Christian Adventist home and thought I understood the meaning of grace and mercy. It seemed quite simple. We didn't lack anything at home, and God kept my family safe from physical harm. That was enough for me to say, "Yes, I see God's grace in my daily life."

But as I got older and became more familiar with the Bible, I realized that God's grace was so much more than just providing us with safety. It was going further, building a personal relationship with God, and accepting Him into my life. This also meant trusting in Him through the low points in my life. It is easy to turn away from God when faced with trials and tribulations, but God never leaves us. He is always there, and so is His grace.

Psalm 23 says, "Surely goodness and mercy will follow me all the days of my life." This verse stands true. No matter what we endure in our lives, God's mercy will follow us.

I pray that we see the countless ways God shows us His grace daily. Whether it's a beautiful flower garden, the morning dew, a good grade on an assignment, or simply having good health. We can find God's grace in the most minor things. We don't need a grand-scale "miracle" to know or believe God exists. He knows our hearts and knows what we need.

Believe in Him, and take time to observe His grace.

APRIL 23

A Flash Flood

Bimal Nowrangi

"For when they shall say, Peace and safety; then sudden destruction cometh upon them."

I Thessalonians 5:3, KJV

It started out as a typical calm summer day for more than 400 students residing in the boys' dormitories at the then Spicer Memorial College, Pune, India. Morning worship and breakfast, followed by classes and work programs, went according to schedule.

After dinner and evening worship everyone had gone to their respective rooms to retire for the night. The general monitor and floor monitors had made their rounds and came to the Dean's office for their nightly meeting with me.

Suddenly, we heard frantic knocking on the door. It was an urgent report: The water level was rising rapidly in the creek (Ram River) that ran next to the dormitory, and we should act immediately. In a few moments, the concrete wall, built to protect the dormitory, was breached, and the swirling flood, knee-deep by now, gushed onto the yard and into our apartment and the lower floors of the buildings. Men's shoes, clothes, pots and pans, and other articles floated out from the rooms onto the yard.

The first thing we did was to rush into the rooms where my wife and children were fast asleep. We picked up the children and hurriedly placed them on tabletops high above the water level. We glanced at the boxes and suitcases containing our clothes but could not save them. Ultimately, we were all safe, but that unexpected flash flood in the dark hours of the night caused severe damage and destruction.

Let us remain vigilant and prepared. The Lord may return at any time, day or night!

April 24

Sing Unto The LORD A New Song

Biju Thomas

"I will sing a new song unto thee, O God; upon the psaltery and an instrument of ten strings will I sing praises unto thee."

Psalm 144:9, KJV

My father, Mr. M.M. Thomas composed 72 Malayalam Christian songs while working as a teacher at the SDA school in Kottarakara, Kerala, India. These songs inspired generations of students who came to study at this school.

He not only composed the songs but sang them as well. My childhood memories are full of the beautiful melodies that filled our home each day as we woke up to the sound of praises to God. Our hearts were lifted up and inspired by an experience that I simply cannot express in words!

Some of the songs he composed touched my heart, and I recall some of the words with fondness: "The love of Jesus is so sweet, that I can't really express it in words. The moment I became His child, the kingdom of heaven became my birthright. What a privilege to be bought with the precious blood of Jesus Christ and call Heavenly Canaan my eternal home."

Such a beautiful flow of praise and rapture is like the expression of David in the Psalms. "And He hath put a new song in my mouth." Psalm 40:3

Salvation and song are inseparable. To have a personal relationship with God is to have a new song planted in the soul. When a person is in fellowship with the Lord, that person has a new song in his heart. Let us sing songs of praise to the LORD day and night.

April 25

Sleep in Peace

Soosan Varghese

"Behold, He who keeps Israel; Shall neither slumber nor sleep."

Psalm 121:4, NKJV

It was the end of the school year. Bye-bye, eighth grade! Hello, summer vacation! I bid farewell to my friends at the boarding school and went with my dad to the bus stand.

The bus started on time at 6:30 pm. We should be home around 2:30 am, so I dozed off on my dad's shoulder. At 10:30 pm, I woke up to the sounds of commotion. The bus had broken down, and we were stranded in the middle of nowhere! Since it was hot on the bus, we all alighted and sat around on the ground.

My dad instructed me to spread a bed sheet on the ground, and I went to sleep again. When I woke up, the man sitting close to us said to me, "Young lady, do you know that your dad never sat down the whole night?" I looked at my dad. He just smiled as if to say, "Not to worry. Everything is alright." I looked down and saw his swollen feet through his sandal straps. He had sat up all day on the bus to get to the school and stood all night watching over me. He did not want to sit and risk falling asleep while I, his precious daughter, slept among strangers.

How much more does our heavenly Father care?! May we live and sleep in peace, assured that our heavenly Father is watching over us. "I will both lie down in peace and sleep, for You alone, O LORD, make me dwell in safety." Psalm 4:8, NKJV

April 26

Importance of Preparation

Bimal Nowrangi

"Therefore, you also be ready, for the Son of Man is coming at an hour you do not expect."

Matthew 24:44, NKJV

Every year our parents took us to be enrolled in a boarding elementary school. We had to travel by train, and it took 24 hours to reach the destination. We used to wait for this long train ride. We especially liked the rhythmic sound of the wheels on the tracks, the ear-piercing whistle, and the billowing black smoke from the chimney of the old steam locomotives. We would get off at as many stations as possible, and run over to the engine, just to watch the crew shoveling mounds of wet coal into the furnace to heat the water boiler. It was so much fun!

However, we enjoyed the trip because of all the effort that had gone into preparing for it. We were least concerned, but our parents took the full responsibility for that tiring and demanding job.

Long before the journey, my mother would begin making all the necessary preparations. She would pack our clothes, toiletries, shoes, and stationery in our suitcases. She would stay up most of the night before the journey, to cook a variety of food and snacks for the trip. She made sure there were extra amounts because she knew that her growing children would get hungry any time and many times! That's exactly what happened!

I remember those train trips with nostalgia. They were pleasant and enjoyable, but only because of the careful preparations made by our responsible parents.

God has done all the planning. If we make the proper preparations, our journey will be rewarding.

April 27

Passing Score

Rajam Edison

"But looking at them, Jesus said, "'With men it is impossible, but not with God; for with God all things are possible."

Mark 10:27, NKJV

One of the requirements to continue my job was to get re-certified by passing four tests, and all four tests had to be passed separately. I would pass three in my earlier attempts but fail on the fourth by just one or two points, so I could not be re-certified. There seemed nothing more I could do. I had earnestly prayed and done my best, but was still unsuccessful.

It seemed hopeless, and I was just about to give up, when I got a call from the district office. They informed me that for the coming year, they were going to combine the scores of all the four tests to determine the final score. Based on that change, I was counted successful, because my total score was above the passing level. I would receive the certification! I was surprised and thrilled! Help had come in a completely unexpected way. God had indeed answered my prayers.

I have been working in that district for the past 20 years, and even today, it sends shivers down my spine, and I feel the same joy as when God led me in a miraculous way back then. What had appeared to be impossible to me was made possible by God.

Our duty is not to give up, but to cast all our burdens on God. Then pray and trust, and He will work in unexpected ways. Yes, he will even change the final scores for you!

April 28

Symbol of Great Hope

Biju Sunil Thomas

"Because strait is the gate and narrow is the way, which leadeth unto life, and few there be that find it."

Matthew 7:14, KJV

In the year 2016, I had the opportunity to visit the Cape of Good Hope in South Africa. This is a region of breathtaking scenery – mountains rising from towering cliffs, sheltered bays, sandy shores, and serene ocean. Not surprisingly, the Western Cape of South Africa has become a world-renowned tourist destination. From a vantage point, you can see the dark blue waters of the Indian Ocean merge with the bluish-green waters of the Atlantic Ocean – a majestic sight to behold!

The convergence of two ocean currents – one warm and one cold – in the shallow waters, produces unpredictable and turbulent water movements. The treacherous coastline is notorious for nasty weather and violent storms. So, it was first named "Cape of Storms" in 1488. The remains of many shipwrecks are still scattered around the coastline. But the Portuguese King John II, renamed it the Cape of Good Hope – the hope of reaching India once the cape was rounded.

Vasco Da Gama sailed from Lisbon, Portugal and ultimately reached India. After rounding the Cape of Good Hope, he recruited a very experienced sailor, who helped him cross the Indian Ocean to reach his destination. This route was the only correct one; however, it was not easy to traverse.

Similarly, the path to eternal life requires effort and searching to find. But Jesus said he was the "Door" [John 10:7] and the "Way" [John 14:6.] His Cross, the Symbol of Great Hope, is our light, and Jesus Himself is our assurance of heaven.

April 29

The Stranger Among Us

Joseph Eapen

"Then the King will say, 'I'm telling the solemn truth: Whenever you did one of these things to someone overlooked or ignored, that was me – you did it to me.'"

Matthew 25:40, MSG

One day, while stopped at a traffic signal, waiting for the light to turn green, I saw a young man holding up a sign, "Homeless, anything will help." My first thought was whether he was indeed homeless or whether he was trying to take advantage of the stopped traffic to panhandle for cash. Because I couldn't determine genuine need from outward appearances, I offered a quick prayer, asking God to help him in his need.

How should we react to the strangers we face daily? As Christians, we are called to be the hands and feet of Christ to assist the needy to the best of our abilities. In the parable of Matthew 25, Jesus described the services done to the hungry, the thirsty, the homeless, the cold, the sick, and the imprisoned. The righteous do not recall performing any of the services listed because they did not count these deeds as extraordinary. They had not done them to earn salvation or impress God. They were just a part of their way of life.

Just as the righteous reveal their true relationship with God through compassion, the wicked demonstrate their lack of a genuine relationship with God by their cavalier attitude toward the needy.

Let us reach out our hands, be willing instruments in God's hands, and provide whatever help we can to the stranger in our midst. Jesus commends those who do this: "You did it to Me."

April 30

Mother and Baby Elephant

Bimal Nowrangi

"How often have I longed to gather your children together, as a hen gathers her chicks under her wings, and you were not willing."

Matthew 23:37, NIV

It is interesting to visit zoos and see wild animals in their cages. However, it is a totally different experience to watch them in their natural habitat in the wild. We made plans to visit Jaldhapara Safari Park, a conservation park in West Bengal, home to elephants, tigers, leopards, the one-horned rhinoceros, antelopes, and many species of birds.

The safari started in the early morning hours before dawn. We sat atop six elephants, which were going to follow a beaten trail through tall grass and thorny shrubs, and cross a large stream. A huge, experienced male elephant led the team. Among the elephants was a one-year-old baby with a mind of its own who stayed at the back or strayed from the path at will.

When we came to the wide stream, which would take some time to cross, the mother elephant shepherded the errant baby with her trunk to a position in front of her and in the middle of the herd. There, the baby would be safe from unexpected dangers. In fact, the "mahout" (driver) pointed out a large rhinoceros, partially submerged in the water, which we carefully passed, to avoid disturbing and irritating it. We crossed the stream safely and returned to the base camp after an enjoyable sightseeing ride.

We were freshly reminded of the way God watches and protects His wayward children even more closely than a mother hen or a mother elephant.

May 1

WHAT'S IN A TEA BAG?

Cinthya Daniel

"Before they call, I will answer; while they are still speaking, I will hear."

Isaiah 65:24, NKJV

I usually do not keep tea bags at home, but I had one in my kitchen cabinet. It served no purpose, and I had meant to throw it out but somehow never got down to doing it. So, it just sat there.

One Friday morning, my older son had all four of his wisdom teeth removed. He woke me in the middle of the night because it was bleeding from one spot and wouldn't stop despite the recommended firm pressure with gauze. He was visibly distressed. I glanced through the discharge papers, but no other measure was described. So, before searching the internet, I knelt at his bedside and prayed, "Lord, please stop this bleeding."

On the internet, I found that tea bags have been used in such situations. I remembered that I had one in the kitchen cabinet. I quickly got it and followed the instructions on how to use it. It should be dampened, rolled up, and placed on the extraction site.

Of course, I was skeptical. What could this one tea bag do? But to our astonishment, the bleeding stopped in a few minutes and did not recur. We were overjoyed with relief, and looked up with gratitude to our heavenly Father for such a quick and effective answer.

Could it be that God began His answer long before I prayed – when I had kept the tea bag in the kitchen cabinet instead of throwing it out?! Is He not an amazing God who takes care of us even in the small details of life?!!

May 2

Where is Your Light?

Praveen Pedapudi

"Let your light so shine before men, that they may see your good works and glorify your Father in heaven."

Matthew 5:16, NKJV

I was sitting in the car at a signal light, talking to my girlfriend on Facetime. The bright sunlight shone on my face, and I tried to keep the sun out of my eyes without much success. I was frustrated, but she said, "You look so bright in the sunlight!" That obvious remark suddenly stopped my thoughts as if something had struck me.

I hadn't given off any light because I had no light of my own. All I had done was reflect the sun's light – just like the moon, which has no light of its own (and yet we marvel at its beauty!)

Sometimes, we feel God's work is just that – His work. Reaching people is His responsibility. Of course, He can handle it. After all, He is the One with the light, right? But think again!

How many people look directly at the sun? (Don't try it; you may wreck your retina and might even go blind!) It is the light *reflected* from the sun that our eyes can bear, allowing us to see and comprehend our surroundings.

Similarly, looking directly into the light of God's truth is blinding to many. But the light that we reflect will not hurt. It can be tolerated and cause God's great truths to become clear and distinct.

Our conduct – our acts, speech, and behavior – is where God's light will shine through us so that others may see our good works and glorify Him.

MAY 3

GOD'S STRENGTH IN OUR WEAKNESS

Usha Thomas

"My grace is sufficient for you, for my strength is made perfect in weakness. Therefore, most gladly I will rather boast in my infirmities, that the power of Christ may rest upon me."

II Corinthians 12:9, NKJV

I was 11 and in a boarding school away from home, when I accidentally swallowed a large gooseberry while playing with my friends. I choked on it and would have suffocated. In fact, I thought it was my last day on earth! But, by God's grace, I was rescued by my teacher, who was nearby.

Although the fear of choking gripped me from that time onward, I remembered what was done to save me. And because of that, later in life, I saved two others from similar dangers. One of them was a co-worker who was choking when nobody was around. The other was an uncle of mine who had a chicken bone stuck in his throat, and it happened in public when many people were around.

Looking back, I realize I was not an expert, yet these lives were saved. I believe it was the power of God, revealed even in my weakness. On my own, I would not have even attempted to help. God provided the quickness, the right decision, and the strength.

We cannot take any credit for ourselves. All the honor must go to Jesus. His promise is sure: "Fear not, for I am with you; be not dismayed, for I am your God; I will strengthen you, yes, I will help you, I will uphold you with my righteous right hand." Isaiah 41:10, NKJV

May 4

When Nature Speaks

Daisy Sharlin

"For since the creation of the world His invisible attributes are clearly seen, being understood by the things that are made, even His eternal power…"

Romans 1:30, NKJV

When I was a young girl living in Chennai, I often went onto the terrace of our house to talk with God. At moments of sadness, I would look into the starry skies and just talk, sing, and praise God. I have had experiences when nature spoke clearly.

Once, when I was troubled in my heart, I wanted to be left alone to talk with my Lord. I went up to the terrace, conversing with Him the whole time.

Our garden had twelve coconut trees that surrounded the house. Their height reached the second story of the building. It was exceptionally calm and quiet outside that night – not the slightest breeze. All the trees stood very still. I poured out my heart's troubles and pleas. Then I asked if He would please show me a sign that He had heard me.

A little later, the trees with their leaves began swaying by a strong breeze. It got so windy that I had to rush to a shelter on the terrace. The wind blew very hard for about one or two minutes, and suddenly, everything went calm and quiet again. I stepped out of my hiding place. Not a single tree or their leaves moved.

To me, that was a clear sign that God heard my prayers. I thanked God for giving me His assurance, bringing peace to my heart that night. He is an amazing and truly understanding God!

MAY 5

USE YOUR MAP

Selena Kelly Thomas

"Thy word is a lamp unto my feet, and a light unto my path."

Psalm 119:105, KJV

One evening, I had to drive into Washington DC. This was before we had GPS and smartphones. So I got the directions from MapQuest and mapped the route in my mind. It appeared simple enough. At first, the going was easy, through the busy streets of D.C., but then, I noticed a large sign with flashing lights that indicated that the road was closed. I tried a few turns here and there to get back on track but soon realized I was lost. Alarmed and helpless, I wondered what to do next.

Then, I recalled that the printed directions from MapQuest were in my purse. There was also a small map on the page, pointing to specific locations in that area. I checked my whereabouts and was able to identify my location and the possible routes to my destination. My fears were now replaced with a sense of calm and renewed confidence. I did not feel lost anymore.

We embark on life's journey, confident of reaching specific destinations. However, along the way, we face obstacles and road closures. We try our detours and feel abandoned, worried, and discouraged.

The Word of God provides continued guidance, comfort, and hope. Like a map, it helps us get back onto our path. God is our rock and shield, who takes away all our fears. He has promised to see us through and will always be there for us. His Word is truly a lamp to our feet and a light to our path.

May 6

The Joy of Unity

Bimal Nowrangi

"How good and pleasant it is when God's people live together in unity."

Psalm 133:1, NIV

During my high school studies, I briefly lived with my parents on the school campus. Since everyone in the family loved animals, we had many animals and birds with us. We had cows, goats, chickens, pigeons, a parrot, a dog, a cat, and a monkey. Our house was a veritable mini-zoo!

The mooing of the cows, crowing of the rooster, meowing of the cat, barking of the dog, squawking of the parrot, cooing of the pigeons, and squealing of the monkey, were all common sounds. However, they didn't make all their sounds at the same time. That would have been an unpleasant cacophony! We all lived in peace and harmony.

This household peace was disturbed once – when the monkey got out of her leash and began resorting to her "monkey business!" She started doing what monkeys are wont to do. She would grab the pigeon eggs from the pigeon boxes, climb up on the rooftop to dance around there, and play the touch-me-if-you-can game! It was totally chaotic! And nothing could entice her to come down to us.

Now, she loved one thing – going on bike rides on my shoulder or on the handlebar. So, I got onto my bike, pretending to leave. And sure enough, she came hurrying down for the ride! Peace and tranquility were restored. We had learned to understand each other!

God does not require uniformity, but He does desire that all His people engage in mutual efforts for peace, avoid disharmony, and strive for unity of purpose.

May 7

SPEAK TO THE MOUNTAIN

Usha Thomas

"For assuredly, I say to you, whoever says to this mountain, 'Be removed and be cast into the sea,' and does not doubt in his heart, but believes that those things he says will be done, he will have whatever he says.'"

Mark 11:23, NKJV

As children of God, we are given the promise of the power and authority of the Holy Spirit to speak to the mountain to be removed.

In 2021, my left ear suddenly became deaf. It was uncomfortable and disturbing, so I went for a checkup and was told that the cause was ear wax deposits. Once they were removed, things would be alright. He tried to remove them two times, but failed. I returned a week later, and again, he tried twice without success. He said that I might need surgery. On hearing that, I became sad and depressed but decided to try again – this time in an emergency room. Here again, two unsuccessful attempts were made. I then went to another doctor, who was about to give up after his two tries but said that he would try a third time.

All along, I had felt like I was the target of some attack. So, I recollected the words of Isaiah 54:17, "No weapon formed against you shall prosper." I kept repeating this promise as the doctor tried the third time. And then it happened – the deposit broke up, he cleaned my ear, and I could hear again!

At the end of every tussle with the enemy, we can say, "I know in whom I have believed." His power is more than sufficient.

MAY 8

MIRAGE EXPERIENCES

Bimal Nowrangi

"As the deer pants for streams of water, so my soul pants for you, my God."

Psalm 42:1, NIV

It was one of those scorching hot summer days in India. I was riding my motorbike on a familiar road that passed through a long stretch of flat, barren land – no fields, trees, shrubs, or man-made structures. All I could see was a long, straight road stretching out into the distance before me.

Suddenly, in the distance, I saw what appeared like a pool of water on the road. As I rode towards it, the "water" kept moving further and further away, finally disappearing. I then realized that what I had just experienced was a mirage!

It is a naturally occurring phenomenon caused by heated air and refraction of light that appear as shimmering rays, and mimic the appearance of sheets of water just above the ground's surface. Humans and animals, in hot and dry conditions, as in deserts, have been deceived by mirages and have been led in futile efforts to get water, only to end with nothing!

David describes a deer thirsting and panting for water. It may have been due to hot and dry conditions or even because a hunter was chasing it. This picture reflected his own thirst for the living God.

Whatever may cause our thirst, God alone can quench it by supplying us with living water. Jesus said, "He who believes in Me shall never thirst." John 6:35, NKJV

The best news is that the water is real; the relief is real. There are no mirage experiences with God!

MAY 9

LIKE A FLINT

Subodh K Pandit

"I have set my face like a flint, and I know that I will not be ashamed."

Isaiah 50:7, NKJV

When I joined Spicer Memorial High School in 1963, I had the choice of either the SSLC stream (the exam papers were set in India) or the ISC stream (the exam papers were set in Cambridge, England.) I opted for the second. I also noticed that until that time, the ISC results were always nearly the same: only one-second class pass in each batch, and the rest, either third class pass or fail.

My time alone with God was on Friday nights. After the general monitor turned off the lights in the hostel, I would sit up in bed for a few minutes of communion before lying down. During one of those times, it crossed my mind to try to get a first-class pass in the ISC exam, and I prayed about it.

Six months before the exam, I was impressed to set my face like a flint. I decided not to go to any Saturday night function but rather, to spend that time studying. I also asked permission from the floor monitor to study by candlelight after the lights were turned off during the week.

I was seventeen, and there were many times when I badly wanted to go for the functions, but deep inside, I felt supported in my decision. (I faltered once – another story!)

When the results were out, I had a first-class pass in the ISC exam!

While I had set my face like a flint, I knew I had a constant Guide all along the way!

May 10

An Understanding Heart

Subodh K Pandit

"See, I have given you a wise and understanding heart."

I Kings 3:12, NKJV

During my final year at Spicer Memorial High School, Pr. Jesudas was the Dean of boys, in charge of our life in the dorm. We had been studying hard for months for the ISC exams, and one day, our resolve gave way. We decided to quit studying for the night and go for a jaunt outside the campus – against the rules.

We slipped out the back door and made our way to the road, and began our trek towards a mela (an annual festival) a few miles away at Chatrasinghe. I think we looked like jokers on the road, because we were all dressed in our nightly pajamas!! We had worn them to appear like we were getting ready for bed! And now we looked at each other and burst out laughing!

The mela was fun. It was past midnight when we decided to return to the hostel, and began to wonder how we could get back inside.

To our amazement, we found the front door still open. We stealthily walked in, thanking our good fortune, and then ran right into Pr. Jesudas, who had been waiting just for us!!

He called us into his office (I wonder if he felt like laughing at our attire!) but then told us to return to our rooms, and never said a word about it ever after. If he had punished us, we would not have been able to write our exams. He understood.

Thank God for those who are strict but also have an understanding heart!

May 11

The Cat and the Squirrel

Soosan Varghese

"Be sober; be vigilant; because your adversary the devil walks like a roaring lion, seeking whom he may devour."

I Peter 5:8, NKJV

"It was my 8th grade summer vacation, and after completing the morning chores, I was relaxing in my second-floor bedroom in Kerala, India. The leaves of our mango tree brushed against my open window. Two squirrels playfully jumped about on the branches of the mango tree. I then noticed a sudden flurry of heightened activity and heard screeching from the squirrels.

To my horror, I saw Tippu, our black and white cat, pounce on one of the squirrels. He caught the squirrel by the neck and jumped into my room through the open window. I tried to rescue the little squirrel, but Tippu ran under the bed with the squirrel.

I watched in dismay as my cat played with the squirrel. He would let the squirrel go, and as soon as it got out of reach, he would pounce back on it and drag it back to the corner. He would bite the squirrel and toss it back and forth on the floor or in the air. My repeated attempts to rescue the squirrel went in vain. Finally, Tippu jumped out the window with the squirrel in his mouth.

This incident reminded me of the above Bible verse. If we are not vigilant, the devil, who is our enemy, will pounce on us, make a game of us, and eventually devour us. God's grace, which keeps us alert, is also described in the Bible. May we stay vigilant by reading His Word and praying, just like Daniel in the Bible.

May 12

Songs of Praise in the Night

Gladwin Mathews

"I call to remembrance my song in the night: I commune with mine own heart: and my spirit made diligent search."

Psalm 77:6, KJV

A few decades ago, in 1973, I went for a general camp meeting in the forest area of the Dehradun Valley along with a group of students from Roorkee High School. We had gone early as an advance party to prepare the campsite for the main group of campers who would join us later. After finishing our task, we all planned to walk the 7 km to the nearby town of Clement to meet the other group and ride back with them.

Unfortunately, we missed the group, and night was falling. So we began our journey back on foot through the dark jungle. When fears arose, somebody suggested that we pray. We prayed, and on resuming our trip, we found ourselves singing songs and hymns. The darkness made us sing from our hearts, and the music we made became more meaningful and encouraging.

While loss of eyesight can make life dark, we can turn that darkness to advantage. Fanny Crosby, a well-known hymn writer, composed the song "Redeemed! How I love to proclaim it!" She was blind and referred to her blindness in the words, "Who lovingly guardeth my footsteps, And giveth me songs in the night." She did not count her blindness as a tragedy but accepted it graciously and used her condition to bless others.

Dark experiences are a part of life that comes to all. If we relate to them correctly, they can teach us invaluable lessons to encourage us on life's journey.

May 13

Maldivian Expedition – Part 1

Biju Thomas

"If I take the wings of the morning, and dwell in the uttermost parts of the sea; Even there shall thy hand lead me, and Thy right hand shall hold me."

Psalm 139:9-10, KJV

One of the most beautiful places I have ever visited is the Maldives – a group of more than 100 coral islands in the Indian Ocean. The name "Maldives" is derived from the Sanskrit words "Mala Dvipa," which means "Garland of Islands" or "Necklace of Islands."

The photos depict the islands: picture-perfect private villas suspended over striking blue waters, alabaster white sand beaches, kaleidoscopic reefs, and spectacular sunsets. The scenic beauty is hard to even imagine until it is seen in person. It is beautiful but far away!

In April of 2005, I went to the Maldives as a teacher. This was my first experience away from home. My children, 12 and 8, came to the airport to bid me goodbye. I can still recall the scene – my younger child held onto my hand and pleaded with me not to leave her. As a father, I was heartbroken but couldn't change any of the plans that we had made much earlier, after considerable thought and discussion.

As I trudged through the departure lounge, I felt the pangs of separation and loneliness grip my heart. The emotions were acute. So in my distress, I cried to the Lord for comfort, strength, and courage, and He answered me. Throughout my lonely sojourn in Maldives, I experienced the constant, comforting presence of the Lord.

No matter where you go, be assured that God is always there to help and guide you.

May 14

Maldivian Expedition - Part 2

Biju Thomas

"And call upon Me in the day of trouble: I will deliver thee, and thou shalt glorify Me."

Psalm 50:15, KJV

I flew into the capital of Maldives and then got into a tiny fishing boat for the next leg of my journey. We headed to an island called Kendhikuludhoo, 122 miles to the north, across the Indian Ocean. It was boisterous and got rough in the middle of the night. The waves lashed and pounded against the sides of the tiny boat as it rocked from side to side and was tossed up and down. Water splashed onto my face, and I could hear creaking and crackling sounds as the strong waves crashed against the boat's sides. I was terrified.

The only light on board was a dim lamp. All else was eerie darkness. I reached into my handbag, pulled out my Bible, and opened it. My eyes fell on these words: "But the Lord sent out a great wind into the sea, and there was a mighty tempest in the sea so that the ship was like to be broken." Jonah 1:4 KJV

My heart sank as I pondered those words and thought, "Am I going somewhere the Lord doesn't want me to go?" I pleaded with the Lord to help me reach my destination and allow me an opportunity to correct any mistakes I had committed. He answered my prayer in His mercy, and His Mighty Hands guided me to safety through the tempest.

I had called upon Him in my time of trouble, and true to His word, He delivered me. All praise and glory to Him!

When in trouble, remember to call upon God.

May 15

Help of a Friend

Subodh K Pandit

"Nevertheless, you have done well that you shared in my distress."

Philippians 4:14, NKJV

It is a challenge for a medical doctor from India to get licensed to practice in the USA. I felt that pressure. Being new to the system, I did not realize that most graduating medical students apply for their residency programs even before the results of the licensing exams are out. So, by the time I got my results, the date for applying for a residency position had already passed. Now, I would have to wait one whole year to try again.

With prayer, I decided to try anyway. I filled out the application form, got the necessary references, and sent them to Dr. Richard Jesudas in Oklahoma, telling him about my predicament. He approached the residency program director at Tulsa, Oklahoma, and handed over my application.

Although the date had already passed, the Director took the application because it had been handed to him personally by a member of his faculty. Surprisingly, he decided to arrange an interview.

Within a few minutes of the interview, he wanted me in his residency program and told me so. He worked hard to overcome all the many delicate hurdles in such a situation, and finally, I was admitted into the program.

Two years later, when he was leaving Tulsa to join the American Board of Internal Medicine in Pennsylvania, he confessed, "I don't know why I did it for you!"

To me, the starting point was a friend who had helped by personally handing over my application. Be a friend to those in distress. Help someone today.

MAY 16

TRUST HIS GRACE

Soosan Varghese

"My eyes are ever toward the LORD, for He will pluck my feet out of the net."

Psalm 25:15, ESV

Song Sparrows are plentiful among the tall trees in our backyard. I love to hear them sing, "Sweet, sweet, sweet, trill. . .and a chirp, sweet, sweet, sweet again, and a trill. . ."

Some evenings, I sit on our deck just to hear the birds sing. Part of our deck is covered and netted to keep birds and other creatures out. One day, I went onto the deck and found two sparrows inside the covered area! The netted door was locked. I couldn't figure out how they got inside, and they couldn't figure out how to get out! Terrified at my presence, they fluttered their wings and whizzed by me, shrieking all the way.

I propped the door open so the birds could fly out. But they kept flying back and forth inside, sometimes flinging themselves at the net. One of the birds eventually fluttered to the floor between the deck rails. I gently caught it and released it to the woods, where it flew away and rejoined its chorus. In its effort to evade me, the other sparrow flung itself to the walls and net several times. I placed water and grains outside the net door to entice it to fly out. However, this sparrow was not buying it!

I wondered how many times I have tried to evade the guiding, loving arms of Jesus when He tries to get me out of the trouble that I got myself into! May God give us the discernment to recognize His call and fix our eyes on Him.

May 17

Daniel and Nebuchadnezzar's Dream

Biju Thomas

"Daniel answered the king and said, 'No wise man, enchanter, magician, or diviner can explain to the king the mystery he has asked about, but there is a God in heaven who reveals mysteries. He has shown King Nebuchadnezzar what will happen in the days to come.'"

Daniel 2:27-28, NIV

When I was studying in the 8th grade at Spencer Road High School in Bangalore (Bengaluru,) I was chosen to play the role of Daniel in a school event. I was too young to recognize the significance of Nebuchadnezzar's dream or its interpretation. I simply memorized the lines given to me and delivered them on stage as best as I could.

Later, as I grew up, studied the prophecies in the books of Daniel and Revelation, understood their impact, and witnessed the fulfillment of those prophecies, I was amazed at how God used Daniel to reveal His redemptive plan through historical events.

In ancient times, kings expected the wise men in their courts to provide a range of services, including the interpretation of dreams, because they claimed to possess supernatural powers. In this particular instance, Nebuchadnezzar had forgotten his dream and wanted them to describe it before interpreting it. They rightly complained, "There is not a man that can show the king's matter... except the gods, whose dwelling is not with flesh." But when Daniel came before the king, he said, "There is a God in heaven who reveals mysteries."

One of the keys to living strong in today's world is to know that God is in control and that "history" is really "His story!"

MAY 18

HE WILL MAKE A WAY

Subodh K Pandit

"Thus says the Lord, who makes a way. . ."

Isaiah 43:16, NKJV

We had decided to move permanently from India to the USA in 1993 and were keen to take advantage of the offer by British Airways. They had just opened a new route starting from Kolkata, and to encourage potential passengers to take that route, they were making a buy-one-get-one-free offer! It was a great deal, but we would have to buy the tickets soon before they were sold out. We assessed our situation and realized we didn't have enough money to purchase the tickets. We would have to sell our Maruti van right away to have enough. But how would we find a buyer that quickly? We were living in the small township of Hosur and hadn't met many who might be interested. We prayed, "If this is your leading, please open the way."

That afternoon, I was sitting at home thinking about what to do when our gardener came to say that a man was at the gate wanting to see me. I went there, and his first words were, "Sir, I heard you were looking for a buyer for your Maruti van. I know someone who wants to buy it from you!" I stared at him for a moment, dumbfounded. "How did you know that I wanted to sell the van?" All he did was shrug his shoulders. When I mentioned the price, he said, "No problem. Shall we make the deal right now?"

We soon had seven tickets in hand, three of which were free of cost! Relieved and moved, I looked upward, "Thank you!"

No matter your situation, God will make a way for you.

May 19

The Tickets, God!

Subodh K Pandit

"I will guide you with My eye."

Psalm 32:8, NKJV

We were leaving for the USA in three days. I picked up the seven air tickets from the agency in Bengaluru, put them in my briefcase, and placed it behind the passenger seat in the autorickshaw that was taking us around shopping. When we finished shopping and returned to Hosur, I suddenly realized I had forgotten to take my briefcase out of the rickshaw!!

I reported my plight to the ticketing agency early the following day. Their response was devastating! If I did not find the original tickets, I would have to buy seven new tickets (pay for all seven!) and then request a refund for the ones bought earlier.

In desperation, I went to the rickshaw stand to look for the rickshaw. My heart sank! There were scores and scores of similar-looking rickshaws! It appeared hopeless. I went to the police station to report it and returned home. I prayed, "God, You know where the tickets are. Please help!"

The next day, I returned to the police station, to the agency, and to the rickshaw stand and hopelessly looked around. I thought of how many years it would take to save up enough to buy those seven tickets. America now seemed utterly out of reach!

Dejected, I decided to try once more at the agency. As soon as I entered, an agent called out, "Is this your briefcase? The rickshaw driver just came in and gave it to us." I opened it, and all seven tickets were in there! I sang my gratitude the whole way from Bengaluru to Hosur!

Pray when in trouble, and our all-knowing God will answer.

MAY 20

A SINCERE SILENT PRAYER

Gladwin Mathews

"Therefore, I tell you, whatever you ask for in prayer, believe that you have received it, and it will be yours."

Mark 11:24, NIV

In June of 1986, we were called to head a school in the small town of Rohru, in a remote area in the district of Shimla. It had a population of about 6 to 7 thousand. The usual amenities found in larger towns were not to be found – no gas station, LPG cooking gas, taxi service, or telephone or telegram service. It was really remote!

Cooking could be done only on an Indian wood chula (earthen stove using wood) or a kerosene stove. We could not use wood in the building, so our only option was the kerosene stove. Then, I learned that kerosene was rationed to the public, and would be distributed only on certain Saturdays. Dejected, I sat with my eyes moist with tears and whispered, "How much worse can it get?! Lord, please consider my condition and help me find a way so I don't have to buy on the Sabbath."

But we needed kerosene, so I went to the shop and stood in line. When I neared the counter, the shop owner called out, "Oh, Principal Saheb, it is you!" I had not met him before, but he knew about me because his son studied at our school.

He gave me kerosene and said that we could settle the payment later. "Next time, you needn't come. I will make all the arrangements." I thanked him.

God had responded to my silent prayer. "Thank you, merciful God!"

If we sincerely choose to obey Him, God will help us keep His commandments.

May 21

Lesson From a Child

Naveena Mora

"Call upon Me in the day of trouble; I will deliver you, and you shall glorify Me."

Psalm 50:15, NKJV

When I got home, I saw tell-tale signs that my daughters, 3 and 4, had been having a good time in the yard. Excitedly, I went in, hoping to join them in the fun and games. But they were not to be seen anywhere. I asked my mother, who said they had been in the yard just seconds earlier. I went upstairs and checked the bedrooms, the closets, the bathtubs, and under the beds. I went to the basement and even peeked into the washer and dryer – just in case!! They were not at home.

My mother and I then went to our neighbors. I finally called my husband, who told me to call the police. Soon, the whole neighborhood was out looking for them – kids on scooters and bikes, and adults running and driving in the vicinity.

My six-year-old son, who had kept up with my mom the whole time, stopped her and said, "Naani, we need to sit down and pray." And, sitting on the steps of a neighbor's house, he offered a simple petition to God. A police officer arrived and, after a few questions, was about to call for additional help when my father pulled up in front of the house, with a puzzled look on his face. He opened the car's back door and out popped my precious girls!

I had lost my nerve and was terribly anxious and apprehensive. But my son taught me a great lesson of trust through his simple faith.

Let's exercise simple, childlike faith in our God.

May 22

A Child of the King

Biju Thomas

"Our God is a God who saves. He is the King and the Lord."

Psalm 68:20, NLT

It was a challenging time in our lives, and when we gathered for family worship that evening, my father explained the grave situation he was facing. He told us that we needed to sincerely seek God's guidance and leadership in order to overcome the very serious trouble we were facing.

He then asked us to suggest a song we could sing as a family. Without any hesitation, my brother called out, "Let's sing, 'I'm a Child of the King.'" We all burst into laughter! It seemed so inappropriate. Here we were, facing a dire challenge, without a solution in our hands, and we were supposed to sing that we were royal children!! It sounded like a joke!!

But now, when I reflect on it, it is actually very appropriate! Christians are bought with a price and belong to a heavenly family.

I am truly His child, seated with Christ in the heavenly realm, chosen and accepted as a citizen of heaven and a bona fide member of God's household. I am loved by God unconditionally and without reservation. No matter my situation, all God's resources are within reach. He can, and will, supply every need!

The words of that song evoke some precious memories of my childhood:

"My Father is rich in houses and lands, He holdeth the wealth of the world in His hands…I'm a child of the King."

No, we may not look like it, but the reality of the Christian faith allows us to sing the song with confidence and meaning.

May 23

Unfair Burden

Subodh K Pandit

"But He was wounded for our transgressions. . ."

Isaiah 53:5, KJV

It was a holiday, and functions were arranged for the students on the campus.

I was in the hostel that morning, with a syringe filled with water, looking for someone to startle. I found him, and swish! The water caught him right in the face! I laughed, and he nodded at me, with a wait-till-I-get-back-at-you look on his face. Minutes later, he was back with a bucketful of water. Splash! Splash! I was drenched, the hallway was flooded, and in a moment, he was gone!

Just then, the monitor walked by, and seeing the water and my wet clothes, he promptly reported me to the Dean. I was ordered to clean up the mess, and until then, I could not attend the functions outside. It was so, so unfair! I was sour and grumpy while cleaning up the mess that someone else had created!!

Years later, when this episode came to mind, I was stunned: "He was stricken, smitten by God and afflicted." And then, "But, He was wounded for our transgression." Isaiah 53:4,5. The roles were diametrically reversed here! Now, I had created the mess, and Someone else was paying for it. I remembered how bitter and unhappy I had been, cleaning up the mess. But He? ". . .for the **joy** that was set before Him endured the cross, despising the shame." Hebrews 12:2. I felt small and humbled. He had really thought it worthwhile. Otherwise, it couldn't have been a "joy!"

There is a way to find meaning even when bearing unfair burdens!

May 24

Morning By Morning

Gladwin Mathews

"The Sovereign LORD has given me a well-instructed tongue, to know the word that sustains the weary. He wakens me morning by morning, wakens my ear to listen like one being instructed."

Isaiah 50:4, NIV

Since the 6th grade, I have studied in Adventist boarding schools in India, where we were made to wake up at 6 am to attend morning worship sessions. At first, I didn't like it, but as I got accustomed to it, I even enjoyed participating actively in the sessions. To this day, it is my practice to have morning and evening prayers. Mornings are special because the mind is clear and more impressionable after a refreshing sleep.

Such was the prayer life of Jesus. It was His custom to commune with His Father each morning. "Very early in the morning, while it was still dark, Jesus got up. . .and went off to a solitary place, where He prayed. Simon and his companions went to look for Him, and when they found Him, they exclaimed, 'Everyone is looking for you!' Jesus replied, 'Let us go somewhere else – to the nearby villages – so I can preach there also. That is why I have come.'" Mark 1:35-38

Jesus felt it necessary to spend time early in the morning alone with God so that He might receive strength and wisdom from Him for the day. Those were precious moments for Jesus, not only to talk to His Father but also to listen to Him.

David also found this a blessing: "I am up before dawn to pray, waiting for your promises." Psalm 119:147.

Let us start each day right with prayer, morning by morning.

MAY 25

HE NEVER FAILS

Naveena Mora

"Be still and know that I am God. . .The Lord of hosts is with us; The God of Jacob is our refuge."

Psalm 46:10, KJV

Imagine working six days a week, for a total of 60 to 70 hours! That was my husband's work schedule. Our children hardly ever saw him. I barely had any time with him. And it went on year after year. I felt like I was living a married but single life, and gradually sank into loneliness. The harder we worked, the further the goal seemed!

I cried, prayed, and pleaded with God. I got upset and questioned Him. When was it going to end? How would He do it? The answer came, and it was shattering – after 22 years of service, my husband lost his job! Now, my emotions swung in another direction. I became hysterical and frightened. I couldn't accept it when my husband said, "Don't worry. Everything will be okay. We must walk by faith." It was one of the most challenging times in my life. To demand trust at that time was asking me to be superhuman!

Then I noticed that since he was at home, my children and I saw more of him; he took my mother to her doctor's appointments (as she battled cancer) and was able to help with the specialized care that my mother and my daughter required. These were real blessings!

After nearly a year, my husband found a new job, with more time for family, and weekends off so he could come to church. Life now had a new direction!

God answered my prayer but in His time. I needed to trust!

Yes, he will answer our prayers; His ways are better than ours.

MAY 26

GOD'S TELEPHONE NUMBER

Biju Thomas

"Call unto me, and I will answer thee, and shew thee great and mighty things, which thou knowest not."

Jeremiah 33:3, KJV

The Maldivian Archipelago (a string of islands) has an average ground level of 4 feet 11 inches above sea level, and is considered the world's lowest-lying country. It was hit by a devastating tsunami in December of 2004, which left more than 100 presumed to be dead. I reached the Maldivian island of Kendhikuludhoo in April of 2005, just five months later. It is a very tiny island – less than one square mile in area, and situated far out in the Indian Ocean.

A few months after I arrived, we woke up to the island's public address system warning everyone of a tsunami heading in our direction. Panic spread, as the memory of the previous tsunami was fresh in everyone's mind.

My roommate, a Muslim, said that we needed to pray for protection, because there was little hope of survival should it strike our island. He went to pray in the mosque, the only place of worship on the island, while I sat outside our place and prayed for mercy and protection. We spent nearly the whole night in prayer.

God answered, and the waves caused by the tsunami did not sweep over the Maldives that night. We were kept safe from disaster! It seemed like we had a direct phone line to God, and He had promptly picked up and answered.

God's "phone number" is found all over the world. It is a 24-hour service, and is within easy reach of everyone. Make sure you remember this at all times.

May 27

God Chose The Method

Subodh K Pandit

"Him shall He teach in the way He chooses."

Psalm 25:12, NKJV

The financial burdens were growing, and we still had some ways to go before being licensed to practice medicine in the USA. The income from our residency program was barely keeping us afloat, and we knew bigger expenses were on the way.

I had already gone through the Internal Medicine course of studies in India and wondered if I should request a one-year waiver so I could take the board exams a year earlier. That would be a huge relief financially.

With a prayer in my heart, I approached the Program Director in Tulsa, Oklahoma, with my request. He said the approval would have to come from the American Board of Internal Medicine. I would have to apply there, and he was willing to help write the letter.

Soon after, he was called to become the Executive Secretary of the American Board of Internal Medicine, and he moved to Pennsylvania. By the time my request reached the Board, he had taken up his position as the Executive Secretary.

So, as the Program Director in Tulsa, he had helped me with the letter, and now as the Executive Secretary of the Board, he responded to the request he himself had helped draft!! Of course, I was granted the one-year waiver!! Relieved and delighted, I did the board exams and was successful.

When I think about this episode in my life, I find myself chuckling at the way God chose to answer my prayer. "Our heavenly Father has a thousand ways to provide for us of which we know nothing." EGW

May 28

Everlasting Arms of Protection

Biju Thomas

"Our God is a God who saves! The Sovereign LORD rescues us from death."

Psalm 68:20, NLT

I was twelve and still in school when my father sent us on our first journey by ourselves. My grandmother, brother, and I were to visit an uncle who lived quite far away.

We got onto the bus going from Bangalore to Mysore. While on the highway, we suddenly heard a loud bang, and our bus shook violently. Our bus had collided head-on with an oncoming bus, started rolling backward towards the side of the road, and then skidded down a steep incline, before settling at the bottom of the valley.

My brother and I didn't sustain any major injuries, but we were perplexed and didn't know what to do. The people all around us were screaming and crying for help. Our grandmother was badly hurt with a gash on her lips. She was bleeding profusely and crying out for help, and we felt totally helpless. All we could do was pray and plead with God.

As we looked around, not knowing what to do, the people from the nearby villages came rushing to help. They came with their trucks and tractors and carried the injured to the nearest hospital, where they were treated.

We were in strange surroundings and entirely unfamiliar with the local language, but the people willingly helped us in our desperate need. I felt they were like angels sent from heaven. And when I look back on this incident, I am reminded again of the everlasting arms of protection, which faithfully uphold and protect us along the way. Thank you, God!

May 29

Constant Protection

Subodh K Pandit

"Fear not, for I am with you…"

Isaiah 43:5, NKJV

We were three energetic and inquisitive boys, living in Salisbury Park, Pune, India. Between us and a village to our south, was a pond, which the village folk used as the water source for their daily needs. It would get filled to the brim during the rainy season, but get shallower at other times.

One day, when we walked down to the water's edge, we noticed a hole in the embankment. We curiously peeked in and saw two snakes coiled up. We took it upon ourselves as a duty, and unanimously decided to kill them. But the snakes were deep inside.

First, we stood in a circle and prayed. Then, we picked up pieces of rock and flung them into the hole. One of the snakes came dashing out, but we were ready with rocks in our hands. We got it with just two attempts.

The other snake wouldn't come out. This called for ingenuity on our part. After a few moments of intense brainstorming, we came up with a foolproof plan. My friend would reach in with his hand and pull it out, while my brother and I stood on either side of the hole with rocks in our hands, ready for the head.

One, two, three, Go! He reached in, pulled it out, and as soon as the head appeared, two rocks came down on it with unerring accuracy. Our job had been accomplished!

Today, my heart nearly stops, just thinking about our foolhardy adventure!!

I know God's watch care was constant in our lives, for without it we wouldn't have survived!!

May God's protection be with you today and always.

MAY 30

GOD'S PROTECTION

Gladwin Mathews

"And these signs will accompany those who believe: In my name they will drive out demons; they will speak in new tongues; they will pick up snakes with their hands; and when they drink deadly poison, it will not hurt them at all; they will place their hands on sick people, and they will get well."

Mark 16:17,18, NIV.

In 1984, we were living on the campus of the Roorkee Higher Secondary School, with its sprawling grounds spread over hundreds of acres. Certain areas of the campus were known to be infested with cobras, and our house was in such an area.

One evening, when I got home, I felt uneasy and sensed that danger might be lurking nearby. I went to the back door and cautiously opened it, and there was a cobra coiled up just a few feet away! I silently closed the door and fetched the rod I had kept for just such an emergency. I slipped out again, brought it down accurately, and pinned the neck of the cobra. But it fought back so hard that I had to put my whole weight on the rod to keep it in place. I called out to my wife to get help. Our neighbor came running over, and together, we soon had the upper hand. My wife said, "I had just come in through the back door!!"

Psalm 91 speaks of the protection that God provides those who put their trust in Him. It describes the work of angels and explicitly mentions the cobra. God is our protector, and He has repeatedly shown His care in our lives.

May you be protected by God's angels always.

May 31

God's Amazing Love

Biju Thomas

"Can a mother forget her nursing child? Can she feel no love for the child she has borne? But even if that were possible, I would not forget you."

Isaiah 49:15, NLT

In 1997, my mother was diagnosed with a cancerous tumor, and the doctors told us that she had only six more months to live. We were thrown into despair and fell on our knees and pleaded with God to extend her life.

A surgery was scheduled to remove the tumor, and as she lay on her hospital bed after the surgery, with tubes running all over her body and unable to speak, she gave up all hope. But God, in His mercy, touched her and provided her a miraculous recovery.

In 1998, she emigrated to the USA, and became a citizen in 2005. Ever since moving to the USA, she worked tirelessly with one goal uppermost in her mind – to bring her children to the USA. Of course, there were hurdles and challenges, but she braved them all for the sake of her children. For 21 years, her love for her children gave her the patience, endurance, and strength of faith to keep pleading with God to open the way. In June 2019, the answer came, and we traveled to the USA to join her.

She met us at the airport with excitement that could not be contained! She welcomed us with open arms and tears of joy.

Her steadfast love had endured for decades!! We couldn't compare it with anything else on earth! And yet, God's love for us far exceeds a mother's tender love for her children! Thank you, God!

May you be surrounded by God's love today.

JUNE 1

WITH A PRAYER IN MY HEART

Gladwin Mathews

"God is our refuge and strength, an ever-present help in trouble."

Psalm 46:1, NIV

When we moved from the Midwest to Virginia, we first lived in a rented two-bedroom apartment. After two years, we realized we needed a bigger place, and I began looking for a single-family home. While driving around in the neighborhood, I saw one put up for rent by a realtor. I prayed and then called the realtor who showed us the house. We liked it and signed the agreement. While signing it, I off-handedly mentioned to him that I would be interested in buying it if the owner ever wanted to sell it.

Two years later, we got word that the owner wanted to sell the house, and that we had the first preference to make an offer. I contacted a loan agent who arranged a good deal for us. It included having to pay the "closing costs." But I didn't have the money to pay the amount. I turned to God, because I didn't want to lose such a good deal, and at the same time, I didn't have enough money.

The next day, the agent called and said everything had been worked out, and I would not have to pay the costs upfront to close the deal. I heaved a sigh of relief and joy. What seemed like an impassable barrier, had been passed. The way was opened for us to have a house. Thank God!

The way around us may be filled with obstacles, but the way upward is always open! Keep that path unobstructed, and we will always be filled with hope!

June 2

God's Mysterious Ways

J S Navarose

"When the master of the feast had tasted the water that was made wine, and did not know where it came from (but the servants who had drawn the water knew,) the master of the feast called the bridegroom."

John 2:9, NKJV

God's miracles come in unexpected ways, through unlikely people, and at surprising moments, even to those who trust in Him.

In 1992, we made plans to upgrade Bangalore Spencer School to a Pre-university College. So, we submitted the necessary documents to the Karnataka State Education Department. We knew it would take a lot of underhand payments to push our file through the different stages, and we didn't have the money. So, we just waited.

One day, the local MLA (Member of the Legislative Assembly) called me to his office and showed me the permit to upgrade the school, but said he would hand it over on payment of a considerable sum! I made a copy of it, handed it back to him, and returned home, wondering how to cross this seemingly impossible hurdle!

Sometime later, an ordinary-looking person came to the school asking for a favor. He said he would help the school in return. Not expecting much, I showed him the copy of the permit and mentioned the price demanded by the MLA.

Three days later, he was back. And lo and behold! In his hand was an authentic authorization from the desk of the State Education Minister, permitting us to upgrade the school! And he did not demand any payment!!

God had worked in an unexpected way, through an unlikely person!

Our task is to place our trust in Him!

JUNE 3

DIVINE INTERVENTION

Gladwin Mathews

"I will tell of the kindness of the Lord, the deeds for which He is to be praised, according to all the Lord has done for us – yes, the many good things He has done for Israel, according to His compassion and many kindnesses."

Isaiah 63:7, NIV

My dad had been sick for some time in India. Since he was alone, we decided to bring him to the United States. My sister would accompany him on the flight, which had a 5-hour layover in Paris. During the transit, he suddenly became very ill and nearly collapsed. The hostess called for emergency transportation, and he was rushed to a hospital. His condition was serious, and treatment was started immediately, including a transfusion of two units of blood.

We could not have much contact with them when they were at the hospital. We also knew they would need money, but did not know how to send it to them. That period was very stressful for everyone.

After more than two weeks, he had regained enough strength to resume the journey. The hospital asked for payment before discharging him, and it was an enormous amount – beyond anything they could afford! Praying silently, my sister confessed that they didn't have that much money. To her amazement, they decided to write off the entire bill! And my father made it safely to the USA.

We often hear the words, "Divine Intervention," which could be a miraculous healing or just people being in the right place at the right time. Both happened in the case of my dad. It was Divine Intervention!

May divine intervention be evident in your life today.

JUNE 4

SHUTDOWN ON SABBATH

Daisy Sharlin

"You shall keep my Sabbaths. . ."

Leviticus 19:30, NKJV

I was the only SDA nurse in the Emergency Department (ED) in that hospital in Singapore. It was easy to arrange the shifts so I would not have to work on Sabbaths. But some nurses felt it was unfair that I got to have every Saturday off to attend my church, while they had to take turns on Sundays to attend theirs.

One day, the manager called me, brought up the issue, and put me on duty on a Saturday. Not wanting to cause any trouble, I decided to comply. However, I carried my Bible and Sabbath School book with me.

In the ED, a nurse came to see me read the Bible, then others joined her. We fell into a conversation about my belief in the Bible Sabbath. I said that I wished the ED remained empty so we could all observe the Sabbath. Some laughed, "So, now we all in the ED must do as you do!!" When they left, I prayed, "If it is Your will, please keep the patients away from my unit."

Weekends are hectic in Singapore due to drinking and alcohol-related accidents. The EDs get full quickly. As we waited for the first patient, the IT Department sent an urgent message. A technical problem caused all the systems in the ED, including the reception area, to shut down. I could hardly believe my ears! Patients were redirected via ambulances to other hospitals, and our ED remained absolutely quiet the whole time.

I felt as if God had sent a message, not just to me, but to all my colleagues, doctors, and receptionists!

God will open ways for us to keep his commandments if we genuinely seek to do so.

June 5

A Generous Life

Gladwin Mathews

"Each man should give what he has decided in his heart to give, not reluctantly or under compulsion, for God loves a cheerful giver. And God is able to make all grace abound to you, so that in all things at all times, having all that you need, you will abound in every good work."

II Corinthians 9:7,8, NIV

In April 2020, I received word from India that about 240 daily laborers were helplessly stranded, with no place to stay, and no money or food for their families. Many of them had small children who immediately needed milk and other supplies. Covid-19 was a real threat, and the need was urgent!

Their dire condition touched my heart. The person who had called for help, was willing to pitch in and reach out to them personally. So, I immediately raised some funds and sent them over as quickly as possible. It was sufficient to feed them and also get the much-needed supplies to combat Covid-19. Those unfortunate families were helped, and I had the wonderful sense of having been of help!

I have been doing a personal ministry in Punjab, India, for 12 years now, and I can testify, without any hesitation, that I have experienced great joy and happiness in my life. Giving and sharing through the ministry has resulted in many individuals and families being helped, which has brought about changes in me from the inside out! Indeed, it is "more blessed to give than to receive!"

God's motivation in giving to us is love. Let us emulate Him, and give back to Him and to those in need.

JUNE 6

IN HIS TIME – PART 1

Anonymous

"He has made everything beautiful in its time. . ."

Ecclesiastes 3:11, ESV

I was sitting in the plane's window seat and gazing down at the clouds beneath me, on my first trip to the USA.

Over twenty years earlier, to the day and month, I had run barefoot on the hot melting tar road to reach my college for the practical exam in Chemistry. I was being ill-treated at home and intentionally made to be late for the exam. The bus I caught took me only half the distance, and I had to run the other half to be on time.

I was very hungry and thirsty and noticed that I had about 15 minutes to go before reaching the college. So, I stopped under a tree to catch my breath. Suddenly, a lady from a nearby shop approached me and gave me a glass of cool lemon juice and a big piece of peanut candy. I had never seen her before and said I had no money to pay for them. She patted me on my shoulder and said it was okay.

"When the poor and needy seek water, and there is none, and their tongue is parched with thirst, I the Lord will answer them, I the God of Israel will not forsake them." Isaiah 41:17, ESV.

God had promised to answer when times were hard, and when I was in need, He arranged for a stranger to meet my needs. Blessed be His name!

Though I suffered much hardship as a young person, here I was, over twenty years later, flying to the US. What a God of deliverance!

If you are going through hardships, hang on to God, He will deliver on time.

JUNE 7

IN HIS TIME – PART 2

Anonymous

"He says," Be still and know that I am God; I will be exalted among the nations, I will be exalted in the earth." The LORD Almighty is with us; the God of Jacob is our fortress.

Psalm 46:10-11, NIV

When I reached the chemistry lab, I was 45 minutes late. The supervisor from the university took one look at my swollen, tear-streaked face, and without a word, allowed me into the lab to take the exam. When I reached my desk, and opened my ink pen, I was shocked to find the tip broken off. I did not have an extra pen! Just then, an attendant reached my desk and handed me a pen. I wondered how he knew that I needed a pen. This Bible verse crossed my mind, "Be still and know that I am God." When I got the results later, I had scored 47/50!

Looking back, I realize I had no way of dealing with the problems alone. Three strangers (the lady from the shop, the supervisor, and the attendant) showed me kindness at crucial moments on that one day when I was struggling under a heavy burden of grief, torture, and oppression. It helped increase my faith in God and hang on to life.

It is my testimony that God pulled me out of the depths of despair. He may answer our prayers in 2 seconds, 2 hours, or 20 years! He will not allow burdens more than we can bear. So, when we face pain and cruelty, let us submit everything to God. He will solve our problems and bless us abundantly in His time!

JUNE 8

THE WITNESS OF BLOOD

Gladwin Mathews

"This is He who came by water and blood – Jesus Christ; not only by water, but by water and blood. And it is the Spirit who bears witness, because the Spirit is truth."

I John 5:6, NKJV

In June 1986, I was called to serve as Principal of the SDA school at Rohru, a predominantly Hindu community, some distance from Shimla. My wife and I were the only Christians there. One morning, I opened my front door to see drops of blood leading all the way around the house. It was a sign that somebody was upset with us, and had attempted to cast a spell on us. I wasn't alarmed. I took a bucket of water and washed the blood away.

The next day, while conversing with the parents of children who were studying in our school, I mentioned the drops of blood. The mother laughed and said that such incidents were quite common, and then added, "But you are a Christian and believe in God. Don't worry; nothing will happen to you or your wife!"

I was surprised to hear such a testimony from a Hindu. It affirmed my faith in the living God, and reminded me of the awesome God we serve whose sacrifice of blood is more powerful than any spell that may be cast on us.

Hindus have the concept of blood sacrifice similar to the Christians. As the book of Leviticus is to the Old Testament, and the book of Hebrews to the New Testament, so is the Yajurveda to the Vedas. I thanked God for the opportunity to talk about the blood sacrifice that really counts.

JUNE 9

GOD'S UNCONDITIONAL LOVE

Cinthya Daniel

"Can a woman forget her nursing child, and not have compassion on the son of her womb? Surely they may forget, yet I will not forget you."

Isaiah 49:15, NKJV

While living in India, I had the luxury of going to my parents' home during the fifth month of my first pregnancy, and they were absolutely delighted to have me there! Every morning, I found my mom at the kitchen table preparing various home remedies such as barley water, drumstick soup, and exotic juices. She would ask me what I wanted, and lovingly prepare every meal – nutritious South-Indian breakfasts, my favorite curries for lunch, and real yummy dinners. She made me the center of all her activities; and would even rush home during her lunch break to serve me with warm food!

Four weeks before my due date, I suddenly developed a bout of pneumonia, and had to be hospitalized. Even there, my mom was always at hand. Whenever I felt hungry, like clockwork, she was right there with a warm drink or a snack. She seemed to know exactly when I would be hungry. I asked her how she knew, and she replied with warmth and kindness in her voice, "That is the beauty of a mother's love!" I was very fortunate to have experienced that love.

I thank God for the healthy baby boy He gave us when the due date came. And I praise Him for mothers who reflect God's unconditional love!

God's love for us surpasses human parents' love by far! He set us apart to be His own, gave us His Son, and loves us with everlasting love!

June 10

The Garden

Gladwin Mathews

"Now the Lord God had planted a garden in the east, in Eden; and there he put the man he had formed."

Genesis 2:8, NIV

I have a kitchen garden where I love to sow seeds, prepare seedlings, and plant vegetables and fruit trees. Seeing the fruit of my labor blossom in various colors gives me great joy. I love to see the colorful birds, beautiful butterflies, and naughty squirrels that come to dig up the garden when they visit!

The beauty, the activity, and the constant growth seen in the garden, remind me of God as my Creator, my Provider, and the Source of the mercies that surround me daily. Working and spending time in my garden helps me see God's wisdom, care, and love on display. It helps me physically and economically and allows time for reflection – to think of all my silly mistakes. Even in the midst of suffering that results from my blunders, goodness still flourishes! From the warmth of the sun, to the flowers in my kitchen garden, to the melodious songs of birds, and the fluttering of delicate butterfly wings, His love is revealed, and I thank Him for revealing His truths to me! Through the gift of Eden, Adam could see that God was a generous Provider and a lover of the beautiful!

Let us pay close attention to what is all around us. God is sowing His truth daily, and I pray that our hearts will be prepared like good fertile soil, ready to receive Jesus, and be rooted, watered, and established in His garden of love.

June 11

Get Thee Behind Me Satan - Part 1

Daisy Sharlin

"Whenever I am afraid, I will trust in You."

Psalm 56:3, NKJV

I was very excited When I got the opportunity to work in an Emergency Department (ED) in Singapore. The ED had 12 observation rooms. For reasons unknown to me then, the manager cautioned us during the orientation process, that we should always go to the rooms in pairs. Later, my colleagues informed me that many atrocities had been committed in that area during World War II, and that the observation rooms were haunted.

Out of curiosity, I went onto the internet and checked it out. The hospital was previously the "British Military Hospital," where the Japanese soldiers had killed many staff, patients, and even children. Some escaped through underground tunnels. Others tried to hide in bunkers but were found out, taken to the football field outside, and gunned down. During our orientation, they showed us the bunkers with some items still in place!

My excitement regarding the new job turned into fear and sadness. When I started work, my worries grew as I experienced unusual manifestations!

One day, the call bell rang from room 1, but when I glanced up at the CCTV, the room was empty! I went over and deactivated the alarm, but it rang again as I returned to the nurse's station. After a few attempts, I called the security personnel, who advised me to ignore such happenings. However, I was very disturbed. I recalled Psalm 56:3, "Whenever I am afraid, I will trust in you." The words seemed to apply precisely to my situation.

Trust in God, and he will remove our fears.

JUNE 12

GET THEE BEHIND ME SATAN – PART 2

Daisy Sharlin

"Submit yourselves therefore to God. Resist the devil, and he will flee from you."

James 4:7, KJV

The Emergency Department used to be the pediatric unit where the Japanese soldiers had committed many atrocities during World War II. In our conversations, my colleagues would report seeing images of soldiers on the CCTV, the sound of soldiers marching, and the sound of children crying.

Room 12 was previously used exclusively for patients affected by the radiation accident in Japan. Hence, it was currently unused, but we had to perform routine room checks, including this room. It always smelled like Jasmine flowers, no matter how it was cleaned! And I was told to walk backward when leaving the room!

One day, when Room 4 was empty, the TV turned on. I turned it off, and as I closed the door, it came on again! Then I heard my name being called. Thinking that my colleague had called, I responded, "Coming!" But when I reached her, she hadn't called.

Such experiences were frightening and were taking an emotional toll on me. So, I called my mother crying, and told her how unbearable the experience was. She reminded me that Christians had an armor – Psalms 23 – and if I should ever face fear, I should loudly say, "Get thee behind me Satan!"

I started doing exactly that! And all the weird, abnormal activities stopped. After that, I would sing a song to Jesus whenever I had to go to those rooms alone. I continued working peacefully in that ED for the next five years!

Resist the Devil, and he will flee from you.

JUNE 13

SEEKING THE BEST FOR THE CHURCH

Gladwin Mathews

"Mordecai the Jew was second in rank to King Xerxes, preeminent among the Jews, and held in high esteem by his many fellow Jews, because he worked for the good of his people and spoke up for the welfare of all the Jews."

Esther 10:3, NIV

I have been attending the Southern Asian Seventh-Day Adventist Church (SASDAC) for the last 22 years, and I can testify that we have many in this church who have played the role of Mordecai. Some honored their Lord in the high places of affluence and influence where God placed them, and testified for Jesus before great men.

Others had a much lowlier role, but equally important in the sight of God. They prayed for the weak, the doubting, the tempted, and the unfortunate. They interceded for those who were out in the darkness, and pleaded to bring them to His light.

I have watched as Pastors, Elders, Deacons, Deaconesses, and others offered their talents for the good of others, and imparted their wealth of learning to build them up. Even the very least have sought the welfare of God's people, and have given until they could give no more! They had one goal – to finish the great commission, reflected in the motto: "To know Him and to make Him known."

We have an actual, real-life example of working for the good of the church: every member did whatever he could, with whatever he had, and wherever he was. The result was a wonderful edifice, built for the glory of God – the SASDAC! Let us prepare ourselves for His kingdom and say, "Come Lord Jesus, come!"

June 14

Father God

Anita B.R. Mohan

"For whoever calls on the name of the Lord shall be saved."

Romans 10:13, NKJV

It was the morning of April 26, 2022, just a couple of days after we had returned from India. I left home for work just like any other day. I had gone about 3 miles, and the signal light ahead was green, so I went forward. But at the crossing, I saw a car from the opposite direction suddenly make a left turn right into my path. It was too close, and I didn't have time to brake or turn away. An accident was inevitable. At that moment, all I could do was call out "Yesappa!" It means "Father God," in my language, Tamil.

The collision was hard. The impact pushed my Jeep out to the side of the road, and I hit a large post, which fell on the other side, and not on the car. The door was jammed, and the firefighters who came to rescue me had to break it open to get me out.

I was in shock, and began to shiver, and was sobbing by the time my husband reached the scene. The vehicle was totaled, and the damage looked so bad that everyone thought I would have to go to the ER for treatment. But I was not hurt at all! No bones were broken. I did not have a scratch on my body!

I had called upon His name, and He had sent His angels who had kept me under His wings of protection. Our Father God protects us from known and unknown harm and seen and unseen dangers.

JUNE 15

THE FLOOD IS UPON US!

Gladwin Mathews

"The waters rose and covered the mountains to a depth of more than twenty feet."

Genesis 7:20, NIV

Scientists who don't believe the Bible, treat the story of Noah's flood as a fairy tale. But others believe that it really happened.

One evening, my Hindu friend and I were walking along the side of a tall mountain, in Rohru, that showed layered bands of rock, similar to the ones in the Grand Canyon in the USA. "Do you know how these layers formed?" I asked.

"Yes," he said. "There is a story in the Hindu Scriptures which describes a universal flood. God had told Manu, the first human, that the world would be destroyed in a great flood. A big fish, called Matsya, who was the first incarnate of the God Vishnu, pulled the boat in which Manu was riding, to a safe harbor. Manu then re-populated the earth with people."

I then narrated to him the Biblical account of how the great underground water reservoirs had exploded, and heavy rain had come down and destroyed all life on earth. I also mentioned the reason God sent the flood, as well as the identity of the survivors, who then re-populated the earth. God gave humans a sign, the rainbow, that a similar flood would not destroy the earth.

Jesus described another type of flood that would come upon the world at the end of time – a flood of severe trouble and anguish. He said it would be terrible, unlike anything experienced before it. It is of the utmost importance that we build a faith strong enough to withstand that flood.

JUNE 16

THE VOID

Naveena Mora

"For the Lord Himself will come down from heaven, with a loud command, with the voice of an archangel and with the trumpet call of God, and the dead in Christ will rise first. . .we. . .will be caught up together with them in the clouds to meet the Lord in the air."

I Thessalonians 4:16,17, NIV

Almost ten years ago, my family and I went through a deeply painful experience. After a long battle with cancer, my mother was called to rest in July 2013. I knew it was bound to happen, and yet, when it did, I was not prepared for the emotional trauma. I felt lost and utterly helpless. The finality of it! It was so permanent! I would never see her again! Many times, I would go into my closet and weep! I had lost my best friend.

I watched my father suffer as he went through his loss. Often I would hear him weeping in his room as he cried and "talked to her" in his grief. The void we all felt was almost unbearable! I questioned God, and those questions seemed to fill my conversations with God.

But gradually, we learned to cope with that void, finding ways to console each other. One day, while sharing our memories of our mother, I thought of the verse in the Bible that talked of seeing our loved ones again. It was in I Thessalonians 4:16,17 – a wonderful, comforting promise! And I found peace, knowing that a day will come when I will see my mother again. So, until then, I will wait and cling to Him and His words.

Remember His promise when you miss a loved one resting in Christ.

JUNE 17

I Will Lift up My Eyes to the Lord

Anonymous

"I will lift up my eyes to the hills. From where does my help come? My help comes from the LORD, who made heaven and earth."

Psalm 121:1, ESV

I was returning to the USA from India with my two children. My son was three years old, and my daughter was eight months old. I was alone with them. On the first leg of our flight, my daughter developed a fever. I gave her some medication, but it continued and would not subside. She then started vomiting and began to have diarrhea too. She looked very sick, and soon became weak and limp. The flight attendant said we would have to stop at Amsterdam as the child was getting dehydrated. She would need medical treatment in a hospital right away.

I took my daughter to the restroom, knelt, lifted my baby with both arms and, from my heart, I prayed and cried out to God on her behalf. I distinctly remember hearing the words of Psalm 23 in my ear: "Yeah, though I walk through the valley of the shadow of death, I will fear no evil; For you are with me. . ."

Strengthened in my heart, I came out of the restroom and asked the flight attendant for water, sugar, and salt. I mixed all three in a feeding bottle and gave it to my daughter. She began to drink rapidly, and soon, the fever subsided, she didn't vomit again, and the diarrhea stopped.

We continued our journey without stopping in Amsterdam, and arrived back home on schedule. Thank You, Jesus, for answering my desperate cry.

Lift your eyes to Jesus; In Him is our help.

June 18

Showing Christian Love

Gladwin Mathews

"So in everything, do to others what you would have them do to you, for this sums up the Law and the Prophets."

Matthew 7:12, NIV

When I was a child, I had the opportunity to visit my maternal uncle in Lahore, Pakistan, along with my mom and other siblings. Many relatives lived there, so every evening, we were invited to one of the homes for a family function. Before we left for the functions, my mom would instruct us on how to behave: "Listen, don't forget to say 'Salaam' (greet) to everyone and be respectful. Obey your elders and show them respect. Wash your hands before you eat. Accept whatever they give you, and don't make a fuss."

We were all one family, and this was a way to express our love and togetherness in practical terms. Words alone wouldn't be enough, and we needed instructions to translate words into actions.

Hebrews 13:1-8 has a similar set of instructions for Christians. Admonitions given there cover various aspects of private and public life, and religious and social life, that distinguish the Christian, who knows the truth, from others. Our behavior should be in line with that truth.

The character of the Christian is shown by his daily life. "Those who have genuine love for God will manifest an earnest desire to know His will and to do it. . .We are commanded to love one another as Christ has loved us. He has manifested His love by laying down His life to redeem us." EG White, Sanctified Life, chapter 10.

May we have concern and respect for others, faith in action, and love at work.

How God Helped Me

Saharsh Isaac

"But the very hairs of your head are all numbered. Do not fear therefore; you are of more value than many sparrows."

Luke 12:7, NKJV

I am now eight years old, but I was seven when this happened. I had a headache and felt sick. So I was given the special privilege of sleeping on the couch, having my favorite soft drink, and even missing school. The special privileges, especially missing school, were fun, but the headache was not fun at all. It was quite bad. So I prayed to God. The headache came on and off during that day, but the next day, it was gone! It felt really good to be well again!

I had prayed about my headache because I know God cares about our minor problems too. He doesn't want me to miss school, and He doesn't want me to miss out on playing with my friends.

I was thrilled when my headache was gone. Now, I could go out and play with my friend, Sammy, who lives in my neighborhood. It is so cool to play with friends. (Another time, I will tell you how cool playing with friends is.) After my headache was gone, I also got to go back to school, learn, and play with my other friends again. God had heard my prayers, taken away my headache, and made me feel well again.

Jesus, who cares about every hair on our heads and every sparrow in the field, indeed has the time to hear and answer all our prayers, whether about small or big problems.

JUNE 20

GOOD SAMARITAN AND THE GOOD SHEPHERD

Daisy Sharlin

"I am the good shepherd. The good shepherd gives His life for the sheep."

John 10:11, NKJV

My grandfather was a great storyteller. When I was a little girl, I would sit by his side and listen to numerous stories of his life. Many of them were from when he was in the army during World War II.

Most evenings, the soldiers would drink and party. However, my grandfather would not participate in those activities. A British officer noticed it and inquired about his decision. The officer was impressed with his integrity and loyalty to his beliefs. So he removed him from the frontline and put him in charge of the stockroom. He did not have to carry arms. Thus, he possibly escaped being killed in battle.

One day, while in the war zone, he was instructed to go and collect some supplies. While driving in the army jeep, he noticed a soldier wounded and lying on the ground. He stopped the jeep, went to check, and discovered he was an enemy soldier. His colleagues begged him to leave the soldier alone. But my grandfather could not turn away. He covered him, carried him to the jeep, and took him to his supply room. There, he cleaned his wounds, fed him, and hid him for many days, at the risk of his own life! My grandfather said that this was his bravest act as a soldier! He had been a Good Samaritan!

Jesus, our Good Shepherd, not only risked His life but gave it so that we may live! Thank God for good samaritans and the Good Shepherd!

JUNE 21

GOD SPEAKS

Lillykutty Joseph

"I will instruct you and teach you in the way you should go; I will guide you with My eye."

Psalm 32:8, NKJV

This happened decades ago, when I was a student at the Lowry Memorial Junior College in Bangalore (Bengaluru,) India. My sister was the Dean of the girls' hostel, and I was staying with her in the house near the hostel.

One day, I felt impressed to go home. It was an unusual thought because we were not close to any school holidays. But it was so heavy on my mind that I decided I simply had to go.

I left the campus, boarded the overnight train, took a connecting bus, and reached my hometown by noon the next day. Before walking home, I stopped by the local market and bought some fruits and vegetables.

When I reached home, I found my mother in bed, very ill with chickenpox. Chickenpox gets much worse in adults compared to the condition in children. She was in a weakened state because she had developed vesicles from head to foot and needed a lot of help. My dad was elderly himself and couldn't give her the care and support she crucially required. They didn't inform the children because we were all in different stages of our lives and far from home.

I stayed home and took care of my mom until she was well enough to take care of herself. God, in His mercy, had compellingly impressed me at just the right time so I could care for my mom when she needed help.

God always acts promptly! Let us obey Him when He speaks to us.

JUNE 22

OBEDIENCE

Anita B. R. Mohan

"Now therefore, if you will indeed obey my voice and keep My covenant, then you shall be a special treasure to Me above all people; for all the earth is Mine."

Exodus 19:5 NKJV

Years ago, Sabbath Services were held at a park or dam, every now and then in our churches in Tamil Nadu. They were all-day events with potluck, afternoon discussions, and quizzes. We, as children, were required to sit with our parents and not wander off by ourselves.

One such event was planned near the Manjalar Dam, about 75 km from Madurai. It was a beautiful day; the service was wonderful, out in nature; the potluck was enjoyable, and then it was time for the afternoon discussions.

My friend and I, eleven and nine, didn't want to sit for the discussions at that time, so we sneaked out to explore the area. We came across a canal flowing in full force from the opening in the dam. Out of curiosity, I decided to step into the water. The moment I did, I was swept away by the powerful undercurrent. I heard loud screams from some people, and my friend immediately jumped in, and somehow, dragged me out. She was only 11, and I believe she was given extraordinary power and wisdom to pull me out of that strong current. I was safe!

We had disobeyed, but God was still watching over us with love and care, providing the needed strength in time. How much more will He do for us, His "special treasure," if only we obey and keep heeding His call!

June 23

For the Widow and the Fatherless

Gloria Moses

"He executes justice for the orphan and the widow, and shows His love for the alien by giving him food and clothing."

Deuteronomy 10:18, NASB

I had finished 6th grade when my elder sister, my younger sister, and I, along with our mom, moved to a house a short distance from my late grandfather's old residence. My mom was a widow and had a hard time supporting us. We didn't have goats to provide milk for us, so my mom would buy milk from the agricultural department about 2 miles away. The person who brought us the milk, also delivered milk to others. Since we were the last house on his route, he would give us all the remaining milk in his container, which was more than my mom had ordered. And he refused to take any payment for the extra milk. So, we had plenty of milk, although we didn't own a cow or goat. With that milk, my mom gave us hot milk, yogurt, yogurt-rice, and buttermilk to drink.

The person would also bring ripe guavas, and my mom would buy them from him. He brought many of them, so we had plenty of delicious guavas. We could see a bright smile on his face when he gave us the milk and guavas. He knew my mom was a widow who was trying hard to care for her family. He was a stranger and himself poor, but he was helping us the best he could.

God sent a stranger to help my mom and us. God takes care of widows and orphans.

Let us always remember to help those in need.

June 24

Even the Smallest Prayer

Anita B. R. Mohan

"Therefore I tell you, whatever you ask in prayer, believe that you have received it, and it will be yours."

Mark 11:24, NIV

A week had passed since we proofread my cousin's wedding invitation. It had been designed online, and sent to the printers in India, who print it and then send it to us here in the USA.

On Sunday morning, my aunt called my husband and said there was a mistake in the card. I nearly went into a panic! It was already Sunday. India's time zone is hours ahead, and we had planned for the cards to arrive within the week. What were we to do?!

My husband sent an urgent email to the printers asking if a change could be made, and whether we could still get the cards by the due date here in the USA. It seemed that only a miracle could get it done. And we needed a miracle! This was a once-in-a-lifetime occasion, and I didn't want the invitation cards to be printed with that error.

I couldn't see how it could be done in time. So I kept praying the whole day. On Monday morning when I checked the email, I saw the welcome news! The printers had responded, "Sure, we will do it!" We got the cards the same week, in good time, just as we had planned.

We hear stories of big prayers answered very impressively. But our God listens to, and answers, even the smallest prayers. What a wonderful, understanding God!

Let us go to God in prayer, even for little things. He cares about all our needs.

JUNE 25

CALL AND ANSWER GAME

Bimal Nowrangi

"He shall call upon Me, and I will answer; I will be with him in trouble; I will deliver him and honor him."

Psalm 91:5, NKJV

I was five years old when my father took me for a school picnic near a waterfall. Everyone was enjoying their time out there. Some were swimming; others were merely dipping their feet in the crystal-clear stream. My father and I decided to play the game of hide-and-seek. My father called it the "call-and-answer" game. The one hiding would call out, and the other would quickly assess from where the call had come, and "catch" him before he moved away and hid himself again.

There were many rocks, trees, and shrubs around, and it was fun! But to my dismay, I discovered that he moved so fast that I simply couldn't catch him. On the other hand, when it was my turn to hide and call, he would catch me much too quickly!

I began to get frustrated, and even came to the point of crying, because I was not able to find him. But on hearing me cry, he quickly reappeared from his hiding place, reassuring me that he was still nearby, and the game was still on!

In my life, there were times when I did not feel God's presence near me. I had called, and His answer had not come as I had hoped. But I knew then and know now, that He is always near, and He answers in His own way, in His time. But in every case, it is for our best.

Wait on the Lord; His plans are better than ours.

JUNE 26

ANGELS OF THE LORD

Nilima Nowrangi

"For he shall give his angels charge over thee, to keep thee in all thy ways. They shall bear thee up in their hands, lest thou dash thy foot against a stone."

Psalm 91: 11,12, KJV

While at Spicer Memorial College, my husband was the Dean of Men. There were two separate three-story dormitories, and we lived in the Dean's apartment. Our three children were born while there. We were fortunate, and considered our children to be safe while they played in the yard, because they were always under the watchful eyes of the more than four hundred dormitory students.

One day, our three-year-old daughter wandered away, and while playing behind the dormitory, she fell into the concrete laundry tank there. Some very kind and alert students saw what had happened and quickly pulled her out to safety.

Another time, our two sons, ages 3 and 4, wandered away from their designated play area in the yard. I looked around, and could not locate them. Suddenly I heard their tiny voices calling me from the balcony on the top floor. I looked up and could barely see the tops of their little heads. When I asked them how and why they got up there all by themselves, the older one confidently replied, "For he shall give his angels charge over thee, to keep thee in all thy ways!!" He had learned it as a memory verse in his Sabbath School class.

As a mother, I could have been anxious. But I clearly saw God's protection in how He had sent His angels to protect our three little children from various types of harm and danger.

JUNE 27

THE GREAT COMMISSION

Gladwin Mathews

"Abraham lived a hundred and seventy-five years…and he was gathered to his people."

Genesis 25:7-8, NIV

(I chose this verse only for the number 175! Here's the story.)

Both my parents, Pr. and Mrs. E.G. Mathews were ministers of the Gospel, spreading God's word in the northern parts of India, particularly in the Punjab. They were earnest and passionate in their ministry. I grew up watching them closely. I accompanied my dad a few times. He would go to previously unentered territories every year, organize meetings in peoples' homes, and follow the meetings in the homes with 3 to 4 weeks of public meetings.

One such experience was in a remote village close to the Indo-Pak border. It was new territory, and only a family of four came the first night. Two more neighbors came the next night. Another three came the following night. Word quickly spread, and more and more came every night. He had to arrange for a bigger tent and a larger "daree" (a carpet upon which the people were accustomed to sit and listen.)

At the final meeting, almost the whole congregation accepted the message he had brought. The next day, they all went to a nearby river for the baptism. The water was cold, but he didn't mind it. He had thought the service would be over fairly quickly, but they kept coming into the water to be baptized. He stayed there from midmorning, baptizing them until late afternoon. In that one day, he had baptized 175 people into God's kingdom!

He came out of the water, cold, numb and tired but happy at having a part in the Great Commission!

JUNE 28

THE GREAT COMMISSION – PART 2

Gladwin Mathews

"Therefore go and make disciples of all nations, baptizing them in the name of the Father and of the Son and of the Holy Spirit."

Matthew 28:19, NIV

Among the 175 newly baptized members was a young man pastoring a non-SDA congregation in that area. Initially, he was unhappy that the meetings were held there, and also about the fact that many in his congregation were attending the meetings. He was alarmed and voiced his displeasure. However, my dad continued visiting them and giving them Bible studies regularly because he saw they were genuinely interested in learning from the Bible.

Gradually, word spread, and when members of his own family decided to be baptized along with the others from that congregation, the pastor also became interested. Sometime later, the pastor came to my father and confessed that he believed the messages taught from the Bible by the SDA church and wanted to be baptized. My dad was more than happy to baptize him.

Upon being baptized, he lost his job, but my dad made arrangements via the church administration and helped him get to the seminary program run on the SDA School campus in Roorkee. He went through the course there, and when he graduated from the seminary, the SDA church employed him. Along with my dad, he returned to work among the people of that area. They both worked hard, fulfilling the Great Commission, spreading the news of God's kingdom, and bringing many to the light of the Gospel.

Let us follow in Jesus' footsteps as my dad and others did.

JUNE 29

GROWING IN FAITH

Gladwin Mathews

"Start children on the way they should go, and even when they are old, they will not turn from it."

Proverbs 22:6, NIV

I am a PK (Preacher's Kid) and the fourth of six children. We obtained our early education from our mother, who ran an Adventist school in the Dera Baba Nanak area in the Punjab. My parents had studied at the Adventist school in Roorkee, and they always advocated sending children there for their early education.

When it came time for us to go to boarding school, all of us siblings attended that school. When it was time to leave for college, my mom admonished me, "Son, you are now going to college, so make sure you stay focused. Study well, always pray, and don't worry about the fees." I don't know how my parents managed their expenses and my college fees. But I know they trusted God and believed in His providence, which instilled faith in me. My dad always said, "Don't worry, God will take care." And God took care of us!

My response was to make them proud of me. I completed my BLA degree, and then a double MA, while attaining the honor roll throughout. I joined the faculty at Spicer Memorial College, and served as Assistant Dean of Men and Assistant Professor of Religion and Industrial Arts. Then, I moved to the USA to join the Lake Union Conference as a Bible Worker and Youth Leader. I eventually completed my doctoral studies.

I can see that the seeds planted back then by my parents, true to God's promise, had sprouted and grown. Praise God!

Let us train our children to grow in God's path. He will keep them there.

JUNE 30

FLOATING IN THE WATER

Anita B. R. Mohan

Call upon Me in the day of trouble; I will deliver you, and you shall glorify me

. Psalm 50:15 NKJV

My aunt's father owned a farm on the outskirts of Tiruchirappali (Trichy) in Tamil Nadu. To water the paddy field, he had built a huge tank, the size of a swimming pool. When visiting India from the USA, it was our custom to spend a day at the farm, play in the water, and enjoy a home-cooked meal.

On one such occasion, while we all were there, my 3-year-old cousin sat on the steps at the water's edge, playing with her toys. Everything was fine, until someone noticed a cloth floating on the water and pulled it out. It wasn't just a cloth; it was my cousin floating face down on the water! She had probably fallen asleep and silently slid into the water while we were busy having fun.

One of my aunts, who was a nurse, immediately turned the nearby bullock cart on its side, placed my cousin on the wheel, and spun it around until she threw up all the water, and came back to consciousness. We were relieved – a tragedy was avoided!

Sometimes in life, we seem to be getting along comfortably, even when away from God, until a crisis occurs. But, like our family was present to rescue my cousin, we have our elder Brother, Jesus, who is willing to rescue us, pull us out of the "water," give us "CPR," and bring us back to "consciousness" – a life with Him.

May we open our hearts, and ask Jesus to lead us in His paths today.

JULY 1

TO GOD BE THE GLORY

Makeda Garland

"I can do all things through Christ who strengthens me."

Philippians 4:13, NKJV

As a first-time mom, the excitement of starting a family was all I ever wanted. As I prepared for the arrival of my child, I devised my plan. I had done my research and mapped out the whole process – exactly how I wanted everything to go!

On the day of the delivery, things seemed to go according to plan until the monitors began to beep, and the nurses and doctors huddled together, talking among themselves. I knew that something wasn't right. I closed my eyes and began to pray, asking God to keep me through whatever was happening. When I opened my eyes, the doctor said that the baby's heart rate was dropping and that I needed to go for an emergency C-section to get the baby out as soon as possible.

C-section?!! This was not part of the plan! I hadn't researched this and had no clue what this meant for me or my baby! As a flood of emotions swept over me, I knew I would have to trust God and lean entirely on Him. I prayed the whole time I was being transported to the surgery room, and by the time we reached the room, I felt a sense of assurance and peace. God was in the room with me!

The surgery went well, and today, I have a healthy two-year-old child. God was right there with me in my time of fear and uncertainty. Looking back, I realize that all the events were timed and executed according to God's plan. To Him be the glory!

When facing unexpected events, trust that we can do everything through Christ.

July 2

A Timely Help

Anita B. R. Mohan

"Give, and it will be given to you. A good measure, pressed down, shaken together and running over, will be poured into your lap. For with what measure you use, it will be measured to you."

Luke 6:28, NIV

It had been seven years since our last visit to India, and I really wanted to go back there. However, accumulating paid leave was a challenging prospect in the place where I worked. We were short-staffed, the patient volume was high, and the workload was so heavy that we hardly had time to take a break or even to drink water! The year 2017 was tough on me because my health condition caused me pain for most of the day. At times, I would cry, but I kept pushing myself because the work needed to be done. The Chief Therapist would sometimes pull me aside and have prayer for me.

I hadn't thought that the upper levels of management were paying attention and had noted my commitment. I had felt I was merely doing my part in that busy environment, but the CEO had noticed my work all along. The following year, 2018, I was awarded 40 hours of extra paid leave. That was a whole week that I could take off! With that additional leave, I could plan our trip to India to visit my family and father-in-law after long seven years.

Let us look for ways to help others, as we never know who needs our help, how that help will affect them, and what an effect it will have on us as well.

July 3

The Good in a Bad Day – Part I

Vivian Ruiz

"And we know that all things work together for good to them that love God..."

Romans 8:28, KJV

Yesterday was just a bad day. A series of unfortunate events, one after the other, made it so, and I found it hard to maintain my calm and cheerful disposition. Amid one of those "unfortunate events," when I urgently needed to make a phone call, I realized my phone was not working. My younger son, Mani's phone, had also run out of power. And now, I had no way to make a call.

Just then, Mani saw one of our neighbors, a pleasant lady who would smile and wave at us on the rare occasions we met. She was very helpful, allowed us to use her phone, and patiently waited for us to complete the call. Most of the people in our neighborhood are somewhat distant and do not mingle at all. But that small encounter opened the opportunity for us to become better acquainted and a little closer to one another as neighbors.

As I reflected on the day over dinner with Mani, I had three thoughts. 1. Events in life happen for a reason. 2. The reason may not be apparent at the moment. 3. The reason may not be only for you, but for others just as much.

I enjoyed getting to know my neighbor, although what brought us together was a problem. We can find a blessing in every situation because everything happens for a reason. May God help us to find good in all the circumstances of life.

July 4

The Good in a Bad Day – Part 2

Vivian Ruiz

"In everything give thanks: for this is the will of God in Christ concerning you."

I Thessalonians 5:18, KJV

My younger son, Mani, and I were having a bad day. A little after our neighbor helped us make the much-needed calls, we had to wait at the Metro station for almost an hour! Once again, an unhappy situation!

While waiting, I noticed a gentleman needing help with the fare card machine. He had put in his last $20 bill but hadn't gotten his ticket and was trying to explain it to the attendant. He spoke only in Spanish, and the attendant knew only English! I walked over and helped translate the conversation. I helped the gentleman fill in the form to get his money back. The attendant then gave him a pass that permitted him to reach his station and get to his home in Virginia.

I reflected on the lessons I was learning. Events that seem horrible at the time, are not always as horrible in the light of a new day. Our misfortunes can be turned into what is good fortune for others. In addition, I experienced a certain joy as I used my knowledge of a second language to help someone in need. The sense of fulfillment that resulted from assisting the gentleman seemed worth all the trouble I had faced that day.

We cannot expect a smooth life without troubles, irritations, and discomfort. We are bound to face many challenges in the future. May God help us to appreciate what is positive, even in our "unfortunate" events.

JULY 5

JESUS OPENS DOORS

Anonymous

"I cried out to God with my voice. . .and He gave ear to me."

Psalm 77:1, NKJV

After completing high school, I had a great desire to go to college – to Spicer Memorial College. I wrote to my father expressing my wish, but he replied that he did not have enough money to send me to college and was planning to get me married. I was deeply disappointed and went to God in prayer. I then wrote to the college president, requesting admission as a self-supporting student. A few weeks later, I received the reply – I was granted admission. I was overjoyed! But there was more to come. Soon after, a family member wrote to me that they would pay my tuition for the entire four-year course at the college. My prayer-answering God had opened a door!

However, there were other costs besides my tuition fees. I worked hard, and God blessed me – I was on the honor roll every semester. Based on that academic achievement, I was granted the Lowry Scholarship. The faculty members noticed my diligence and appointed me as a paid hostel monitor. I also qualified for a scholarship given to those from a lay household. Further, I enrolled in the student work program, which gave me added financial help.

I did not suffer or lose time in college due to lack of funds. With all these supplemental avenues of income and help from family, I completed my studies on time.

I had cried out to God, and He paved my path in a wonderful way. His grace is truly amazing!

Cry out to God in prayer, and He will open doors for you that you never knew existed.

JULY 6

Mice Holes

Bimal Nowrangi

"Learn a lesson from the ants, you lazy person! See how hard they work."

Proverbs 6:6, EASY

Ants and bees are insects known to be industrious, disciplined, and work very hard. Other creatures like animals and birds also work hard to care for their families. I have watched them with awe and great interest.

In the elementary school I attended, all the students were required to participate in manual labor. This work program was meant to teach us the dignity of labor. One of the places we were put to work was the farm – the rice and wheat fields.

While harvesting rice and wheat, we noticed many holes in the ground, dug by field mice. We would dig into those holes, looking for mice to get rid of them because they were known to destroy our crops. In these holes, we found not only mice, but large amounts of grain. The mice harvested the grain even before us, and stocked them for their rainy day! The holes were granaries as well as homes for the mice. Some of them were ingeniously blocked from the inside to keep out intruders. In some, we found up to 5 pounds of wheat or rice – enough to last until the next harvest season!! It seemed like they had calculated their needs, taking into consideration the effort and energy needed to gather the grain.

We were created a "little lower than the angels." (Psalm 8:5). How much more disciplined and industrious we should be, in taking care of our families and preparing for our future! Let's learn a lesson from the mice holes!

JULY 7

LET GO AND LET GOD – PART I

Veena Alfred

"Glory belongs to God், whose power is at work in us. By this power He can do infinitely more than we can ask or imagine."

Ephesians 3:20, GW

On a cool April evening, walking down the street, I felt envious of the people seated on restaurant patios and enjoying themselves. I tried to show strength and toughness on the outside, but I was hurt, sad, and disappointed inside. Every restaurant owner there knew my son because he owned the most successful restaurant on that street!

I had learned that my precious, charming son was an addict! He had successfully kept his secret until his (late) elder brother broke the devastating news to me. A whirl of thoughts went through my head: denial, questioning my role as a parent, and trying to figure out where I had gone wrong. Through it all, I kept pleading with God.

I sought professional advice and remembered reading a book, Tough Love. And then, trusting in God, I decided to take action, for if I didn't, I felt he would simply waste away and die! The time had come, and I was walking down the street to see him.

I met him in front of the restaurant, with many eyes looking on. When I told him that he should go through a rehab program, he declined my offer. I then summed up all my courage and gave him an ultimatum. He could either take my offer, or break the relationship with me.

Tears flowed as I walked away, for I dreaded the consequences. Nevertheless, I knew I had to let go and let God!!

Are you going through a painful experience? Let God take control. He is all-powerful.

July 8

LET GO AND LET GOD – PART 2

Veena Alfred

"This is what the Almighty Lord, the Holy One of Israel says: 'You can be saved by returning to Me…'"

Isaiah 30:15, GW

With sweaty palms and a tear-stained face, I counted the hours from Wednesday until that Friday evening, the deadline for his response. I would walk around and pace in silence, constantly praying and, with tears, earnestly claiming God's promises.

Just before the deadline, the phone rang, and I heard his voice, "I will go anywhere you want me to go!" I could hardly contain myself! All I said was, "I'll pick you up tomorrow!" I knew I would have broken down if I had tried to say anything more!

I picked him up and started for the rehab center in Pennsylvania. I was instructed not to engage in conversation or stop anywhere. We drove in complete silence the whole way. It was excruciating.

The campus had beautiful grounds and buildings, and my son looked a bit relieved. We went through the admission process, and we parted coldly. Back home, I prayed he would not leave the program.

After a week of detox, he began to sound upbeat about the program. I visited him, as permitted, and attended the 5-day training session for parents, during which I got to know my son better. He talked, and I listened. We talked, cried, and hugged each other often. This was crucial for his recovery.

Finally, the program was done! The first stop coming back was at the SASDAC sanctuary. God, who had brought him thus far, would carry him through!

Have you strayed away from God? He says if you return to Him, He will gladly accept you back again!

July 9

God Saw Us Through – Part I

Gladwin Mathews

"Even though I walk through the darkest valley, I will fear no evil, for you are with me; your rod and staff, they comfort me.

" Psalm 23:4, NIV

I will never forget the fateful day/night of August 4, 1965. We lived in Dera Baba Nanak, very close to the Indo-Pak border. My parents had gone by bus to Amritsar, miles away, to buy school supplies. Around 4 pm, we heard, via the radio, that the enemy had bombed Amritsar, and bus services from Amritsar were suspended.

After 4 hours, I went to the local bus stand to inquire, and learned that buses were still not coming in from Amritsar. We were hungry, but there was no food at home, and shopkeepers had closed their shops after news of the bombs. So we just went to bed hungry. At about 10 pm, my parents finally arrived. Much relieved, we ran to them and hugged them. My parents then got us some food, after which we prayed, and went to sleep.

At about 4 am, we woke up to the thunder of blasting bombs. We were sleeping outside our house, and when we looked up, the sky seemed to be on fire! Bombshells were streaking across the sky, and the blasts shook the whole town. My dad quickly led us into the house, gathered us in his arms, and began to pray. We were crying out of sheer fright. He then said, "It's a war. But don't worry. God will take care of us." Two hours later, the local police inspector was at our door.

When frightening events happen around us, let us not fear, for God has promised to be with us.

July 10

God Saw Us Through – Part 2

Gladwin Mathews

"Do not be anxious about anything, but in every situation, by prayer and petition, with thanksgiving, present your requests to God. And the peace of God, which transcends all understanding, will guard your hearts and minds in Christ Jesus."'

Philippians 4:6,7, NIV

The police had come to our door seeking the help of my dad, who was well-known and well-respected in the town. They wanted him to accompany them as they went through the town, trying to calm the people's fears. He agreed and went with them.

He returned about 7 hours later and, with my mother and aunt, began to prepare to leave town. He filled the chicken feeder and two large bowls of water for the 200 chickens my mother had raised. My mother then gathered food supplies and utensils, which my father loaded onto his bicycle. He took a long look around and began to pray – for the people of the town, for the army, and for us, who were about to start on a journey on foot. He closed all the doors and locked the front entrance with a padlock. We set out south and east, moving away from the border to the next town, Batala, more than 30 km away!

When we came to the main road, we joined hundreds of others who were also leaving home and moving away. One could see fear on their faces and tears in their eyes. There was a sense of desperation, but everyone kept moving. It was a shocking scene! We walked for hours, hoping to get away from danger.

The scripture says there will be more wars in the future. May you feel the presence and peace of God when going through terrifying situations.

July 11

God Saw Us Through - Part 3

Gladwin Mathews

"Trust in Him at all times you people; pour out your hearts to Him, for God is our refuge."

Psalm 62:8, NIV

Amid the horror, there was a silver lining too. As we passed through the villages and towns, the residents organized themselves and came out with food, water, and refreshing "lassi" (buttermilk!) I remember a Sardarji, imploring us to have a meal, some lassi, and rest before continuing the journey. All distinctions of caste, creed and religion were thrown aside. It was a heart-touching experience. We ate, had lassi, and rested for about an hour before hitting the road again.

We still had some ways to go when I heard my dad's name called out by a man in a truck. He belonged to the church where my parents had ministered! He pulled us up into the truck, but the driver wouldn't allow my dad's bicycle on board. So, he stayed back to come later with his bicycle.

We reached Batala at about 11 pm, completely exhausted. My mother spread a sheet on the ground, and we slept on the roadside. I woke up at about 2 am because someone called my name. It was my dad. He had been searching for us. Wherever he saw a group of people resting on the roadside, he would go by and call out my name. Finally, he found us. It was wonderful to be together again! Eventually, we reached our aunt's place safely. I experienced God's protecting hand over us, and it strengthened my faith in Him.

We may go through difficulties. However, God asks us to trust in Him at all times.

My God Hears

Maya Foster

"Now this is the confidence that we have in Him, that if we ask anything according to His will, He hears us."

I John 5:14, NKJV

In November 2022, I underwent a surgical procedure on my arm. It seemed to be healing well, but one day, I felt excruciating pain, and the doctor said that a deep infection had set in. It was serious. He scraped out the infected tissue, leaving a large hole, and informed me that it would take a long time, maybe even months, before the wound would heal.

I did not have the courage to look at the gaping hole. My daughters said it was at least two inches deep. A family friend, a nurse, came daily to change the dressing, but even after a week, there was hardly any improvement at all, and the severe pain continued.

One night, I took it to God in prayer. With tears rolling down my cheeks, I asked God for healing. I prayed for a long time, but after that, I felt calm and fell asleep.

When I awoke the next morning, I noticed my dressing slipping off repeatedly. "What now?!" I asked aloud, wondering what was happening. When the nurse saw the wound that evening, she was utterly surprised! She called my daughters to ask what had been done because the hole was almost gone!! I couldn't control my tears of joy and couldn't stop praising God. He had touched my arm and brought healing to my wound. It was a miracle that reaffirmed my trust in the Lord. My God answers prayers!

Let us confidently ask God to meet our needs and then, trust His promises.

JULY 13

WE SHALL TALK AGAIN SOON

Bimal Nowrangi

"You do not even know what will happen tomorrow. What is your life? You are a mist that appears for a little while and then vanishes. Instead, you ought to say, 'If it is the Lord's will, we will live and do this or that.'"

James 4:14,15, NIV

We had been friends since 1956, when we had enrolled in the second grade of an elementary school in India. When in boarding school, he helped me with many of my activities of daily living. He was several years older than me, and treated me like his younger brother. He even helped me fetch water for my needs from a nearby deep well.

After elementary school, we went to high school and attended the same college. Our paths parted when we graduated from college and entered our different careers.

I tried to get in touch with him for over a year. One day, recently, after a gap of 45 years, we connected, and talked for over an hour about our bygone days. We ended our conversation saying we would talk again soon. We looked forward to another conversation. That was our wish, but it was not to be.

A little later, he lost his life in a tragic road accident. Our paths would never cross again, and we would never talk again on this earth.

Sadness and grief call for sober reflection. Only God knows the future and our final parting time. So, let us use our precious passing moments, whether few or many, solely for His glory, praise, and honor. Let us live on this earth for the good of others.

July 14

Ants

Anonymous

"Strengthen me according to Your word."

Psalm 119:28, NKJV

I have many physical limitations that prohibit me from lifting, reaching up to high places, bending down, and even walking. Despite this, I try to do my best and not ask for help from others, including my children.

I keep my kitchen and home clean – free of food crumbs and other particles on the floor or the counters. Imagine then, my dismay when I saw an ant crawl across the floor! One ant meant many others were around, and when I looked, I found a long line of them! I had to get rid of them immediately. This meant I would have to clean out everything in the kitchen – the pantry, the shelves, and so much more. It was a challenge, more like a war! But the real challenge was my disability. The work was taxing, and I would have to do the whole thing myself, because I didn't trust anyone else to do it correctly! It brought me to the verge of tears, but I didn't want to ask for help – they were only tiny ants, after all!

I knew I didn't have what it would take to get the job done. So, I prayed for help, strength, and endurance. All were mercifully granted, and I finished cleaning the kitchen exactly how I wanted it done. I had prayed, and God gave me strength.

This experience taught me how limited I was in my mobility, and even more importantly, that God listens to, and answers, all our prayers. Nothing is too small in His sight, not even prayers regarding tiny little ants!

July 15

Surviving The Polio Pandemic

Pansy Chintha

"My grace is sufficient for you. . ."

II Corinthians 12:9, NIV

(This is the story of a friend of the author, written with permission)

On a beautiful day in the 1940s, a young couple's joys were mixed with fear, for they were anticipating their first child, a precious gift from God, but could not help feeling a tinge of anxiety about the unknown. But at 1 am, she came into the world, and joy overtook all fear. They couldn't take their eyes off the beautiful, delicate face and thanked God for this priceless jewel!

They watched over her day and night during those early days. They then took her to Sabbath School, where she learned songs of God's love, and as she grew, they taught her how unconditional that love was! Faithfully and earnestly, they gave their best for their precious baby.

And then tragedy struck! During the polio pandemic of those days, she contracted the dreaded disease. The heartbroken parents agonized before God and prayed for healing. But as in the case of Paul, healing did not come.

However, she was given strength and grace, to overcome every hurdle that came with the paralysis. She never gave up, but always maintained a sweet and cheerful disposition, as an extraordinary witness to God's unfailing promises. God had a particular task for her – she was destined to carry her candle into the dark world and light it with God's love! The witness continues to this day!

Father GOD, Thank you for your love and grace, sustaining us despite difficulties. Amen.

July 16

Patience and God's Grace

Gladwin Mathews

"Yet the Lord longs to be gracious to you; therefore he will rise up to show you compassion. For the Lord is a God of justice. Blessed are all who wait for him."

Isaiah 30:18, NIV

I had just finished high school and was preparing to go to Spicer Memorial College, but I realized that I didn't have enough money. So my dad suggested earning money by selling books as a colporteur. I applied, along with one of my friends, and was given the town of Jodhpur as our territory.

An experienced person went along with us to help us on the first day. It was tiring work, but we didn't have any success. The next day, he left us to work by ourselves. We had no sales that day either.

On day three, we worked for two hours going from door to door and had no sales. We had prayed every day but were still empty-handed. By now, we were low on money, with just enough for another two days. We knew we had to keep going.

At about 4 pm, we took a break under the shade of a tree, encouraged each other with prayer, and then decided to tackle the bigger houses. At the first big house, the gentleman listened patiently as we said everything we had memorized in our training session. He then thought for a moment and said, "I will take this whole set of books." We were overjoyed, not only because it was costly, but also because it was such an encouragement to us.

Yes, the first sale took some time, but God had a plan for us.

When things don't take place at the speed we expect, let's wait on God.

July 17

On Fire for God

Pansy Chintha

"For I know the plans I have for you," declares the Lord, "plans to prosper you and not to harm you, plans to give you hope and a future.".

Jeremiah 29:11, NIV

The young man's first love was his Master's mission – a passion to spread God's wonderful Gospel wherever possible.

On this particular day, he had set out to visit someone who had taken Bible lessons by mail and now needed to have a personal visit. The last bus stop was miles away from the student's home, but undeterred, he set off on foot, having to cross a dense jungle. With a song in his heart and a prayer on his lips, he pressed on until he reached his destination. The student warmly welcomed him into his home, and they sat down for a diligent Bible study.

It was late by the time it was over, and the two set out on foot with a lantern in hand. A short way into the jungle, a pair of bright eyes stared at them. Could it be a tiger? It shook them, but they kept right on, placing their faith in God, who would protect them.

After crossing the jungle, the student returned with his lantern, and the young man walked on in the darkness. Suddenly an arm touched him. Not a soul was around. But that touch made him pause, and in that moment, he realized that if he had taken another step, he would have fallen into a deep well just in front of him.

That young man was my dad, Pr. Anandarao Undru. God certainly had plans to prosper him!

God has plans to prosper each one of us. Let us do His will each day.

WALK IN THE LIGHT

Susy Mathew

"Your word is a lamp to my feet and a light to my path."

Psalm 119:105, NKJV

We lived in a little village in South India, where I grew up in a Seventh-Day Adventist home with very loving and God-fearing parents. At 6 am every morning, and again in the evenings, they would faithfully call all of us children for a time of worship. No matter where my father had to go during the day, he made sure he was home in time for family worship before we slept. This consistent pattern instilled in us the concept of God's faithfulness and His commands.

I left home at the age of 18 for higher education and then a career. I studied in a non-Adventist institution, and then worked in foreign countries. During those years, I was far removed from other Adventists. At times, I could not attend Sabbath services, but my upbringing kept me steadfast, and I always had special regard for the seventh day as Sabbath. I chose to keep all the commandments of God, and I took extra effort to keep the day sacred to the extent possible, in the circumstances at that time.

While living on secular campuses and working in those environments, the going was sometimes challenging. But, time and again, I was reminded of the verse in Psalm 119:105, which said that His word was a light, and if we walked in that light we would not stumble.

It has been a wonderful ride! If no more tomorrow I should see, then for today and all my yesterdays that You gave me, I thank you Lord!

May God help us to walk in His light daily.

JULY 19

God's Watchcare

Pansy Chintha

"For He shall give His angels charge over thee to keep thee in all thy ways."

Psalm 91:11, KJV

It was a cool, crisp November morning in Pune, India. Six of us children, 5 to 10, living in the City Church campus gathered to play. After some time, when we had played all the games we could think of, my sister, Suhasini, came up with an exciting idea. We would all climb a tree!

The only tree within reach was a drumstick tree. Now, drumstick trees are not sturdy, and their branches are pretty fragile. But we didn't know that! My adventurous sister took the lead, and the rest followed. All six climbed the tree one by one and were seated on various branches. Sitting at the top, Suhasini pretended to be the train engine driver. To add a sense of movement to the sound of the train, she started shaking the branch vigorously. Suddenly, the fragile branch gave way, and we all came down with a big thud! She screamed, and my parents, who came running out, took one look at my sister's face, full of blood, and picked her up and rushed her to the nearest hospital. Her tongue had deep cuts in three places, and it looked like it was in three pieces, but the doctors were able to sew them up.

We were more thoughtful the next few days as we prayed for her recovery. If it wasn't for God's protecting hand holding her up, she might have lost her tongue that day.

Father in Heaven, we praise and thank you for your promise that no evil will befall your children. Amen

May God's angels keep us in all our ways.

JULY 20

RUNNING AWAY

Gloria Moses

"I am with you and will watch over you wherever you go, and I will bring you back to this land. I will not leave you until I have done what I have promised you."

Genesis 28:15, NIV

When I was in the 4th grade, the SDA school in Divlapitiya, Sri Lanka, closed down. My mother enrolled me in the local Singhalese medium school, but I did not know Singhalese at all! I didn't want to go to school.

So, my mother took me to the Lakpahana SDA boarding school in Kandy. I clung to her legs as she was leaving. So, she introduced me to Suganthi, who was two years older and would take care of me. I ended up staying, but was unhappy, and I tried to run away from school almost daily. I didn't know that my home was very far away and that it would require walking a long distance and then riding on three different bus routes. I thought that if I could reach the main road, it would take me straight home. So, I tried slipping out of the campus unnoticed, but Suganthi knew my plans and informed others about it. Several teachers lived along the path leading to the main road, and every time I headed out, they caught me and brought me back to the school.

Back at home, my mother spent sleepless nights picturing my face as I clung to her legs. Unable to bear it any longer, she came and took me back.

I know anything could have happened to me while alone outside the school campus. Thank you, God, for protecting me!

God's protection is over us even when we engage in dangerous pursuits in our ignorance.

JULY 21

DARK AND LONELY ROAD

Galdwin Mathews

"No evil will happen to you."

Psalm 91:10, CEB

In 1986, I was working at the Rohru SDA School, and also taking care of the Sandhaur Basa SDA church, about 7 km away. To get there, I would go part of the way on my Rajdoot motorbike and then cross the Pabbar river in a basket – a "jhoola," hung on a thick metallic cord that spanned the river.

On this particular trip to Sandhaur Basa, after a lovely service, lunch, and nature walk, I decided to return home. It was nearly dark by the time I crossed the river. After a few kilometers, my bike's headlight flickered and went off. Then the engine died out. I was still moving but did not know where I was going. On my left was a mountain, and on my right the river, with no barrier between the road and the river! So, I stopped. I tried to kickstart the engine but to no avail. I got off the bike, began to feel the road cautiously with my foot, and realized I was at the edge of the road! It was pitch dark. It was so dark that I could hardly see my bike; I could only feel it! How would I ever get home?!

I bent my head and silently prayed, pleading with God to guide me. Then, I sat on the bike and decided to try once more. I kicked, and the engine started! I turned on the headlight switch, and the light came on! Deeply grateful, I drove home safely.

God's promises are sure. He takes care of His own. When in trouble, call upon God, and He will take you through.

July 22

Healing Remedy

Gloria Moses

"So do not fear, for I am with you. Do not be dismayed, for I am your God. I will strengthen you and help you; I will uphold you with my righteous right hand."

Isaiah 41:10, NIV

As a child, I was always playful. I played with my sister outside if it was not raining. If it was raining, we both would play inside. I would venture out alone if no one else was available because I wanted to keep playing.

One day, when I was out by myself, climbing up the various trees that lined our compound and enjoying the fruit, I noticed a fruit that looked like a delicious guava. It looked tempting, so I ate it, but it was not a guava. It was not edible at all! It produced a strong reaction and caused itching, rashes, and swelling all over my body.

I was in a serious condition and was taken to the doctor, but the treatment didn't seem to help. I suffered for several days, during which my mother prayed for healing. On hearing of my condition, my aunt said she knew of a home remedy that could help and advised my mother to try it. When she did, the rashes, itching, and swelling subsided, and I soon returned to normal. It was such a relief!

I believe God sent His help, like the balm of Gilead, in the form of a home remedy and relieved me of my distress. God has promised those who trust Him, that He will "rise with healing in His wings."

Let us trust Him to heal us of all our maladies.

JULY 23

HEDGE OF PROTECTION

Gloria Moses

"Though you search for your enemies, you will not find them. Those who wage war against you will be as nothing at all."

Isaiah 41:12, NIV

My mother and three of us - her daughters, lived in a house with a main gate and a road leading from the gate to the house. Across the gate were many shops and houses, and it was well-known in the community that no men were in our house. It was always frightening. Some mornings, we would wake up to see the gate open, the chicken coop broken into, and things missing.

Tony was a dog that lived on the technical institute campus where my sister Deborah studied. He was a ferocious dog and was known to attack people. They wanted to get rid of him, so my sister brought him home as a watchdog for us.

After we got Tony, my sister picked up the courage and decided to stay up all night to keep watch. She walked around the house with Tony by her side, and then, when she felt sleepy, she woke me up at 2 am and asked me to keep watch. I, too, walked around a few times and then fell asleep in a chair on the porch. I woke up to Tony's sharp barks, and knew someone was at the gate. After a few moments, he stopped barking.

Nobody stole things from our house after that. My mom was able to raise chickens and sell their eggs as a source of income for us because Tony was our protector.

God is our great Hedge of Protection against any source that may pose a danger or harm to us.

JULY 24

THE STUNT

Gloria Moses

"For He will give His angels concerning you to guard you in all your ways."

Psalm 91:11, NIV

During the mid 1950s, my family lived in Divlapitiya, Sri Lanka, at my (late) grandfather's place, along with my uncles and their families. My uncles had a rice mill, which required a cemented portion of land, about an acre, where the rice could be spread out to dry in the sun. Once the rice was packed away, the cement floor was available for us children to play on.

One evening, while playing hide-and-seek, I hid in the back of my mom's truck, which was parked nearby. I stayed hidden even towards the end of the game. I then decided to come out, and jumped out, but didn't realize that the sharp metal hook that held the back door was hanging exposed. It caught the back of my knee, and went right in, and held me in mid-air, leaving me hanging upside down. Everyone except my sister Rose thought I was doing a stunt to make them laugh. She heard my cry of pain, and above all the laughter, she called out to my mother and others to come immediately. I was held up, and the hook was removed, but I had been badly injured and was taken to the doctor to be treated.

Among the children, only my sister recognized what was really happening, and called for help. I am sure the injury to my knee would have been much worse if I had been left hanging there, because it appeared to be a funny stunt!

God took care of me, and may He always protect you.

JULY 25

God's Plans - Part-1

Bimal Nowrangi

"People make plans for what they will do, but it is the Lord who leads them in the right way."

Proverbs 16:9, EASY

After several years of patiently waiting, praying, and planning, my wife and I were able to travel to India and to a picturesque city in Europe. During our three-week itinerary, we visited 10 cities, 6 Adventist educational institutions and several churches. We boarded 11 different flights, passed through the security and immigration systems of 7 airports, spent a total of over 42 hours in the air, and flew over 21,500 miles. It was very demanding but very rewarding as well!

We were able to visit places where our childhood and professional career years were spent. We were able to enjoy local food, seasonal vegetables, and fruits we had not tasted in years. We met families and friends we had not seen in ages. We walked through the campuses and halls of the schools we had studied in and graduated from. We heard about their growth, development, and challenges. We sat on the pews in the school chapels, and participated in Sabbath worship services, reflecting on how God had led everyone thus far.

Our planning was meticulous, but everything did not always happen exactly as we had planned. On the other hand, God rewarded us with a few pleasant surprises we had not anticipated! He alone knew what was best for us.

Our trip began and ended well because we had submitted our plans in His hands from the beginning. Our faith was reconfirmed that God will continue to be in full control of all our current as well as future plans.

When the unexpected happens, trust God to lead you in the right direction.

JULY 26

GOD'S PLANS - PART-2

Bimal Nowrangi

"For I know the plans I have for you," declares the LORD, "plans to prosper you and not to harm you, plans to give you hope and a future."

Jeremiah 29:11, NIV

My wife and I had great experiences during three weeks of recent traveling. We had great food. We met many old and new relatives and friends, and even went on several sightseeing tours. While we had good times, we also had some close calls.

While in Zurich, Switzerland, we took a tour bus for sightseeing. We saw famous old churches, castles, universities, and the famous lake Zurich. We also saw the famous ETH university of science and technology built in 1855, where Albert Einstein studied and later became its professor.

After loading our bus on a ferry, we crossed the lake and headed to have the thrill of a cable car ride to reach the top of the hill. When we reached the cable car base station, we were told the cable car that was to take us had got stuck halfway with 2 passengers in it! That sounded tragic! Our tour guide told us that in his entire career of many years, this cable car had never broken down!

We were told to abandon our plans of riding the cable car, but we somberly reflected on some pertinent questions, because we were next in line. What if we had taken the ride? How long would we have remained stuck, hoping for rescue? What would the rescue operation have involved?

I have only one response: I thank God for his farsighted plans that prevented us from experiencing great inconveniences, difficulties, and even tragedies.

May God protect you in your going out and coming in today.

JULY 27

GOD'S PLANS-PART 3

Bimal Nowrangi

"Put your plans in front of the Lord, so that what you want to do will go well. The Lord causes everything to have its proper result."

Proverbs 16:3,4, EASY

During our 3-week travel itinerary, my wife and I saw numerous positive signs of God's leading.

During Sabbath worship service at Spicer Adventist University, we were greatly surprised to meet a former student after over 50 years! She had been brought from a foreign country by her father, a diplomat, to study in the Spicer Elementary School at the age of 3.

Visiting the east, I was especially delighted to see the house where I was born, and the pond on the school campus where I was baptized by my father! My wife stood by the river where she was baptized.

Precious memories of over sixty years flooded our minds as we walked through the dormitories, classrooms, and chapels. We recalled how during the heavy monsoon rains, our school used to be closed so we could plant rice seedlings in the leech-infested, knee-deep muddy and slushy paddy fields! We thought of the several minimally paid and basically trained teachers, who diligently and patiently, imparted knowledge and wisdom to students like us!

We clearly saw how God had planted the desires in the hearts and minds of both the expatriate pioneers and local leaders, in establishing training centers for the future workers in God's vineyard.

I thank God for his assurance and declaration: "For I know the plans I have for you, plans to prosper you and not to harm you, plans to give you hope and a future." Jeremiah 29:11 NIV

July 28

God's Plans-Part 4

Bimal Nowrangi

Whatever your hand finds to do, do it with all your might, for in the realm of the dead, where you are going, there is neither working nor planning nor knowledge nor wisdom."

Ecclesiastes 9:10, NIV

While my wife and I had many pleasant experiences during our 3-week trip to India, we recall having a few disappointing moments too. We were surprised to see many changes. Familiar paths had become wide streets. Roads and cities had become congested. New buildings had replaced memory-filled ones. Most people we met in the schools and churches were unfamiliar to us. Small children had grown and had taken up positions of responsibility. We did not easily recognize one another!

We love many tropical fruits like custard apples, jackfruits, wood apples, mangos, lychees etc., but since they were not in season, we missed them.

Our saddest experience was missing many of our childhood friends, who had gone to school with us and had also worked alongside us for years. We were told that some had retired and were living spread out in various communities. Many had passed on and were now resting from their worldly labors. Somber memories came to mind as I stood by my grandfather's resting place, and my wife visited her mother's resting place.

While visiting all the resting places, we were reminded of the serious responsibilities of those who are still alive. God has a plan for them before they are called to rest. He wants that, "While it is still day, we must continue to work… and we must do his work. We must work now because it will be night soon." John 9:4 EASY

July 29

God's Plans-Part 5

Bimal Nowrangi

"Here on earth, we who are believers do not have a city that will always be our home. But we are waiting for God's city that will come."

Hebrews 13:14, EASY.

We had many wonderful experiences during our 3-week trip to India. One of the best experiences we had was while we were flying. While distance and altitude don't matter to God, it certainly mattered to us. We felt we were 40,000 feet closer to Him!

Our old as well as new friends provided us with the best hospitality they could afford, and we could have expected. We were given very special treatment. They took extra pains to furnish our rooms with comfortable beds, mosquito nets and safe bottled drinking water. They provided locally made cooling devices to deal with the summer heat. The food was tasty, primarily because the vegetables were organically grown and prepared the way our parents and grandparents did!

We were visiting the country of our birth and early life. I stood in front of the house where I was born. My wife and I stood on the spot in the school campus where we had first met as students and friends! As precious memories flooded our minds, we stood there with mixed feelings, like sojourners in their own homeland. We felt very homesick, and remembered what Jesus had said: "There are many rooms in my Father's house. I will go now so that I can prepare a place for you there…After I have prepared a place for you, I will return. Then I will take you so that you will be with me. You will be where I am." John 14:2-3 EASY.

May we all always be ready for that city prepared for us.

July 30

God's Plans-Part 6

Bimal Nowrangi

"Since, then, you have been raised with Christ, set your hearts on things above, where Christ is, seated at the right hand of God. Set your minds on things above, not on earthly things."

Colossians 3:1,2, NIV

After spending three happy weeks in India, my wife and I returned to the United States via Zurich, Switzerland. After spending two short days in Zurich, we took a brief 55-minute Swissair flight to Geneva, enroute to Washington D.C.

It was a smooth flight on a picture-perfect spring day. The nearby hills and meadows were covered with lush green grass and trees. While taking off from the runway we could see beautiful houses, grazing cows and sheep below. As we began to climb, we could see clouds above us in all forms, shapes, and sizes. Then suddenly, piercing those clouds, we found ourselves cruising above them. It was an exhilarating and breathtaking experience!

We were at a level higher than the highest place on earth! We were above the clouds! Just then, for a moment, we were reminded to keep looking still higher and forget the earthly things we had left below. Along with the things on land like houses and grazing cattle, we were reminded to also leave behind our cares, worries, and difficulties that are normally found below the clouds. We were glad that the clouds blocked the view of the troublesome things below.

After a short 55-minute flight, our Swissair LX 2804 landed in Geneva airport, but our reassuring thoughts lingered on, inspiring us to continue trusting that "God is our refuge and strength, and ever-present help in trouble." Psalms 46:1, NIV.

Let us set our hearts and minds on heavenly things.

JULY 31

GOD'S PLANS-PART 7

Bimal Nowrangi

"I have told you these things, so that in me you may have peace. In this world you will have trouble. But take heart! I have overcome the world."

John 16:33, NIV

After having flown in airplanes for several years, I have generally overcome the fears and anxieties of flying. The little concerns that remain have to do with the experience of being on the plane during its take-off, landing, and especially during moments of turbulence. I am glad that even my remaining fears have been reduced after logging in a total of over 40 hours of being in the air and watching the captain handle turbulent moments.

Turbulence is caused by sudden changes in air currents and atmospheric pressures, making the plane shake. These dynamics can result in a sudden loss of altitude causing anxiety to the passengers. Taking deep breaths through the nose and exhaling slowly, is known to help reduce anxiety. Wide-bodied aircraft are known to handle turbulence better due to their size and mass.

We did experience occasional turbulence during our flights, especially while heading towards Abu Dhabi. Every time turbulence was expected, the captain would announce it and instruct everyone to fasten their seat belts.

Life also is full of turbulence. God alone can give us the instructions to cope with our anxieties that cause turbulence in our daily lives. He promises all of us that "…To him that overcometh will I give to eat of the tree of life, which is in the midst of the paradise of God." Revelation 2:7, KJV

Christ alone can provide us with daily strength to overcome the turbulence we face in life.

August 1

Turbulence

Biju Thomas

"Are not two sparrows sold for a farthing? And one of them shall not fall on the ground without your Father. . .Fear ye not therefore, ye are of more value than many sparrows."

Matthew 10:29,31, KJV

While working as a trainer at Amazon, I had to travel to many locations around the globe. My very first appointment was to train personnel in the principles of Risk Management in Cape Town, South Africa. The first leg of the flight was a 3-hour flight from Bangalore (Bengaluru) to Dubai, followed by a 9-hour flight to Cape Town across the Indian Ocean.

This was my first international journey, and I was filled with apprehension as I boarded the plane for the 9-hour flight. My fears became worse when the flight attendant ran through the safety regulations and instructions on what to do in case of emergencies. "In case the plane lands on water. . ." were the least reassuring words to a first-time traveler!

Out over the Indian Ocean, I experienced turbulence on an aircraft for the first time. The plane shook violently, throwing out baggage and other stuff from the overhead lockers. People began screaming, and I recalled the warning, "If the plane lands on water!" It sent all kinds of dreadful imaginations through my head!

Then I remembered that I could reach out to God from anywhere in the universe. So I breathed a silent prayer to God. After a few more minutes of severe vibrations, the atmospheric conditions improved, things calmed down, and we had a smooth flight the rest of the way.

We have a special source of comfort and reassurance in God, during times of "turbulence!"

AUGUST 2

THE DOUBLE RAINBOW

Biju Thomas

I do set my bow in the cloud, and it shall be for a token of a covenant between me and the earth. And it shall come to pass, when I bring a cloud over the earth, that the bow shall be seen in the cloud.

Genesis 9:13,14, KJV

Cape Town is a colorful city that is picturesquely situated between a bustling harbor and the iconic Table Mountain. I was in Cape Town for nearly a month, and saw some of the most beautiful rainbows in the sky. On a particular day, I saw a double rainbow, stretching across the waters and the Table Mountain.

Double rainbows are a majestic and fascinating natural phenomenon. The secondary rainbow is created by a second reflection of light within the raindrop, and the order of colors is reversed compared to the primary rainbow.

One of the loveliest sights in God's creation, each of the seven colors composing the bow stands out in its individuality, and yet each smoothly merges with the color next to it. In the midst of life's storms it is often hard to spot a rainbow, because this sign of hope appears only after the storm.

The rainbow is the guarantee, a visible token, given by God Himself that He would never again deluge the whole earth with a flood of water. It is His signature upon the covenant that every time a cloud passes over the earth, there will always be a beautiful rainbow in it! To the believer, there is a rainbow, in every dark cloud. How good it is to remind ourselves that God will never break His promise!

AUGUST 3

WALK THIS WAY

Soosan Varghese

"Your ear shall hear a word behind you saying, 'This is the way, walk in it.'"

Isaiah 30:21, NKJV

It was a pleasant summer evening. My then-teenage daughter and I went on a walk on the paved trail through the woods near our house, with JJ, our golden retriever, on his leash. JJ loved going on walks with our family. If we wore our walking shoes without inviting him, he would get his leash in his mouth and beat us to the door!

There was hardly anyone on the trail that evening. We had planned to walk about 2 miles and return home. We had just walked about half a mile, when a young male cyclist zoomed past us. As soon as the cyclist passed us, JJ turned around and pulled us to return home. We tried to pull him back to complete our walk, but he pulled even harder, and proved to be stronger than both of us put together. This was very unusual behavior for our dog. I remembered that dogs have a sixth sense regarding danger, and even evil intentions of people. Maybe he sensed something ominous. We decided to follow him home.

A few days later, we read in our local newspaper that, in that area, there was a young man on a bicycle, attacking women in secluded spots. The cyclist we saw matched the description in the newspaper.

The Scripture verse above is about our spiritual walk, but I believe God sent us a message that day through our dog JJ, and protected us from danger. Thank you, Jesus!

May God help us perceive His messages and stay safe.

AUGUST 4

THE TABLE CLOCK AND THE THIEVES

Gladwin Mathews

"The eyes of the Lord are everywhere, keeping watch on the wicked and the good."

Proverbs 15:3, NIV

During the war between India and China in 1962, my parents worked in "Shikar Manchian," a village in the Punjab. The majority of residents were daily laborers. They felt the effects of the war as their economic condition rapidly deteriorated, and worse, winter approached. Those were desperate times, especially for the poor.

One morning, as my dad was reading his morning newspaper, there was a knock on the door. He opened it to see three turbaned men standing before him, with their hands folded. After the greetings, they said, "We've come to say sorry." My dad had never met them before, so he was completely surprised, and asked for an explanation.

"Padri Saheb! We know you conduct meetings and bring home offering from the people. We have tried to rob you the past two nights. The first night we looked in and saw someone staring at us with greenish eyes. We ran back in fear. The second night as we entered the room, we saw the same eyes staring at us from the table top! We fled, but now we cannot sleep. Your 'Rabb' (Lord) is watching over you, and we fear He will punish us. We've come to say sorry!"

My dad forgave them and prayed for them. He smiled as they went away, because the two "greenish eyes" was the radium in the table clock which brightly glowed at night!

Let this remind us that we are always under the watchful eyes of God, to whom the night is as the day! (Psalm 139:12)

AUGUST 5

VIRTUAL LIFE

Anonymous

"Finally, all of you, be like-minded, be sympathetic, love one another, be compassionate and humble."

I Peter 3:8, NIV

It was just another day when I was scrolling through my social media posts, about five years ago. A post from my non-Christian classmate immediately caught my attention. Among his expressions was a hint that he had made a decision to end his life. I was alarmed and wanted to help him immediately, but didn't know how, because I had hardly interacted with him before.

Then I realized that our college group interacted on WhatsApp. I reached out to a few friends who I knew to be trustworthy, and we discussed my fears. Almost instantly, word spread to his friends and members of his immediate family. This support group made sure nothing went wrong.

Sometime later, I received a thank you note from his parents, and later, one from him: "May YOUR God Bless you and your family." My name is a very common Indian name, and does not point to my Christian faith, but he probably made that out by the expressions I had earlier posted online.

His words, "YOUR God," conveyed and repeated to me the truth that OUR God is the one true source of blessing, and He wants us to be a blessing to all without any discrimination.

Today, we are immersed in the world of social media. We simply read and move on. But we are called to be like the Good Samaritan who recognizes peoples' needs and helps them with compassion.

Our journey on earth is short. Pray for eyes to identify people who need our help even in the virtual world!

August 6

Alone and Afraid

Lillykutty Joseph

"It shall come to pass, that before they call, I will answer; And while they are still speaking, I will hear."

Isaiah 65:24, NKJV

In April of 1973, I was on my way home for summer vacation from Spicer Memorial College, Pune, India. Heavy rains had caused floods in Kerala, and the train could not go beyond Kochi. I boarded a bus that would take me to a town, Panthallam, where I could get a connecting bus to my hometown, Vallicode. It was getting very late, and I was alone and afraid.

Most of the travelers in the bus were men, and some of them invited me to their homes, but I was not comfortable going with strangers. When we reached Panthallam, the bus to Vallicode also arrived. It was actually late by an hour, due to the floods, but right on time for me! Yet, it would be past 10 pm on reaching Vallicode, and I would still have to walk another two miles to get home. How would I carry my luggage and walk that distance alone in the dark? I knew there could be snakes, stray dogs, and even drunk men on that road.

But as soon as I stepped out of the bus, a man walked up to me and asked if I was Lillykutty, the daughter of Thomas Sir. It was my Hindi teacher from eighth grade, who lived close by! He said he had been impressed to come to the bus station. He went and got his servant boy to help with the luggage, and walked me home right away.

I knew it was God's provisions. Let's trust Him.

August 7

Roadside Magician and God's Word

Gladwin Mathews

"For great is the Lord, and greatly to be praised; He is to be feared above all gods."

Psalm 96:4, ESV

During the summer holidays in 1980, I decided to work selling books as a colporteur. It was hard work but I kept at it.

One day, after working all day, and not making any sales, I was ready to return home, when I saw a crowd gathered on the other side of the road. Curious, I walked across, and saw a magician entertaining the crowd with his magic tricks. The tricks were not sleight of hand, but were real magic done by supernatural agencies.

I had a little time on my hands, so I put my bag down, and stood there to watch. Suddenly, he stopped, looked into the crowd, and then moving his eyes toward me, said, "There is something here that is interfering with my magic. I am not able to overcome it. I cannot proceed." Then he walked over to me and said, "Bhai Saheb, this is my bread and butter. I sense that you have something that is hindering my magic. Please leave and go away from here."

I was amazed and embarrassed. So, I picked up my bag ready to leave, and as I began to walk away, I remembered that I had a Bible in my bag! Black magic and the Bible do not go hand in hand.

The experience that day strengthened my faith in the power of God's Word as a real force. God had a purpose for me to go to that crowd and show me and the magician which power was stronger!

August 8

Brave Eight-Year-Old Girl

Gloria Moses

"A father of the fatherless, a defender of widows, is God in His holy habitation.

Psalm 68:5, NKJV

Our dad passed away a month before my younger sister, Rose was born. After his death, our family went to live at our (late) grandfather's place in Sri Lanka. Later, in the mid-1950s, my older sister was sent to an SDA boarding school.

Rose and I attended a school close to our home for a while, but then, it closed down. So, I too was sent to that boarding school. Rose was only eight years old and in the third grade, when my mom enrolled her in a school about 25 miles away. She had to take multiple public transport buses and then walk about half a mile to get to her school. My mom went with her for several days, showed her which buses to take, and how to get to the school and back.

After my sister was confident about the buses and the route, my mom let her travel by herself. But our fear was always whether she would get onto the correct bus going and coming, because at the bus stand, there were several buses at any given time, going in various directions. However, she bravely did the routine and got home safely every day. God was with her, guiding and protecting her. He is the father to the fatherless.

After one semester at the boarding school, I left and joined my younger sister at her school, and after that, we traveled together.

I thank God for answering my mother's prayers and keeping us safe.

Are you in need of the courage to do something? God gives us courage. Look to Him.

August 9

I Am Your Child

Anonymous

"See, I have inscribed you on the palms of My hands; Your walls are continually before Me."

Isaiah 49:16, NKJV

Some time ago, I had a terrifying vision that my children were taken away from me, and my husband was caught between helping me and saving our children. It gripped me and affected my emotions. It caused such stress, that I prayed and asked God to please explain what He wanted me to know. I felt as if God was trying to tell me something.

A few months later, my kids misplaced the offering envelope with the offering in it. We searched in vain for it. Something was definitely not feeling right, and I left the church in tears. Again, I wondered if the experience was supposed to teach me something.

Within the next two days, my vision became a reality. My children were taken away from me, and my husband was put into a dilemma. I begged him to go and save the children, and he did. They were safely returned to us.

Two months later, the lost offering envelope was found in the church where our children had left it, with all the money intact.

Putting all the experiences together, it seemed that God was preparing me regarding what was to happen, and that through them all, He would show me that He is still in charge of my life.

If a thing has been given to us and is meant for us, God will bring it back to us, even if it is taken away for a while. Let us be confident in Him.

August 10

Miraculously Saved - Part 1

Gladwin Mathews

"For He will command His angels concerning you to guard you in all your ways."

Psalm 91:11, NIV

My brother, Edwin, and his family were touring Israel in December 2022. The family had planned to spend their Christmas vacation in Israel. He rented a car to travel around, and things were going well until about a week before Christmas.

They were on their way to the Mount of Ascension on December 17 and were passing through a tunnel, when they heard loud honking behind them. A speeding car was bearing down on them. As they exited the tunnel, they heard a loud crash, and watched in horror as that car rammed into three cars just behind them, and then kept coming toward them. In that split moment, Edwin prayed, "God help us!" And suddenly he realized that his car was being pushed over to the left of the curb and brought to a halt. He had not turned the steering wheel nor pressed the brakes!

Recalling the incident, he said he was sure God had sent His angels to move the car just enough to the left and save them from a catastrophic, and possibly fatal, accident. They lifted their hearts in praise and thanks to God for this amazing miracle which protected them from harm that day.

God's word promises that He will send His angels to guard and protect us in all our ways. We can trust His promises. Let us thank Him for His protection.

August 11

Miraculously Saved- Part 2

Gladwin Mathews

"Even though I walk through the darkest valley, I will fear no evil, for you are with me: your rod and your staff, they comfort me."

Psalm 23:4, NIV

My eldest sister's wedding was set for June 16, 1972. This was the first wedding in the family, and everyone was very excited. All the arrangements were being made according to the local Punjabi tradition. As was the custom, a big, fat he-goat, along with bags of "maida" (refined wheat flour,) sugar, rice, lentil, and large copper pots (degh) were brought to the house. Mounds of firewood were procured for the "chulla" so that the special sweets could be made exactly according to recipe. The ladies gathered to sing wedding folk songs and dance every night, for a whole week prior to the bridal shower. Excitement was in the air!

Three days before the bridal shower, my sister had to go to the local bazaar to do some shopping. I decided to accompany her. As we were walking through the narrow streets of the town, and passing a three-story building, three bricks from the top came down just in front of her, barely missing her head! Even if one brick had struck her, it would have caused havoc, and ruined the entire wedding plans!

We were dazed and shaken. We quickly finished shopping and hurried back home in silence, deeply grateful to God for His protection over us. He had kept us, and especially my sister, safe from certain disaster. Thank you, God!

God is with us wherever we go. We do not have to fear any evil as long as we submit to Him. His angels protect us.

AUGUST 12

"IF WINTER COMES?"

Biju Thomas

"There is a time for everything. And a season for every activity under the heavens."

Ecclesiastes 3:1, NIV

I lost my father in 1989 when I was young. I was deeply disappointed, disheartened, and devastated. I didn't know how to withstand such a loss, and couldn't think of facing the challenges of life without him. Throughout his last days, he had tried his best to turn our thoughts to our Eternal Father, who will always uphold us in our distress, and provide us divine comfort to overcome our deepest grief.

Despite being Christians who believe in the Resurrection, when we are faced with the prospect of death, our spirits sometimes plunge to uncontrollable depths of despair, and we are prone to lose all hope.

In "Ode to the West Wind," Percy B. Shelley ends his poem with, "If winter comes, can spring be far behind." I learned this classic poem in college; and whenever I'm in despair, the lines ring through my mind. They are imbued with hope and a spirit of optimism, and they encourage one to never lose hope.

In literature, winter depicts adversity, trials and gloominess; whereas spring symbolizes freshness and hope. Just as in the cycle of nature, so in life's seasons, sorrow is followed by joy.

The loss of a loved one through death is one of life's most intense challenges, and the pain can be overwhelming. If you are in a season of winter, remember that your time of enduring pain, and yet trusting in God, will not be in vain. The Resurrection Day is not far behind!

AUGUST 13

GOOD GIFTS

Vidhya Melvin

"If you, then, though you are evil, know how to give good gifts to your children, how much more will your Father in heaven give good gifts to those who ask him!"

Matthew 7:11, NIV

It was winter 2022, and to escape the cold weather, we planned for a vacation in warm and sunny Florida. One of the things on the to-do list was to book a rental car for our stay there.

As parents, we thought it would be great to get a car with three seats in a row, so all three of our children could sit together as we drove around exploring the place. However, the car rental company could not guarantee that, and said that we should be prepared to adjust with whatever vehicle was available at that time. Yes, we recognized that, but in our hearts, we really wished we would get one with three seats in a row, for the sake of the children.

When we landed in Florida, the car we got had three seats in a row! It was such good news!

I have a prayer journal in which I write down every testimony, so when I feel low, I can read my own testimonies, which remind me that God is still in control.

Months later, as I read through this testimony, it suddenly struck me: We are sinful humans, and yet we try our best to give the best to our children. It would go beyond our imagination to think of what our sinless Christ is willing to give us.

Let us trust Him in our life's journey.

AUGUST 14

A Humble Cry

Gladwin Mathews

"And whatever things you ask in prayer, believing, you will receive."

Matthew 21:22, NKJV

In 1998, we planned a one-day trip to Malawali and Bhaja caves and waterfalls, for the Pathfinders at Spicer College. They had done an excellent job the whole year doing several ministries, and as the Pathfinder Director, I wanted to show them some appreciation. It was a popular destination, a few miles away and was easily reached by train.

As soon as we reached the place, the excited students ran ahead to the waterfalls, and by the time I had reached it, some were jumping into the water and some had gone to the top of the falls. Before I could call them down, one of them slid down along with the water and hit his head on the rocks below. Blood began to flow out of his ears and nose. I froze! This was an emergency! I whispered in desperation, "Lord! Please intervene and save him!"

We pulled him out of the water, and rushed him toward the railway station. On the way, there were a few men partying, who had come in their jeep. They stopped their partying and gave us a ride to the railway station in their jeep.

Back at Spicer College, arrangements had already been made to take him directly to the hospital, where he was promptly evaluated and treated. It took a few days, but he recovered well.

I thanked God for hearing my simple but earnest prayer, and saving the boy's life.

We have a prayer-hearing and prayer-answering God!

August 15

Manual for Life

Vidhya Melvin

"The fear of the LORD is the beginning of wisdom, And the knowledge of the Holy One is understanding."

Proverbs 9:10, NKJV

As I was looking forward to celebrating my son's 4th birthday in May, I wondered if there was anything in the Bible that could relate to May. For one thing, the month has 31 days, and the Book of Proverbs has 31 chapters. This book came to mind because my husband and I had decided to teach our children wisdom from that book. One of our favorite verses was Proverbs 9:10, which is quoted above.

On one particular day, I was feeling sad and was brooding over some issues I was facing. When my son came home from school, I tried to shake off my feelings, and perk up. I served him lunch and began to play with him. But he sensed that I was not in my usual bright and happy mood. So, he came to me, gave me a hug, looked up at me and said, "Mommy, Jesus is with you!" That's all I needed to hear! It lifted up my spirits and made my day! I was thrilled that my son had the "knowledge of the Holy One." He recognized that when Jesus is with us, we need not worry, no matter what may be troubling us!

The Bible and the book of Proverbs are like the manuals that come along with gadgets and appliances, explaining how best to use and maintain them.

May we remember to read our manual for life daily and follow the instructions given in them.

AUGUST 16

GOD'S HEALING GRACE

Gladwin Mathews

"Is anyone among you sick? Let them call the elders of the church to pray over them and anoint them with oil in the name of the Lord. And the prayer offered in faith will make the sick person well. . ."

James 5:14,15, NIV

On March 24, 2023, my friend, Jai Singh (Sunny,) whom I had known from my high school days in Roorkee, India, became very seriously ill. His heart rate dropped suddenly, and he stopped breathing for a while. He was rushed to the Holy Cross Hospital. His heart was not pumping well, his body was overwhelmed with a deadly infection and his vital organs were beginning to shut down.

We could do nothing but pray for him and follow his condition with the reports from his wife who was with him in the ICU. At the end of the first week, I visited him. He did not recognize me, but I placed my hand on him and offered up a petition to God on his behalf.

He fought for weeks in the ICU, and during that time, the pastors of the church and I visited him regularly. In fact, the whole church community kept praying for him, hoping for a miracle.

Then, I received a text message from his wife telling us the great news that Sunny was responding! Once he was stable, he was transferred to the Adventist HealthCare White Oak Medical Center, where Pr. John Daniel and I visited him and prayed for his complete recovery. He then made good progress until his discharge and return to his home.

Our faithful God answered our earnest prayers. He will answer yours, too.

August 17

Truly Blessed – Part I

Joel David

"Know therefore that the Lord your God is God; He is the faithful God, keeping his covenant of love to a thousand generations of those who love and keep his commandments."

Deuteronomy 7:9, NIV

Deep down in one of the southern states of India, Tamil Nadu, there is a village called Pragasapuram. The name means "place of light." The church in this village observed the seventh day as the Sabbath for generations. They followed the instructions given by Moses in the Scriptures. A trumpet would sound, signaling the time for the assembly, and the people would gather to worship their God. This church is known as "Nattusabai," which means "Village Church." Interestingly, the local railway station is called, "Nazareth!"

My grandfather, Mr. N.T.N. Nallamuthu grew up in this village and attended this church. He lived there but conducted his business in the neighboring island nation of Sri Lanka.

Pr. J.S. James was one of the first missionaries to come to Pragasapuram with the Adventist message in 1907. When the message spread among the Nattusabai members, my grandfather was one of the seven members to be first baptized there.

He was benevolent as well as devout. He closed all three of his businesses in observance of the Sabbath, and conducted church services for all his employees there. My grandfather and grandmother were blessed with three sons: my uncle N.T.N. Asirvatham, my father, N.T.N. David, and his younger brother, N.T.N. Chelladurai. God richly blessed all his endeavors, and in turn, he willingly and joyfully gave all glory to the heavenly Father.

When God leads us to truths in His Word, let us diligently keep them.

AUGUST 18

TRULY BLESSED – PART 2

Joel David

"I will instruct you and teach you. . .I will guide you with my eye."

Psalm 32:8, NKJV

My grandfather's sudden death at the age of 56, left the family devastated. My grandmother was left with the burden of raising three young sons. Times were hard in those days. She would go to the church, sit at the door, and pray for God's guidance. She often went hungry herself in order to give food to her children. My father and his younger brother quit school and went to Sri Lanka to make a living. There, they faced nearly insurmountable difficulties, trying to start a business.

But even through those difficult times they were faithful with their tithes and offerings, and God blessed them. They got into an agreement with the government, and paddy was sent for processing to the two mills that they owned. Their business prospered and they became well-known as Christians who were generous to the poor, and who kept Sabbath on the seventh day.

The brothers married two sisters who were teachers, and, living in harmony, they raised twelve children in the fear of God. Sabbath services were held in the mill, then at home, and then the brothers built a church in Ja-Ela, Sri Lanka, which still stands today, and also operates a school.

In 1983, during the ethnic violence in Sri Lanka, God protected us and enabled us to provide shelter and food for about 100 people for several months. The family then decided to move back to India, where we started all over again. Through it all, we have experienced God's faithfulness, unfailing love, and bountiful blessings.

Let us praise God for guiding us and providing for us through the ups and downs of life.

AUGUST 19

STRANDED IN THE SNOW – PART 1

Gladwin Mathews

"Though I walk in the midst of trouble, You preserve my life. . ."

Psalm 138:7, NIV

On February 26, 1991, I was traveling from Jalandhar in the Punjab to Rohru in Himachal Pradesh. I had to be at Rohru by February 28 to re-open the school, since I was the principal there. Due to the wintry conditions and narrow, winding roads, I knew it would take more than just one day to make the journey. So, I divided it into two legs, and stopped for an overnight break at the Shimla Sanitarium and Hospital where my sister lived.

The next morning it was snowing heavily. I walked to the bus stop, with a coolie (porter) carrying my suitcase, to catch the bus to Rohru. We started at about 9 am. We climbed higher and higher into the mountains, and at the town of Kufri, we came to a halt. The snow was coming down heavier, and the wind had made it into a blizzard. We could not proceed.

We waited for the snow to stop, but it kept on. We hoped to continue the journey and urged the driver on, but he said he wanted to wait for vehicles coming from the opposite direction, to make sure that the road conditions ahead were safe for us.

Hour after hour, we waited, and finally, at 2 pm, one vehicle came down the hill. The passengers had grown restless by then, and now pressured the driver to start moving. Reluctantly, he started the bus. By now, it was getting dark, but we were still some distance away from our destination.

Yes, even amid trouble, God preserves our life. Blessed be His name!

AUGUST 20

STRANDED IN THE SNOW – PART 2

Gladwin Mathews

"But those who hope in the Lord will renew their strength. . .they will run and not grow weary; they will walk and not be faint."

Isaiah 40:31, NIV

Our driver had reluctantly re-started the bus, going up the snowy hill towards Rohru. After traveling about 60 km, we reached a steep point, and suddenly felt the bus skidding sideways. We hit a huge rock on the side of the hill and stopped. If we had gone the other way, we would have plunged into the deep ravine, causing fatal outcomes for sure. It was dark, and the snow kept falling, so we stayed right there. The next morning, those who were familiar with the area left the bus to go on foot. We waited for help the whole day but none came. I had no food, only a little water, which I gave to a small child who was crying. Soon it was night again.

The next day, the driver suggested that we follow those who were leaving, and get to the nearest hotel. With a prayer on my lips, I picked up courage and walked 12 km in the snow to reach a restaurant. I ate some food and then walked another 9 km to the next village.

In the distance, I saw a bus probably ready to go. I prayed that it would not leave until I got there. As I neared the bus, I saw the driver get in, take his seat and turn the ignition on.

With numb feet, I climbed in, closed my eyes, and thanked God for keeping me safe through the blizzard!

May God keep you safe even in unpredictable and inclement weather conditions.

August 21

An Anniversary to Cherish

Biju Thomas

"And now these three remain: faith, hope and love. But the greatest of these is love."

I Corinthians 13:13, NIV

My wife and I celebrated our 31st wedding anniversary last year (2022.) It was a joyous occasion as we looked back over the years and recounted God's guidance in our lives. Through every step of the journey, God had taken us by the hand and led us. Yes, there were many challenges that we faced, but through His grace they were overcome. The overriding emotion we felt was a deep sense of gratitude towards the Almighty for His Amazing Grace!

The occasion was doubly special because both our children had grown up, had jobs, and now were able to give us gifts from their income. The sense of satisfaction we felt on receiving those gifts was truly wonderful – more than our words can express!

To add to that joy, the children had been making updates on the profile pages on social media to express their love and solidarity. My daughter placed a picture of my wife and I holding hands, and wrote these words under it: "Thank you for showing us the meaning of True Love all these years. Please continue holding hands together, for the rest of your lives." We couldn't hold back the tears of joy and gratitude which flowed down our cheeks!

No, we are not a perfect couple. But if we reflect the Love of God to our children in spite of our limitations, then the purpose of our lives as parents has been fulfilled!

May the Lord Jesus help us to love each other like He wants us to.

August 22

Ask

Lillykutty Joseph

"For everyone who asks, receives;. . ."

Matthew 7:8, NKJV

In 2008, my sons, Praveen and Ranjith, were in their final year at the medical college in Manipal, India. That year, one of the final exams was slated to fall on the Sabbath day. There had been an understanding among the professors in charge of scheduling the exams that in such cases, they would change the date. This time however, the Board announced that the date would not be changed, because it was getting too cumbersome to make such changes for "stubborn" students.

My sons decided to skip the exam, knowing full well that it would be considered as having received a failing grade in the exam. I encouraged them, "Keep preparing as though you will take the exam. God will make a way! We don't know how, but He will!"

At that time, I was working at the General Conference Office in Silver Spring, MD, USA. My co-workers and I prayed earnestly for God's intervention. I decided to write to the President of the Loma Linda University in California and ask for help, as it was affiliated with the college in Manipal. I asked my children to collect all the necessary documents, and the names of the personnel responsible for scheduling the exams.

Before all the documents were collected, it was time to pay the exam fee. When my children went to make the payment, the clerk said, "You win! We just received word that the exam scheduled for the Sabbath has been moved to another date!"

We asked and received. Praise God! May that be the experience for all of us today and always.

AUGUST 23

GLORIFY GOD-PART 1

Suhasini Cherukuri

"Call upon Me in the day of trouble, I will deliver you, and you shall glorify Me."

Psalm 50:15, NKJV

More than 20 years ago, when my husband and I were driving home from work, we stopped to pick up our children from our cousin's house. Just as we were about to leave, my husband felt dizzy. I got him a cup of water, thinking he was tired. But he slid down onto the couch and passed out. We immediately called for the ambulance and got him to the emergency room.

On evaluating him, the doctors informed me that he had a ruptured brain aneurysm. It was bleeding, and if the bleeding did not stop, there was little chance of survival. My life came crashing down! I did not know how I would be able to handle the situation. My children were small, and I was a stay-at-home mom. How would I financially support my family? How was I going to care for my children all alone? What was life going to be like from then on?

He survived, but the doctors cautioned me that he would probably live only another six months to a year. During that time, he would be in a wheelchair. Since I had three children on my hands, I would not be able to take care of him at home, so I would have to place him in a facility with full-time professional care. I couldn't think of doing that!

I turned to our community for support, and to God for healing. He had an answer. He always does! Let us trust the promise from God in Psalm 50:15

AUGUST 24

GLORIFY GOD -PART 2

Suhasini Cherukuri

"I will praise You, O Lord my God, with all my heart, And will glorify your name forevermore."

Psalm 86:12, NKJV

The doctors had predicted that my husband may not live for more than one year and it would be better to place him in a facility where he would be attended to the whole day. I simply could not bring myself to do that! So, I made my own decision.

I brought him home to our beautiful family atmosphere, and he gradually recovered, but was mostly confined to a wheelchair. However, he learned to walk a bit, could talk normally, and fully regained his mental functions.

Contrary to the predictions of the doctors, he lived for over 20 years! We were able to travel, go to church regularly, and even attend church camps! He lived to see all three children graduate from college, and establish their different careers. On the whole, life was beautiful, and we cherished all the blessings and the good things in life that we thought we had permanently lost.

He lived a full and happy life – grateful for every day he lived. We saw how God had His hand over us and took care of everything.

Twenty-plus years after his stroke, my husband's earthly journey ended in 2020. We have the hope of the resurrection morning, when we will see our loved ones again. Until then, we will look back at our lives and always remember how God has led us. We will praise God at all times for His gracious care and blessings.

May we all always glorify the name of Jesus for His grace toward us.

August 25

Thorn in the Flesh

Anonymous

"And He said to me, 'My grace is sufficient for you, for My strength is made perfect in weakness.'"

II Corinthians 12:9, NKJV

At his birth, my son had a large "birthmark" on his face. The doctors called it a hemangioma. We probably could have left it alone, hoping it would disappear on its own as he grew up. But because it was quite big, when he was about three, the pediatrician gave us medicine to apply on it. Instead of getting better, it opened up and became infected. Surgery was now recommended to remove the infected tissues and prevent spread of the infection.

He had to have three surgeries, which finally stopped the infection, but the hemangioma was still on his face. I kept praying for complete healing, but the hemangioma did not change one bit!

Then, one day, at the pediatrician's office, I noticed a child with a tracheostomy – a surgical opening formed at the base of the neck into the windpipe. A tube was placed there to help the child breathe. Another child probably had Down's syndrome. I felt deep sympathy for them. My son's problem seemed so much smaller! My prayers changed, and I stopped asking for the correct treatment for my son's hemangioma. If God wanted to remove it, He could very well do it. I would leave it in His hands.

My son is now an adult. The hemangioma has not disappeared, but he is not bothered by it, and doesn't want any treatment for it. He has completed his studies and is serving the Lord.

His grace is sufficient. May His strength be made perfect in our weakness.

AUGUST 26

LIFESTYLE EVANGELISM

Gladwin Mathews

"In the same way, let your light shine before others, that they may see your good deeds and glorify your Father in Heaven."

Matthew 5:16, NIV

While serving as Principal of the SDA School at Rohru, Himachal Pradesh, I was frequently visited by government officials who had their children enrolled in the school. They would stop by on their way home, to inquire about their child's progress. One of them was an Executive Engineer who respected us and greatly supported the school. Sipping over "coffee," we would talk of the development of the town and Adventist education.

One evening, he invited us over to his place. He was not at home when we got there. His wife welcomed us and said, "My husband told me not to offer you tea, because he never had tea at your house. But he always had "coffee" which tasted different from the usual kind we buy. So, he asked me to find out what kind of coffee that was. He had gone all over town looking for it but hadn't found it."

I smiled and told her that it was a different kind of "coffee" called "Soya coffee," manufactured at the Adventist institution, Spicer Memorial College. It was caffeine-free and healthy. I offered to bring her some when I next visited Pune. When I did bring some and shared it with them as promised, they were more than pleased!

Recalling that incident made me realize that, during our visits, I had silently shared the principles of health, which are an integral part of the message of our church.

May the deeds of our lives be the witness to our faith.

August 27

Good Samaritan-Part 1

Biju Thomas

"By this shall all men know that you are my disciples, if ye have love one to another."

John 13:35, KJV

It was March of 2021. COVID-19 had hit me in a major way, and I was mostly bedridden. I was now slowly recovering and needed a walker to move about. I couldn't go to work due to my disability and was mentally shattered. One day as I lay in bed depressed and dejected, I heard the phone ring. I slowly reached out and picked it up. I did not recognize the number but was impressed to answer the call.

The person at the other end mentioned his name, and then said, "I heard from the church pastor that you are passing through difficult times, so I came to provide some help. I am just outside your home." I was shocked, not knowing what to say, because I had never met him before!

When I finally did find my voice, I said, "Sir, I am afflicted with COVID, so, for your safety I will not be able to open the door and meet you, but I will be grateful for any help you provide."

"OK, I understand," he said. "I have an envelope that I will leave at your doorstep. You can pick it up after I leave." I thanked him and he left after placing the envelope at the door.

Praise God for His faithful and generous stewards who are imbued with His principles and are willing to lend a helping hand to those in need!

May God help each of us be Good Samaritans to someone in need.

August 28

Good Samaritan-Part 2

Biju Thomas

"The next day he took out two denarii and gave them to the innkeeper. 'Look after him.' He said, 'and when I return, I will reimburse you for any extra expense you may have.'"

Luke 10:35, NIV

The gentleman outside my door said he had come to know about my difficulties, and came to my home, called me over the phone, and placed an envelope at my doorstep. It contained a gift from him and his wife, to help me tide over my very difficult condition of recovering from a serious case of COVID-19.

I waited for a few minutes, and when I heard him drive away, I slowly got out of bed and made my way to the door with the help of my walker. I picked up the envelope and opened it. There, to my amazement and awe, was his gift. I slowly counted 600 US dollars! I stood there stunned! To one with no income and unable to move, who was struggling mentally and financially, this was huge! It came as a gift that left me speechless!

And it came from a person I had never met, nor heard of before! I could hardly believe that he would be willing to go this distance to help someone he had not been acquainted with. To me, in that dejected and depressed condition, he was truly like an angel from God! To this day, I pray for this kind-hearted soul and thank God for him.

By the grace of God, we can all be like angels, helping people in need. May God touch our hearts so we would all be like the Good Samaritan!

August 29

Five Years Later!

Gloria Moses

"My grace is sufficient for you, for my power is made perfect in weakness."

II Corinthians 12:9, NIV

In the mid-1950s, my family moved to a house that was located at the border of the land that belonged to my (late) grandfather, in Divlapitiya, Sri Lanka. My dad passed away when I was two years old. To supplement our limited income, my mom planted a vegetable garden, and raised goats and chickens to provide milk and eggs for us.

A small stream separated our land from that of our neighbors. The water was crystal clear, and my siblings, cousins, and I went fishing there. In those peaceful surroundings, we played, caught dragonflies and plucked flowers from the field.

One day, one of our chickens crossed over to our neighbor's field and ate some rice kernels there. The neighbor was so enraged that he killed the chicken in the presence of my mother and took it to his house. All my mother could do was helplessly look on.

One day, five years later, our neighbor was at our door. He had come to apologize for what he had done. He said he had been sick ever since cooking and eating our chicken. He gave my mom some money to compensate for the chicken and then asked her to pray for his healing. My mom began to pray for him every day. God heard her prayers, for he returned later and said he felt fully healed!

I thank God for watching over us – a widow and her fatherless children. His grace saw us through.

May you, too, find God's grace sufficient in all circumstances.

August 30

ROBBED BUT SAFE

Gladwin Mathews

"For I am the Lord Your God who takes hold of your right hand and says to you, 'Do not fear, I will help you.'"

Isaiah 41:13, NIV

During a semester break at Spicer Memorial College, a colleague and I were asked to attend a workshop for chaplains, to be conducted near Nagpur. We boarded the Nagpur Express at the Pune railway station. I had the middle sleeper berth. Around 2 am, I was awakened by loud shouts and crying. People were running back and forth. An old couple was stabbed in their legs and robbed. A newlywed couple was robbed of all their cash and jewelry. It was chaotic and frightening!

I woke up and saw a young man standing near my berth, with a homemade sword in his hand. "What's going on?" I asked. As soon as he saw that I was awake, he pointed his sword at me and said, "Maal nikal!" meaning, "give all the stuff!" He grabbed the front pocket of my shirt. In immediate reflex, my right hand also went to that pocket. At that, my wristwatch flashed in the light and seeing it, he yanked at it. It came off my hand and he ran with it towards the door.

There must have been a gang of about 10 of them, terrorizing and robbing the passengers. Meanwhile, the train started slowing down because someone had pulled the chain. As soon as it stopped, they all jumped out and disappeared in the darkness.

I was robbed, but thank God, my colleague and I were kept from harm!

Let us live without fear for Jesus is holding our hand.

August 31

God Works Miracles

Jaya Biju

"And whatsoever ye shall ask in my name, that I will do, that the Father may be glorified in the Son."

John 14:13, KJV

I had the privilege of attending the Lowry English Church at Krishnarajapuram in Bangalore (Bengaluru) for nearly 15 years. During that period, I met and interacted with some of the most wonderful people in the Adventist community.

The melodious songs by the young children who lived in the hostel, and the dedicated pastors who cared for the congregation, made the worship at that church exceptional. Many times, in my distress, I would go to this sanctuary and cry out to the Lord, and He would be faithful in answering my heart's cry. This was my experience and I shared it with anyone who came there.

In 2018, a couple married for many years came to worship there. Their one great desire was to have children, for they had none. The wife especially was sad and depressed. It broke my heart to see her grief. I shared my testimony with her, saying, "If you kneel and pray in this sanctuary, trusting in God, He will answer your prayer." I assured her that I would also pray for her. Soon after that, I left India.

I went back to India recently and visited that church. I met the lady there and was happy to see that she was pregnant! She told me she had faithfully come to the sanctuary and prayed, trusting in God. And God had answered her prayer!

Let us ask for blessings in Jesus' name, knowing He will do what's best for us.

SEPTEMBER 1

MIRACLE BIRTH

Anonymous

"Obey me, and I will be your God and you will be my people. Walk in obedience to all I command you, that it may go well with you."

Jeremiah 7:23, NIV

I was pregnant with our second baby. The first few months were difficult, with severe nausea and vomiting. It was only after the fifth month that I was able to eat a little. About that time, I felt impressed to stop eating meat and fish. I believed it was God who was prompting me.

At times I would be woken up in the middle of the night and impressed to kneel and pray for the baby in my womb. I did it every time I was impressed, even at 2 am!

One day, I slipped and fell in the bathtub, and was taken to the hospital. My blood pressure was found to be unsteady, and the baby was in the breech position. I was rushed to the operating room for an emergency C-section. After the surgery, the doctor, who was not a Christian, came to my room and said, "Do you know that your baby girl is a miracle baby?" I asked her why she said that. She replied, "You were headed for a dangerous condition called pre-eclampsia. If the surgery had been delayed even half an hour, the baby might have come out stillborn!"

Then I remembered that in our extended family, we had had seven stillbirths among the baby girls.

Thank you, Jesus, for prompting me to change my diet and to pray even at odd hours, and for the gift of a daughter.

Let us obey God at all times.

SEPTEMBER 2

THE LIGHT OF SRI LANKA

Biju Thomas

"Ye are the light of the world. A city that is set on a hill cannot be hid."

Matthew 5:14, KJV

During my days at the Spencer Road School, Bangalore, a trip was planned to visit Sri Lanka. First, we took a train to Dhanushkodi, a pretty port town overlooking the pristine, blue waters at the confluence of the Indian Ocean and the Bay of Bengal. The next part, from there to Talaimannar in Sri Lanka, was by boat, a ferry, which took about three hours to make it across. In those days, it was a great tourist attraction!

It was an exciting trip for me, a 13-year-old, on his first venture to a foreign country! I still remember how thrilling the whole journey was! But my best memories were of the campus of Lakpahana, the Adventist boarding school there. The whole campus was lush, with a vast number of trees, most of them laden with fruit. And shrubs and flowering plants of every color and hue were found all over. It was both picturesque and peaceful, and produced a sense of calm that made it a very attractive campus to live on.

"Lakpahana," in the Sinhalese language, means "Light of Lanka." For nearly 90 years now, this institution has been a source of light and guidance to the local population.

My beautiful memories of Lakpahana and the meaning of the name reminded me of the words of Jesus in the verse quoted above.

I pray that each of us will be a light to the world, spreading the love, peace, and beauty of Jesus to all we meet each day.

September 3

Gospel Concert Amidst Guns

Gladwin Mathews

But the Lord is faithful, who will establish you and guard you from the evil one.

2 Thessalonians 3:3, NKJV

In November of 2012, I organized a "Gospel Music Concert & Youth Festival" at the Fateh Garh Churian SDA church, where my dad had been the pastor for more than 20 years. We had advertised it widely because we wanted the various SDA youth groups, as well as others to attend and participate. We hoped to share our message with all the surrounding communities.

Prior to my travel from the USA, I was informed that two personnel from the Bureau of Investigation of the Central Government of India had visited there and made inquiries about the meetings. I was keenly aware that Christians and churches were being targeted in some places by radical groups.

I prayed and then consulted my dad. He suggested that I obtain written permission from the local authorities. It was arranged and obtained.

The Youth Festival was held on a Sabbath day. People arrived and took their seats. The groups were ready to go on stage and start the concert, when a jeep pulled up at the church. A smart, impressive-looking gentleman in a gray safari suit, stepped out of the jeep, followed by two police officers with guns in their hands. He walked toward the gathering. My heart began to pound. He came straight toward me but then smiled and said, "I am a Christian government officer. I heard about this event, and have come to attend it!"

I praised God for His mercy and His assurance of constant protection!

May God's protection be with us today and always.

SEPTEMBER 4

STRANDED BUT BLESSED

Lillykutty Joseph

"And my God shall supply all your needs according to His riches in glory by Christ Jesus."

Philippians 4:19, NKJV

In 1978, I was working as a secretary in the office of the Pathfinder Director, at the Southern Asia Division headquarters in Pune, India. That year, the Annual Pathfinder Camporee was held in Bangalore (Bengaluru.) As part of the organizing staff, I attended the Camporee, and then decided to visit my family in Kerala, before returning to Pune.

Heavy rains had caused flooding, and the train could not continue past Ernakulam in Kerala. It was a long way to my hometown. All the passengers got off the train and headed for the bus station, hoping to find buses to their destinations. To my disappointment, no bus was going to my hometown. I had no option but to stay there among the crowded passengers and wait until the right bus was available.

Then, in the crowd, I saw somebody I knew – an Adventist pastor! He had found a bus that could take him to his hometown, and he graciously invited me to stay with his family until the bus service to my hometown resumed.

When we got off the bus, we had to wade through water that came up to our hips! He carried his luggage and mine, and we made it to his home. I was blessed with his family's hospitality for a whole week, until the waters receded and I could go home.

I thank God for providing a "family of God" that helped in time of need.

Let us be confident in Christ, for His riches will always supply our needs.

SEPTEMBER 5

OUR IDENTITY IN CHRIST

Gladwin Mathews

"But you are a chosen people, a royal priesthood, a holy nation, God's special possession, that you may declare the praises of him who called you out of darkness into his wonderful light."

I Peter 2:9, NIV

When I came to the USA in 1999, I joined the Lake Union Conference as a Youth Leader and Bible Worker. I first stayed with a longtime friend from India. After working for a few months, I had saved some money, and wanted to buy a car before winter set in.

One Sunday morning, my friend and I went car shopping at a used car dealership. I found a 1990 Ford Taurus that I liked. We did a test drive, and everything looked good, so I decided to buy the car.

The sales agent said the price was $3,500. I pulled out $1,500 in cash, and placed it before him. He counted the notes and said, "But this is only $1,500! I had mentioned $3,500!" And with that, he put the money down on the table.

I told him that I was working as a missionary at a low level salary, and that much of my work was done on a voluntary basis.

"Which church do you work for?" he asked. And when I said, "The Seventh-day Adventist Church," he quickly responded, "Oh yes! I know them well! I think I can give you the car for $1,500!"

I thanked God for showing me some tangible benefits of being identified with the church!

Our identity in Christ offers us so much more! Let us always live as God's holy nation.

A Priceless Ingredient

Biju Thomas

"Let all that you do be done with love."

I Corinthians 16:14, NKJV

When I wake up every morning, I go to the kitchen, and find my wife holding up a cup of hot drink for me. It is a very special drink called "kashayam," made with ginger, pepper, jaggery, and some other spices. The name means "medicine!" If I took this drink every day, it would help build up enough immunity and strength to fight any infection.

In view of the Covid pandemic, many, across the globe, have taken to immunity boosters in some form or another.

Kashayam is highly recommended by some nutritionists who claim it to be an effective way of boosting one's immunity. It is claimed to treat everything from coughs and colds to throat congestion, to joint pains, anxiety and stress, to mood swings and depression, to even low blood pressure! Hydration is an added benefit – and not with just any kind of water, but that which contains the special ingredients found in those herbs!

Speaking of special ingredients, think of the enormous amount of money spent on particular brands of coffee because of an exotic ingredient from a foreign place that was added to the blend! Is it really worth all that cost?!

There is one ingredient that whoever brews your morning hot drink, whether wife or mother, adds to the drink each day – and that is "love!" It is priceless! Money could never buy it!!

Paul focused on the hearts of the Corinthians. Without love, their actions would fall far short of God's ideal. May our thoughts, words, and actions be done with Godly love.

September 7

Musician and Blood Sacrifice

Gladwin Mathews

"Now the Spirit expressly says that in the later times some will depart from the faith by devoting themselves to deceitful spirits and teachings of demons."

I Timothy 4:1, ESV

In December 1971, I had come home to my parents in Amritsar for the Christmas vacation. I enjoyed my first Sabbath at the church.

The next day, as I sat basking in the sun, I heard someone across the street talking quite loudly about Moses, and how the Israelites went into Egypt. Then the same voice asked, "Why did they go to Egypt? I understand about the water, but where did the mud come from?" This got me curious, so I looked over the wall. And there sat an old blind and lame man, next to the church gate, talking to himself!

I later learned his story.

He had once been an active church member and a good musician. He played the harmonium and was a song leader in the church. No one could sing Zaburs (Psalms) like him! He knew the Bible well too. But he had wanted to become a great musician and singer. Someone told him he could become one, if he followed the ritual of going to the graveyard at night, practicing there, and offering a blood sacrifice of a chicken or goat. The ritual was demon-worship, and he was told that it would make him a great singer and musician.

There, before me, was the real result of that ritual. This was what he had become by departing from Jesus, and indulging in the worship of demons.

Let us trust in Jesus, and not turn to deceitful spirits.

SEPTEMBER 8

OUR BEST PLANNER -PART I

Vidhya Melvin

"Today, if you hear His voice, Do not harden your hearts. . ."

Hebrews 3:15, NIV

The high school final exam results were delayed in 2004. Because of that, the start of the first year of college at Chennai, Tamil Nadu, was also delayed. This domino effect continued, and the first semester exams, which usually end before the Christmas holidays, were now scheduled for after New Year's Day.

This caused a dilemma regarding where to spend my Christmas vacation. I wanted to go to my native place, Kanyakumari, and spend time with my family. The holiday season is always spectacular there, with the whole area bright with colored Christmas lights.

But my parents wanted me to stay on at the college and prepare for the upcoming exams. I wanted to know God's plan for me during the holiday season, and I surrendered my will to Him. As the holidays approached, my parents asked me to visit my Periyappa-Periamma's (uncle and aunt's) home in Chennai.

On December 25, we spent the whole day in church, fasting and praying. When I returned home, I had a big, heavy dinner. That made me very sleepy, and though my Periamma advised me to prepare for the exams, I went to the study room as if I was going to study, but instead, I hid there and slept on the floor, using my book bag as my pillow.

Suddenly, I woke up to the sound of distinct words, "Get up, open the Bible, and read." I realized it was the Holy Spirit speaking to me.

When God speaks to us, it is best to obey. (To be continued.)

September 9

Our Best Planner-Part 2

Vidhya Melvin

"You shall not be afraid of the terror by night. . ."

Psalm 91:5, NKJV

I had heard the words clearly while sleeping on the floor at my aunt and uncle's place in Chennai: "Get up. Open the Bible and read." I was already tired from the whole day of fasting at the church. Further, I had had a heavy meal. I was too sleepy, and started complaining: "God, isn't this too much for me? I spent the whole day at church, and now You want me to read the Bible again?!

But the voice was more persistent, telling me to read the Book of Revelation. There was a sign of the return of Jesus to happen soon. Now, I was afraid. I got up, read the Bible, prayed, and then shared my experience with my aunt, who told me to pray about it.

We woke up the following day, Sunday, December 26th, and got ready to go to church. We were Sunday-keeping Christians then. As we stepped outside, we saw people running about hysterically, asking, "Did you not feel anything different?" We wondered what all the alarm was about. All the neighbors had felt the earthquake and seen the things in their houses sway, fall, and roll about on the floor! They had run out of their houses, but we had not felt even a tiny bit of all that!

I remembered my experience the previous day, and my earnest prayer, "God, I don't know what You are trying to convey. Please cover our home with your protection."

May God protect us from all terrors by day or night. (To be continued.)

SEPTEMBER 10

OUR BEST PLANNER-PART 3

Vidhya Melvin

"For I know the plans I have for you, declares the Lord, plans to prosper you and not to harm you. Plans to give you hope and a future."

Jeremiah 29:12, NIV

I was in Chennai at my uncle and aunt's house for the Christmas vacation, despite my desire to go to my home in Kanyakumari. I had surrendered my will to God. In spite of being extremely tired the day before, I had got up, read the Book of Revelation, and had prayed, just as the Holy Spirit had prompted me. When the earthquake shook the neighbors' houses, we did not feel a thing.

The unfamiliar word "Tsunami" started flashing on every news channel. The phone networks were affected, and I could not reach my parents immediately. But, a day later, my parents called me. My dad's very first words were, "Makkale (dear daughter,) it is good that you didn't come home for the holidays. It is mentally devastating to see dead bodies strewn all around and family members weeping and frantically searching for their loved ones."

As my dad kept talking, I began to put together how God had prompted me to surrender my holiday plans to Him, and how He planned out my holidays for my best. He knows what is best for each of us.

It's been many years, but as I think of it now, I am reminded of His supernatural qualities. Humans can know about the past and present. Only God knows the future as if it is in the present.

May we always hear the voice of God and follow His plans for us. (Concluded)

SEPTEMBER 11

WHEN GOD SAID NO

Anonymous

"And we know that all things work together for good to those who love God, to those who are called according to His purpose."

Romans 8:28, NKJV

I had been working faithfully and hard at my job, and had been very productive. Soon, an opportunity came my way for a promotion. I was eligible and qualified, so I prayerfully applied for the position. I wanted it badly because I was already performing all the responsibilities that it entailed. I just didn't have the title and the extra compensation that went with it.

I eagerly waited for the decision of the upper management. To my utter dismay and disappointment, I was passed over. I felt I was treated unfairly. But I prayed even more! I didn't want my disappointment to negatively impact my performance at my workplace, or lose the cheerful disposition I had developed with my coworkers and my family. I remembered Romans 8:28, took it to heart, and thanked God for His assurance.

True to His word, God soon opened up another opportunity. I applied for it and was readily accepted. This new job was much easier and a lot more enjoyable! Since it was in the same company, I could keep my seniority and all the benefits intact. To top it all, even the salary I now got was higher than what was offered for the other position.

Indeed, God has a way of working out the best for His children, even when He says, "No!" to some of our requests. All we need to do is follow Him and trust His guidance and His decisions. Blessed be His name.

SEPTEMBER 12

HE WAS SURELY WATCHING

Lillykutty Joseph

"Whoever dwells in the shelter of the Most High will rest in the shadow of the Almighty."

Psalm 91:1, NIV

In the mid-1960s, one of my older sisters and her husband went to another country for higher studies and left their two young children under the care of our parents at our home. I was in the eighth grade, and my sister was in the ninth.

We had a lot of fun with our nephew and niece. We played among the trees in our rubber plantation, collected Lolly berries and cashew nuts from our land, and watched the weaver birds weaving their long, hanging nests and raising their nestlings. We ate ripe, sweet, juicy mangoes plucked right from the trees. We planted zinnias and roses, and watched butterflies drink nectar from the flowers. It was like a little Garden of Eden!

One evening, after worship, my sister and I started doing our homework while our nephew and niece played around. After some time, they grew tired and wanted to sleep, so we sent them off, telling them we would join them later (they were young and scared of sleeping alone!) But then my sister said, "Wait, let's fluff up the pillows and make the bed ready for you to sleep in."

She hurried and went to the bed, lifted the pillow to fluff it, and there, coiled under it, was an unwanted, silent guest – a krait! It is a snake with very deadly venom! Hospitals were located far away, and a bite from a krait could have meant death.

Our awesome God was surely watching! May we rest in His shadow today.

SEPTEMBER 13

CLIMBING THE MOUNTAIN

Gladwin Mathews

"No one who hopes in You will ever be put to shame."

Psalm 25:3, NIV

I loved mountain climbing ever since I was young, especially during high school camps and on road trips.

In 1986, I moved to Himachal Pradesh, to head a school at Rohru, some distance from Shimla. It is situated in a valley from which I could see nothing but snow capped mountains and brooks that joined to form streams that finally merged with the Pabbar River.

Urged by my love for climbing, I decided to go on an expedition to climb one of the mountains. As I climbed and rounded the first bend, the valley seemed to stretch out below me. I climbed higher and could see further – up to three or four miles away. Higher still, and the scene kept expanding and enlarging until, finally, when I reached the summit, I could look east, west, north, and south and see almost the whole town of Rohru spread out before me. It was a breathtaking sight!

"Climbing a mountain" is a metaphor that describes overcoming hurdles and finally reaching the desired goal. It is the completion of a challenging task, and implies that one can experience that achievement only when the top is reached.

It is an illustration of the Christian life. When we first believe in Christ, we see only a little of Him. The higher we climb in our experience with Him, the more we discover the depth and grandeur of His beauty and love.

Psalms 25:3 is a comforting reminder that we won't be disappointed when we hope in God and keep taking the next step.

September 14

He Supplies

Lillykutty Joseph

"My God shall supply all your needs according to His riches in glory by Christ Jesus."

Philippians 4:19, KJV

In 2005, our family moved from Baltimore to the Silver Spring area to be closer to my sister's place and the Southern Asian Seventh-Day Adventist Church (SASDAC.) The housing market was brisk, and houses were going quickly.

We found a home that was just right for us, but after buying the house, I lost my job! Finding a new job was not easy those days! I applied at many places and went for many interviews, but nothing panned out. After my interview at the White Estate of the General Conference of Seventh-Day Adventists, I was told another candidate was selected. If, for some reason, that person did not accept the job, I would be next in line.

I wanted the job, so I kept praying. Time passed, and since I didn't hear from them, I took a temporary part-time position in another company. This helped to keep our family going, and I had time to set up our new home.

One evening, while I was running some errands, I got a call from one of the Associate Directors of the White Estate. They said there was an opening and asked if I would be interested. Ecstatic and grateful, I accepted the offer.

It turned out to be a wonderful experience and a great blessing. I learned Adventist history and led tours of the White Estate for visitors from around the world. This helped strengthen my faith in Jesus and in the mission of the Adventist Church.

Our God supplies all our needs right on time.

September 15

Fast And Pray

Anonymous

"For you formed my inward parts; you covered me in my mother's womb. I will praise You, for I am fearfully and wonderfully made; Marvelous are Your works, And that my soul knows very well."

Psalm 139:13,14, NKJV

I am part of a prayer group at my church. We get together twice a week to pray, which often includes fasting. Sometimes, when the need is grave, we fast for several days in a row.

One day, one of the ladies in the group shared her experience. She was pregnant, and the ultrasound had revealed the baby to be abnormal. The problem was so serious that her obstetrician recommended terminating the pregnancy. But she did not want to do that and said she was willing to accept the baby even if it turned out to be abnormal. However, she requested prayer for a miracle from God. So, we decided to fast and pray for the unborn child.

When she delivered the baby, it was a perfectly normal baby girl! She has grown up like any other child and has participated in many extracurricular activities at school. She was in the top ten in her 12th-grade class of 800! Her parents brought her up in the fear of the Lord, and she is a very active church member today. There are no signs of the abnormality that was seen in the ultrasound!

Our prayer group stands as a testament that fasting and prayer bring us closer to God, and that God hears and answers prayers when His children call out to Him. Let us go to Him in prayer, and live ever closer to Him.

SEPTEMBER 16

TEST OF ENDURANCE

Bimal Nowrangi

"My brothers and sisters, be very happy when you are tested in different ways. You know that such testing of your faith produces endurance."

James 1:2,3, GW

Endurance is the ability to survive and continue going forward with steady effort, despite surrounding difficult situations. Marathons, chariot races, Olympics, and other events allow testing of one's endurance. Some pass the test, while others fail.

In 1975, I decided to tour five South Indian states on my 150cc Lambretta, with my college professor friend as a pillion rider. We started our trip from Spicer Memorial College in Pune, Maharashtra. We passed through the cities of Panaji in Goa, Trivandrum (now Thiruvananthapuram) in Kerala, Bengaluru in Karnataka, and Vellore in Tamil Nadu, before returning to our college. It was a long and grueling journey. We had driven 3,500 miles in 7 days, and by any standards, had passed the test for endurance! Although we were tired, we felt an exhilarating sense of accomplishment!

Life may be long and grueling, and we may encounter many challenging tests along the way, but God will provide us the much-needed power and strength to complete our journey.

Paul's encouraging words for us are, "Let us not grow weary or become discouraged in doing good, for at the proper time we will reap, if we do not give in." Galatians 6:9 AMP. "For you have need of patient endurance [bearing up under difficult circumstances without compromising,] so that when you have carried out the will of God, you may receive and enjoy to the full what is promised." Hebrews 10:36, AMP

Keep going, God is with us.

September 17

You Are Special to God

Jercilla Murmu

"In all your ways submit to Him, and He will make your paths straight."

Proverbs 3:6, NIV

Admission to all the colleges had closed, and I was not accepted anywhere. Feeling discouraged and dejected, I turned to God, earnestly prayed, and even bargained with Him about my final decisions. A few hours after my prayer, I received a letter instructing me to join Manipal Academy of Higher Education in three days! It was thousands of kilometers away, and I needed to start the journey the same night! I did not know the exact location of the place, and did not have the finances for the admission fees.

We first traveled 653 kms to the Kolkata Adventist School, where the principal guided us and told us how to get to our destination. I felt like Abraham, going to an unknown land (Genesis 12:1)

We then traveled three days and two nights by train without any reservations. It was a terrible journey, and all along, I was anxious and fearful of the unknown. However, when we reached Manipal and walked towards the university's main gate, I was surprised to meet my friend's father – the pastor of the Manipal Adventist Church – and two classmates from my high school days! The pastor came along and helped me get registered without paying any fees!

My God had already provided for my needs before I reached the destination. This was the beginning of many miracles God performed in my life.

When all doors seem closed, God prepares and opens other doors for more and greater blessings. Let us submit to Him completely and trust in Him.

SEPTEMBER 18

OUR FRUITLESS LABOR

Bimal Nowrangi

"They will build houses and live there. They will plant vineyards and eat fruit from them. They will not build homes and have others live there. They will not plant and have others eat from it...They will never again work for nothing."

Isaiah 65:21-23, GW

Several years ago, I planted a persimmon sapling in my backyard. After reading the instruction manual, I carefully measured and dug the hole, put in soil and fertilizer, and planted the sapling. I took excellent care of it, and it flourished and became a tree. A couple of years later, I was excited to see some flowers on it. Soon, about a dozen fruits appeared. I now took extra care of the tree and the fruit – fertilizing and irrigating even more regularly.

However, I was not the only one waiting for the fruit to arrive. The bees were there to gather nectar from the flowers and pollinate them. Also, lurking around were ants, bugs, and birds. I noticed a few daring squirrels, frequenting the branches, in anticipation of the soon-to-arrive persimmon!

One morning, to my horror, I saw a few raw persimmons on the ground. They had been pecked by birds and nibbled by squirrels. I felt devastated! I had worked so hard to care for the tree for years, and now I was denied the joy and pleasure of tasting the fruit of my labors.

Our experience will be different in heaven and in the new earth. We will plant and we will eat, because our labor will not be in vain. No one will snatch away our due rewards.

Thank God for His hope and promise.

SEPTEMBER 19

A HOUSE FOR ME

Anonymous

"Now to Him who is able to do exceedingly abundantly above all that we ask or think, according to the power that works in us, to Him be glory in the church by Christ Jesus throughout all ages, world without end. Amen."

Ephesians 3:20,21, NKJV

My family was living in a comfortable house. The only downside was that it was quite far from our church. We wanted to live closer to the church and searched for new listings.

We prayed and asked God to help us find a house that would be ideal for us and closer to our church. Soon, a new listing came up in the perfect location. It was listed as having 3,000 square feet. We bid for it along with two other potential buyers. Our lender approved our loan, while theirs were not approved. Hence, we got the house for a relatively low price.

After the closing transactions were done, the agent realized that the house was 4,500 square feet and was listed in error as 3,000 square feet! It looked smaller from the outside than it really was when you went inside. The rooms were spacious, with all the amenities a family would want. We could not believe what had just happened! We had not asked for such a blessing.

Immediately after closing, the square footage was corrected, and the price of the house shot up considerably, giving us a good amount of equity.

Our incredible God has amazing ways in which to bless His children. Let us trust Him.

SEPTEMBER 20

LOSS OF FIRST LOVE

Bimal Nowrangi

"Yet I hold this against you: You have forsaken the love you had at first. Consider how far you have fallen! Repent and do the things you did at first..."

Revelation 2:4, NIV

One day, as I was driving in the streets of our community, I saw a young man standing by his beautiful, newly purchased, white Toyota Rav4 car. It was spotlessly clean, and he stood there looking admiringly at it. His friends were also standing around admiring it. He hardly paid any attention to his old model car which was parked right in front of his new one. He appeared greatly in love with his new car!

I returned a few hours later, and the young man was still standing by his new car. But this time he was doing more than just admiring it. He was in his shorts, and had a bucket of water and all types of cleaning agents and equipment. He was listening to loud music from the car's sound system, singing, and washing his brand-new car!

I watched him clean his car faithfully every day for the next two weeks. However, during the third week, he washed his car only two times! What was happening? Was he getting tired of washing it, or getting bored with it? Was he beginning to lose the love he first had for his new car?

Let us remind ourselves that, "We all like sheep have gone astray..." (Isaiah 53:6) and that it was God who "...first loved us." (I John 4:19.)

Let us ask God to help us not only to retain, but to increase, our love for Him.

SEPTEMBER 21

GROWING IN GRACE

Jercilla Murmu

"Surely there is a future, and your hope will not be cut off."

Proverbs 23:18, ESV

Gardening is one of my favorite things to do in late spring and early summer. In growing a lush garden, my husband and I pay careful attention to the seeds, making sure they are healthy. The soil is made fertile by adding organic manure, before sowing the seeds. Once the plants sprout, we provide adequate water and plant nutrition. Soon, with all the care given to the plants, we are ready to harvest lots of beautiful flowers and fresh vegetables from the garden.

Apart from the regular garden, I have a particular hobby of dropping seeds in the worst soil conditions (in cracks in the concrete) or finding plants that grow in unusual spots where they were not planted. I discovered that these disadvantaged plants also appeared to be healthy and produced plenty of fruit and flowers. To me, this was an illustration of God's grace.

Sometimes, our lives are like plants that grow in the most challenging circumstances. We may have been born and raised in terrible environments. Our parents may not have afforded the best of food, houses, or clothing. But the blessings of God still come to those who fear Him and put their trust in Him. His love supersedes all our circumstances and makes our lives fruitful. We do not deserve the blessings, but His grace still abounds in our lives.

Let us not get disheartened looking at our circumstances. We can stay assured that there is a future for all in Christ and in God's grace, and our hope will never be cut off.

SEPTEMBER 22

SMALL THINGS ALSO MATTER

Bimal Nowrangi

"The same thing is true for ships. They are very big and are driven by strong winds. Yet, by using small rudders, pilots steer the ships wherever they want them to go."

James 3:4, GW

Last year, our local government officials in Takoma Park authorized a total facelift to our entire community streets. The contractors brought in many types of heavy reconstruction equipment and skilled workers to operate them. One of the first machines they brought in was for scraping off the old black asphalt from the streets. The next ones were for pouring new asphalt onto the streets.

While there were many skilled workers operating the heavy machinery, I noticed that one (sometimes two) was always assigned to just stand at the worksite with a red (STOP and GO SLOW) signpost. Standing, holding, and occasionally rotating the red signs, did not require much skill or training. The specific duty of this worker was to control and direct traffic in the work area. While the task was not as difficult or complicated as heavy drilling or pouring asphalt, it was extremely important for the safety of both the workers and the commuters who were using the streets.

Even so in life, things that appear trivial to us, are often of immense significance in God's sight. In His providence, "God chose what the world considers ordinary and what it despises – what it considers to be nothing – in order to destroy what it considers to be something." I Corinthians 1:28 GW

Everyone is important, and the small things are as important as the big things in the sight of God when used in His service.

September 23

God Still Performs Miracles

Gloria Moses

"Then he took the five loaves and the two fishes, and looking up to heaven, he blessed them, and brake, and gave to the disciples to set before the multitude. And they did eat and were all filled: and there was taken up of fragments that remained to them twelve baskets."

Luke 9:16,17, KJV

In 2016, our senior pastor at SASDAC decided to try a new program of organizing lunch every Sabbath at church, and inviting the visitors to join us. The members were divided alphabetically into four groups, each responsible for one Sabbath, once a month. As the overall team leader, I was responsible for the lunch of about 150 people each Sabbath.

It would go well at times, but at other times, those who had agreed to bring food would forget, and we would run short of food. This is what happened one Sabbath, and the team panicked! Someone then brought a container of sambar, not enough to fill even a quarter of the large serving tray. But as we poured it out, it kept coming in waves until the whole tray was filled! The three of us looked at each other, amazed and spellbound.

The rice too, didn't seem enough. So, we decided to serve the rice rather than have the members serve themselves – just in case! As we served the vegetable rice, the tray seemed to always have the same amount left; and after everyone was fed, we still had a quarter tray left!

Jesus had blessed our food just as He had the loaves and fishes. Let us trust Him. He will meet all our needs.

September 24

You Are Valued

Susy Solomon

"Look at the birds of the air. . . .Are you not of more value than they?"

Matthew 6:26, ESV

Since I had many things in my hand, I placed them on the hood of my car so I could open the car door. I then put them all in the back seat and drove to work. It rained the whole day while I was at work.

On my commute home, I allowed a driver to pull in front of me. At a fire station, the traffic came to a standstill. This driver got out of his car, came toward my car, picked up something from the hood, and handed it to me. To my utter surprise, it was my cell phone that I had left on the hood in the morning!

It had been sitting there the whole day, drenched in the rain! When I called my friend and told her what had happened, she said, "There's no way the phone is still working!"

It was a miracle that it did not fall off the slanting hood.

It was a miracle that nobody stole it while it was in the parking lot.

It was a miracle that a stranger would get out of his car in the middle of traffic to pick up the phone and hand it to me.

It was a miracle that it was fully functional.

That little phone was my means of communication and was essential to me. God cares for little sparrows, and He cares about me and my phone! He will care for all the details of our lives today, even if they seem minor. Let's trust Him.

SEPTEMBER 25

UNDER THE TRAIN

Gladwin Mathews

"Call upon Me in the day of trouble; I will deliver you, and you shall glorify Me."

Psalm 50:15, NKJV

One day, in the mid-1990s, my elder sister planned to travel from Hapur to Jalandhar by train. She purchased a ticket and boarded an express train bound for Jammu via Jalandhar. She didn't realize that this train did not stop at the main Jalandhar City station, which was large and well-lighted, but at the Jalandhar Cantonment station, which was smaller and less lit.

She reached the Cantonment station in the wee hours of the morning and got off the train, but on the wrong side of the platform. It was dark and rainy, and things were barely visible. "I must cross over the tracks quickly to get to the correct side," she thought.

As she walked across in the dark, she was pushed from the back by a train she had not noticed, which was approaching her. She fell flat, face-down, between the tracks. Praying as she fell, a God-given thought flashed through her mind – to keep lying down and let the train pass over her. She just lay there until the train passed over. She had some bruises on her face and back due to the brake hoses of the train that kept hitting her, but she was safe!

A railway guard witnessed the whole scene and came running over to help her climb onto the platform. He helped her clean her wounds and then arranged for transportation to take her to the Ruby Nelson Memorial Hospital for treatment.

God kept my sister's life safe. May we be in His protection always.

SEPTEMBER 26

GOD CHARTS OUR PATHS – PART 1

Biju Thomas

"You saw me before I was born. Everyday of my life was recorded in your book. Every moment was laid out before a single day had passed."

Psalm 139:16, NLT

Nestled between the hills and valleys of southern Kerala is the idyllic village of my dreams. This beautiful village, called Karickom, has a special place in my heart for two reasons. The story of my life began in that village, and my life partner is from there!

The Adventist High School, founded at Karickom, Kottarakkara, is one of the oldest and most beautiful schools in Kerala, India. It is built on a small hill, which came to be called "The White Man's Hill," because white missionaries from America established it.

My father came to this campus as a bachelor on his first job as a Malayalam teacher. He got married in the early 1960s, and a few years later, I was born there as his second son. He stayed for some time in a rented house just opposite another family whose daughter was to later become my wife!

Our family left Kottarakkara for Bangalore (Bengaluru) 404 miles away, when I was an infant, while my wife's parents remained there. I went through my childhood and educational years in Bangalore, while my wife was educated at Kottarakkara. For 20 years and more, we never met, but our paths were destined to cross according to God's will.

God has a plan for every day of our lives. We do not know what the future holds, but we do know that He holds the future, and will bring to completion whatever He begins.

SEPTEMBER 27

GOD CHARTS OUR PATHS – PART 2

Biju Thomas

"The man who finds a wife finds a treasure, and he receives favor from the LORD."

Proverbs 18:22, NLT

Although my wife and I were both born in Karickom, in Kerala, we never lived together there, nor did we ever meet for 20 years because my family moved to Bangalore when I was an infant.

About 20 years later, my father was called to head the Seventh-day Adventist School at Ernakulam as its Principal. It was that time of my life when, as a young man, I was beginning to think of a life partner. I was praying and waiting for God to guide and lead in this crucial matter when, in 1988, she came to the same school as a teacher!

We had been born in homes opposite each other in Karickom but had moved apart in very different directions. We had grown up and gone through our educational years in places separated by hundreds of miles. And now, 20 years later, our paths crossed again. This time, we were aware of the circumstances, for we were now grown up, and we decided to get married in the early 1990s.

Only after our marriage, did I learn that we were born in the same village!! It was wonderful to know that God had guided our lives from the very start. He had orchestrated the events according to His plans, and when we submitted our ways to Him, He had brought it to completion – and made us life companions. The Lord had charted out a plan even before we were born!

Trusting in His Divine plans is the real key to love and companionship.

September 28

My Worries

Abigail Guria

"Do not worry about anything. Instead, pray to God about everything. Ask Him to help you with the things that you need. . ."

Philippians 4:6, EASY

I really enjoyed my preschool, kindergarten, and first-grade education at the Sligo Adventist School. Even though I was very young, I recall having a great group of friends and teachers with whom I participated in various extracurricular activities in a safe environment.

My parents later enrolled me in Beltsville Adventist School (BAS.) My initial concern about transferring to a new school was short-lived because I soon met two former Sligo School friends who had moved to BAS a year earlier. I quickly got into the swing of activities there, and began enjoying sports, music, fundraisers, field trips, and other sponsored activities.

Time flew by, and I was in the 8th grade, my final year. The need to find a good high school began to worry us greatly. I had been in private schools all along, but now I would have to attend a public school.

There, I found myself in a vast school building with a huge enrollment and a strange curriculum and timetable. Between class periods, the corridors were packed with students milling around, nudging and bumping into one another, causing some unsavory scenes.

In the midst of my anxiety, a realization came to me that I had forgotten something, or perhaps Someone, who alone could take away all my worries. I learned to trust in God. In turn, He not only gave me peace of mind, but also constant success in my studies, and I got good grades.

Let's turn all our worries over to God.

September 29

"Where Are My Glasses?"

Abigail Guria

"Open my eyes that I may see wonderful things in your law."

Psalm 119:18, NIV

It was the evening of the 35th anniversary celebrations of our church, SASDAC. The weekend was jam-packed with various celebratory activities, and I was excited and very busy! After the special Friday evening vesper service and orchestral rehearsal, my sister and I went to our grandparents' home to spend the night. I went to bed at midnight and woke up at 6 am since I had a packed day ahead of me.

I hurriedly took a shower, ate breakfast, and began gathering my stuff to go home with my parents, who had come to pick us up. I had a lot on my mind – I had to play in the orchestra, carry the Pathfinder flag during the nationality march, and sing at the social program.

I got my belongings together, but could not locate my eyeglasses! I became anxious. I had placed them in a safe spot before going to bed, but now they were missing. My parents and grandparents joined in the search.

I was on the verge of giving up when my grandmother gathered everyone and prayed to the Lord to help me find my missing glasses. After the prayer, we looked around again, and there it was – in the same safe spot where I had put them!! With a look of embarrassment, I quickly put them on.

We thanked God for opening our eyes. The remaining part of the day of celebrations was truly beautiful.

We serve a wonderful, prayer-answering God! Trust that your prayers will be answered in His time, in His way.

SEPTEMBER 30

FAREWELL MALDIVES – PART 1

Biju Thomas

"How amiable are thy tabernacles, O LORD of hosts! My soul longeth, yea, even fainteth for the courts of the LORD: my heart and flesh crieth out for the living God."

Psalm 84:1,2, KJV

Battered by a tempest, and threatened by a tsunami, the turbulent events during my short stay of 2 months at Maldives, forced me to ponder whether it was worth staying there. Then the probable reason why the Lord didn't want me to stay on in Maldives, dawned on me.

The primary religion in Maldives is Islam. It is the state and official religion of the Maldives. The practice of any other faith is strictly prohibited. Foreigners and migrants are allowed to practice their religious beliefs, but only in private. If you were caught praying or singing, or calling out the name of Jesus in public, you would be punished with imprisonment. Tourists are advised not to bring any religious literature, including the Bible, to avoid any hassle at the Maldives airport.

I had managed to somehow sneak in my Bible but had to read it privately and in fear. I felt very restricted. I was used to having the full liberty of worshiping God while in India, and this was a suffocating experience. I bore it for a few weeks and then longed and craved to attend church. It became so intense that I decided to return to India, where I could worship in freedom and peace. David's words resonated with me. Everything within him – heart and flesh – longed for God. I felt that way too.

May each of us find peace and contentment in God's Sanctuary.

OCTOBER 1

FAREWELL MALDIVES – PART 2

Biju Thomas

"For a day in Thy courts is better than a thousand. I had rather be a doorkeeper in the house of my God, than to dwell in the tents of wickedness."

Psalm 84:10, KJV

The turbulent events in the Maldives and the fact that I could not worship God in freedom and peace, or go to His Sanctuary on the Sabbath day, compelled me to bid farewell to that place. Additionally, my daughter's birthday was fast approaching, and every time I called her on the phone she would plead with me to be home for her birthday.

A few days before her birthday, as if providentially, we had our first vacation at the school where I worked. So, under the pretext of going home for vacation, I decided to pack my bags quietly and leave for home, never to return.

My roommate jokingly said I would reach Male (the capital of Maldives) very quickly if our boat were to be struck by a tsunami en route!

When my flight touched down at Trivandrum, Kerala, a huge wave of joy and relief swept over me. I breathed a prayer of deep gratitude to the Almighty for being with me throughout my difficult sojourn the previous two months, and for bringing me back home in safety, to be reunited with my family.

When I stepped into the Sanctuary of God the following Sabbath, I experienced an overwhelming sense of peace and tranquility. The words of the psalmist in our text are true. There is no place in this world where we may feel more blessed than in the Lord's Sanctuary.

May we all have this experience.

OCTOBER 2

EVEN IN STUDYING CHEMISTRY

Gloria Moses

"Every good gift and every perfect gift is from above, and cometh down from the Father of lights. . ."

James 1:17, KJV

The high school where I studied in Sri Lanka did not offer science courses. Hence, I could hardly understand science when I took the pre-university course in Trichy, India. I tried to memorize the words and write the exams without any basic understanding of the subject, and I barely managed to pass with a C grade.

In college, I opted to take Chemistry as my major subject. It was extremely challenging, and I passed the first and second years with great difficulty.

In the third year, I had a friend who also was struggling in the science classes. We decided to study together. We would write what we knew on a board and then correct each other. We gradually began to understand the concepts of covalent and ionic bonds, and after a while began getting the highest scores in the class. The teacher wondered if we had been cheating, so she would question us during the classes, but we answered correctly. I fell in love with science, and we both received A+ in all the subjects in the final university exam.

I applied to the Madras State Government Laboratory for the Medical Technology course. Discrimination strongly favored those from the upper castes in those days, and my chances appeared very slim. However, there was a Christian in the selection committee, who didn't believe in castes. Based on merit, I was selected.

God helped me understand chemistry and get into the Medical Technology course. He will help you in all your situations.

OCTOBER 3

TO THE LEAST OF THESE

Gladwin Mathews

"Whatever you did for one of the least of these brothers and sisters of mine, you did for me."

Matthew 25:40, NIV

In the early spring of 2023, I had the opportunity to go on a road trip covering the southeast region of the USA. I visited some important landmarks of the struggle for racial equality, including Dr. Martin Luther King Junior's bombed house and the Baptist Church on 16th Street, in which four little girls were killed and more than twenty injured.

While visiting the National Memorial for Peace and Justice in Montgomery, I watched the two-minute video in which eye witnesses described their experiences in their own words. I could not bear to watch it and left the room in tears.

Later, I visited Selma's historic Edmund Pettus Bridge, where the Selma-to-Montgomery March and the historic civil rights struggle in Selma are commemorated.

A tornado hit this area in January of 2023. I saw houses with their roofs blown off. I asked the guide how that small community was holding up. She, an eyewitness and a victim during the civil rights struggle, who had been jailed 13 times by the age of 9, said, "God has been good to us. We have been blessed." I was astounded!

I wanted to help but since I didn't have much to give at that moment, I asked her to contact Selma's Adventist church. I was glad to learn later that the South-Central Conference ACSDR Team partnered with the Selma SDA church and raised funds, especially for the Selma community.

Let us remember Matthew 25:40 and lend a helping hand whenever possible.

October 4

Bike Ride to Munnar – Part 1

Biju Thomas

"Then God saw everything He had made, and indeed it was very good."

Genesis 1:31, NKJV

About 80 miles from my hometown of Cochin (Kochi,) is the beautiful hill station of Munnar, in the Idukki district of Kerala. It is situated in the South-Western Ghats of India. The name Munnar is derived from its strategic location at the confluence of three rivers – Muthirapuzha, Nallathani, and Kundala. The region in and around Munnar varies in height from 4,760 to 8,842 feet above sea level and was once the summer capital of the British Raj in South India.

On December 26, 2004, I took a bike ride to Munnar with my brother-in-law. I was excited, as this was my first bike trip along the winding pathways up those hills. The vast expanse of tea plantations, the streams, the waterfalls, the pristine valleys and mountains, the exotic species of flowers and plants, and the aroma of cool spice-scented air, were exhilarating! It was a breathtaking ride!

Captivated by the beauty around us, we were reminded of the wonderful and mighty God who created such beauty. God's version of beautiful flowers, tasty chocolates, and inviting candlelight dinners, comes in the form of sunsets, moonlight on lakes, the symphony of the crickets, warm wind on our faces, lush gardens, and exotic landscapes!

We had a smooth and uneventful ride up the hills, but along the journey downhill, we were to experience some shocks. Yet, the Lord showed us beauty and was gracious to us. Thank God for His mercies.

Remember to thank God for the beauty of the earth He created for us.

OCTOBER 5

BIKE RIDE TO MUNNAR – PART 2

Biju Thomas

"O give thanks unto the LORD; for he is good: for his mercy endureth forever."

Psalm 136:1, KJV

After visiting Munnar and absorbing the incredible sights of that beautiful hill station, we decided to stop at a small restaurant for a meal on our way back. It was the 26th of December, 2004, and as soon as we entered the restaurant, we heard the shocking news on live television: a major earthquake had struck the west coast of Sumatra, Indonesia.

This had caused a massive tsunami. Waves up to 100 feet, traveling at over 500 miles per hour spread out from there to the surrounding coasts of the Indian Ocean, devastating whole communities, and killing an estimated 227,00 people in 14 countries. It was one of the deadliest natural disasters in recorded history.

Living conditions were utterly disrupted in the coastal regions of Tamil Nadu and Kerala. My hometown was also affected. We were shaken and speechless for a few minutes upon hearing this.

With a prayer on my lips, I quickly got out my phone and called my wife. She responded immediately and assured me that our family was safe and well. A deep sense of gratitude to God welled up in my heart and brought tears to my eyes. God had been merciful to me again, keeping my family safe through that potential tragedy!

God allowed me to enjoy some beautiful sights on my bike trip and provided assurance when I most needed it. While we pray for victims of disasters and lend them a helping hand, let us also thank Him for keeping us safe.

OCTOBER 6

COURAGE AND SUPPORT

Gloria Moses

"Be of good courage, and He shall strengthen your heart, all ye that hope in the Lord."

Psalm 31:24, KJV

My sister, Deborah, was studying in a medical college in India, when I completed high school in Sri Lanka and got ready to follow her to India to study there.

When I went to the Indian embassy in Colombo to apply for a visa, my mother encouraged me to go by myself for the interview. At first, I was afraid, but as the interview progressed, I gained confidence, and answered all their questions in a calm manner, and got my visa. That experience, which my mom encouraged me to go through, helped me to have courage in the future, to do things by myself without fear.

At 17, I took the flight to India alone. There, my sister met me at the airport and then guided me through all the college admission paperwork. I finally completed a major in Chemistry in Trichy. The then-president of the Tamil Section of the Seventh-day Adventist Church took me under his wings and became my local guardian. His family treated me like one of their own and supported me throughout my college days. They helped me navigate the new town, and even provided me a place to stay during short vacations. Looking back, I can see how I was helped all along at every step. I thank God for being constantly by my side, and providing me courage, support, and guidance, through my mom, my loving sister, a caring church family, and strangers.

Let us be assured that God will give us courage and support whenever needed.

OCTOBER 7

GOD IS ALWAYS FAIR

Anonymous

"But my God shall supply all your needs according to His riches in glory by Christ Jesus."

Philippians 4:19, KJV

When I completed high school (10th grade), I stayed at home and bided my time, helping my mom with the housework until I could decide the next step in my studies.

One day, a family going on a trip asked my mom to send me with them to keep company with their children. My mom agreed, and I excitedly packed my clothes for the trip, thinking I would have lots of fun with them.

This family, another family, and I traveled together in one van. When it came time for lunch, we stopped near a beach. There were home-cooked meals for everyone in separate packages, and each one picked a bag. When it was my turn, I was stopped and told to wait. The person went through all the packets, chose one, and gave it to me. I thought she did it to provide me with something special. But when I opened it, I found that mine had an obvious item that was missing. Was that on purpose? Was I being treated this way because I was much poorer than they?

I felt slighted and miserable, and did not enjoy the rest of the day!

When I got home, I told my mom about it. She assured me that God had blessed us with plenty, including more items than we needed. I realized that was true.

As a teenager, I had felt unfairly treated, but I thanked God that He supplies all our needs and is always fair in how He treats us.

OCTOBER 8

THE HEAVENS DECLARE

Biju Thomas

"He who made the Pleiades and Orion, who turns blackness into dawn and darkens day into night. . .the LORD is His name."

Amos 5:8, NIV

When my father served as Principal of the Seventh-day Adventist School at Kolar Gold Fields (KGF,) in Karnataka, we resided within the little school campus. I was pretty young then and learned some of the most beautiful Biblical lessons during those seven years of my childhood there.

Every night, after supper, my father would take us for a walk around the school campus and tell us many interesting stories. Sometimes, he would point to the stars in the night sky and tell us fascinating details about them. He had learned about them during his Master Guide classes at the Adventist School in Kottarakara, Kerala.

He outlined the constellations like the Little Bear, the Great Bear, and Orion, and pointed out the North Pole star, and how to identify it with the help of other stars. In this little village, far from city life, we had no avenues of entertainment, and my brother and I thoroughly enjoyed those walks after supper each night. We would look up in awe and wonder, and imagine the greatness of the God who had created our universe.

In our verse for today, Amos portrays God as the One with absolute control over the vast universe. He told the people of Israel that the LORD was the One who made the Pleiades and Orion; the One who regulated the seasons and the day-night cycles.

The night sky – the heavens – proclaimed this truth of God's majesty and glory. Let us bow down and worship Him!

OCTOBER 9

THANKFUL

Gloria Moses

"Oh give thanks to the LORD, for He is good, for His steadfast love endures forever."

Psalm 107:1, ESV

I studied at Trichy for my bachelor's degree in Chemistry. Due to financial constraints, I would travel by boat, instead of flying home to Sri Lanka for my vacations. It was a long and grueling journey, including riding several buses before and after the boat ride.

In the boat, all the passengers had to fill embarkation and disembarkation forms. After filling mine, there would usually be someone else who would need help with filling theirs. Soon, a line of people would want help filling out their forms. The four-hour boat ride would go by fast, as I helped each one. They were all thankful, and so was I, because the time had gone by swiftly, and I had a sense of fulfillment in helping others!

My mother would pack boiled eggs for the journey, and I didn't have to go to restaurants carrying my luggage, to eat in unsafe places. I thank God that He protected me during all my travels.

My classmates from India loved the nylon sarees from Sri Lanka, and my Sri Lankan friends loved the Indian sarees with bright borders and pallus. I would buy what they needed, and they would willingly pay for them. I made some profit in the process, and had money to buy my books and pay for other expenses. So, everyone was thankful. They got their sarees, and I got the money I needed.

God provided for me in all these various situations and gave us all a reason to be thankful! Let us always thank God.

OCTOBER 10

TIMELY HELP

Gloria Moses

"...God is our refuge and strength, a very present help in trouble...The Lord of hosts is with us; the God of Jacob is our refuge."

Psalm 46:1,7, KJV

After I completed high school in Sri Lanka, my older sister, Deborah, arranged for me to study in India. I left home to join college there. Hence, my younger sister, Rose and our mom lived alone. Rose attended high school in Negombo, about 25 miles away, but because our medium of instruction was not in English, she also attended special English classes closer to home.

Some days, my mom would travel to the city of Colombo to take care of business there. She would sell products from our handloom factory, eggs from our chicken farm, and also sign contracts with construction companies for bricks made in our brick factory. So, when my mom and sister were away from home, the house was left unattended and was an easy target for thieves looking for such opportunities.

One day, after mom had left the house, Rose also went for her English class. She had barely walked half the distance, when her slipper broke. She had to return home to get another pair. When she reached home, she saw a suspicious-looking stranger loitering around the house. As soon as he saw Rose, he ran away. Obviously, he had bad intentions and we would have suffered loss!

I thank God for His care and protection over us, which He showed us in many ways, even when it involved my sister's broken slippers!

Let us calmly trust Him, knowing that God may use seemingly unfortunate events to our advantage.

OCTOBER 11

BE NOT AFRAID

Anonymous

"Have not I commanded thee? Be strong and of a good courage; be not afraid; neither be thou dismayed: for the Lord thy God is with thee whithersoever thou goest."

Joshua 1:9, KJV

On April 2, 2018, I received a call from our Nephrologist. He had reviewed my husband's CT scan, which showed a tumor in his left kidney that looked cancerous. No definite word was given, and so, we spent the next few months going from hospital to hospital, undergoing tests and biopsies, and seeking second opinions.

Those were trying days, full of perplexities, worries and anxieties. It was stressful! Why would God want us to go through an ordeal like this? I would lie awake trying to bargain with God, and we prayed day and night for a miracle. After the initial shock wore off, my prayer turned from "Why God?" to "Please Lord, let it not be cancerous!" We prayed for a consultation with an expert in the field.

Soon we were in touch with the head of the surgical department at Johns Hopkins Hospital. He looked over the CT report and said, "I don't think it's cancer. However, since it is deep in the kidney, we will have to take the kidney out."

My husband underwent a radical nephrectomy at Johns Hopkins Hospital. A week later, the pathology report said that the tumor was benign – a hemangioma, an abnormal cluster of blood vessels – not cancerous!

God answered our prayers in many ways; one of which was to carry us through the period of worry and anxiety. He was always in control.

Let us not fear when God is with us.

OCTOBER 12

BLESSINGS THROUGH A FLOOD

Lillykutty Joseph

"And we know that all things work together for good to them that love God. . ."

Romans 8:28, KJV

My father was a teacher and a good farmer and owned several plots of paddy fields near our home. When I was in the 5th grade, he planted the seedlings late because he didn't get enough laborers to plant them on time. So, when the paddy in the neighboring fields began to mature, ours was just starting to grow. It seemed like a big failure. People made fun: "Look at Thomas Sir's fields this year! What will their harvest be like?"

The monsoon rains that year were unusually heavy, and the paddy fields were completely flooded, making the area look more like a lake.

When the rains stopped and the water receded, the neighbors harvested their paddy, but found to their dismay that it was more husk and less grain. The flooding water had stopped the growth of the kernels, leaving them small at harvest. Since our plants were still growing, we harvested the kernels later and the yield was up to threefold more than usual because the flood had deposited rich soil around them at that critical period of growth.

Rice was scarce that year, and people came from distant places to buy rice from us. My father sold his stock for a discounted price out of sheer thankfulness to God for the abundance He had given us.

My father had always returned a faithful tithe to God, and had been generous in his offerings. God had, in turn, clearly blessed us greatly.

If we are faithful to God, we will be amazed at His faithfulness toward us.

OCTOBER 13

PRECIOUS TO GOD

Lillykutty Joseph

"Precious in the sight of the Lord is the death of His saints."

Psalm 116:15, KJV

It was Friday afternoon, February 13, 1976. I was in the women's dorm at Spicer Memorial College, changing my bed sheets. As I lifted the pillow, I noticed a telegram under it. It said, "Mother serious, start immediately."

I ran to the business office, collected money for the train fare, and then called the Ottapalam SDA Hospital, in Kerala, where my mother was admitted. She was critical, and unconscious. I boarded the train that evening, hoping and wishing to see her alive.

I reached my hometown on Sunday at 2:00 am. My brother-in-law picked me up and updated me on my mom's condition. Before she had lost consciousness, she said that she was going to meet her Savior, Jesus, and that she wanted all her children to be there when He returned. She then named all eight of her children from the first to the last.

When I reached the hospital, I sobbed at the sight of her, unconscious and connected to so many tubes. I kissed her on the forehead and said I was there. She opened her eyes. I asked her for a kiss, and she kissed my face. She kissed my dad and my siblings, too. She stayed alive for one more day.

In His grace, God allowed me to talk to her and hug her, just as I had hoped. As we sang, "Rock of Ages. . .Nothing in my hands I bring, simply to thy cross I cling," she took her last breath.

God's children are precious to Him. Let's confidently trust Him.

OCTOBER 14

SIFTED AND PRESERVED

Gladwin Mathews

"For behold, I will command, and shake the house of Israel among all the nations as one shakes with a sieve, but no pebble shall fall to the earth."

Amos 9:9, ESV

I spent my early childhood years in a rural area of Punjab. During that period, Punjab entered the era of the "green revolution," which began in 1965, with the introduction of high-yield varieties of wheat and rice in the District of Ludhiana, through the Punjab Agricultural University.

The farmers still used the old methods in the rural areas where we lived. Modern methods of farming were still a distant dream. Harvesting was still done by hand, using sickles. Threshing was done manually, and winnowing was done with the sieve called "chhajj," or through the process of blowing away the husk. It was an interesting sight. It depended on a strong wind. The grain would be poured out from a height, and the wind would carry away the light husk letting the kernels of grain fall to the ground.

At home, I had seen my mom use the "chhajj" for sifting. The kernels of precious grain were separated from the unwanted bits of dirt and rock, and retained as valuable food for the family.

Regarding our relationship with God, the sifting comes by divine command and permission. The Lord will graciously and yet firmly separate what is precious from what is not, and the grain will be saved, every single kernel!

However small or insignificant we may think ourselves to be, we are the Lord's, and we may rejoice that we are preserved in Christ Jesus. Let this be the source of our confidence.

OCTOBER 15

UNLOAD YOUR BURDENS

Joel E. David

"Cast thy burden upon the LORD, and he shall sustain thee: He shall never suffer the righteous to be moved."

Psalm 55:22, KJV

One day, I tried to save some pictures on my computer, but it wouldn't let me do it. The pop-up message kept saying, "Storage is full." I was frustrated and had to find ways to add more space before continuing.

Computers are one of the most brilliant inventions known to humans. We can write and save documents, keep accounts in an orderly way and retrieve them anytime, correspond with others by email, listen to music, watch videos, and much more. All the information for these activities is stored in the hard drive, which has a specified and limited capacity. When that capacity is neared, we get notifications about it, and if we ignore the message, the computer stops saving any more data. The system will then function normally only if we delete data to create space.

We operate similarly. We store the burdens of life in our hearts, and over time, it cannot bear any more loads. The emotional baggage we carry expresses itself through our nervous, cardiovascular, and gastrointestinal systems, and even through the state of our skin!

We get angry and frustrated, short-tempered and loud, scatter-brained and unpleasant. We are unable to be kind and patient, and show love.

But God has provided a way to unload our emotional burdens. We can pray to Him and leave our heavy loads with Him. He will delete/unload all the unwanted data, lighten our minds, and help us resume normal function.

Let us cast our burdens upon the LORD.

OCTOBER 16

I STILL SAY BLESSED – PART 1

Kanta Pandit

"The Lord watches over the sojourners; he upholds the widow and the fatherless."

Psalm 146:9, ESV

My mom was 15 years old and studying at a boarding school, when my grandfather, who was a forest ranger, arranged for her to be married. My dad was then a technical engineer in the Indian army. They had four children in all, of whom I am the eldest.

When I was nine years old, and my youngest brother was just one year old, our dad who was stationed at the Ahmedabad army base fell ill. My mom and brothers were with him, while my sister, who was seven, and I, lived with our maternal grandparents in Ranchi. The officers took my dad to the military hospital in Pune, where he underwent four surgeries but eventually passed away.

We were Lutheran Christians, and a Christian family accompanied my mom from Ahmedabad to attend my dad's funeral in Pune. It was four days after the funeral that my grandparents, sister, and I received news of our father's death. We had not seen him for over two years, and although we did not fully comprehend what death meant at that time, it really hurt to think that we would never see our dad again.

The military offered my mom a job and said they would allow all four children to live with her. However, my dad's brother, a colonel in the army, took us home to live with him. We learned to live within our means – the small pension the military paid.

God was with us in our darkest times. May you always feel His presence.

October 17

I Still Say Blessed – Part 2

Kanta Pandit

"Lead me in your truth and teach me, For You are the God of my salvation. .

.Psalm 25:5, NKJV

After our dad passed away, we stayed with our uncle's family in a large house with 12 bedrooms. It was a joint family with many children. The kitchen was outside the main house, and each family made their own food there. Growing up, our mom taught us to live honest lives, without borrowing or stealing.

I attended the Lutheran Mission School, where the medium of instruction was Hindi. I also learned knitting, sewing, and embroidery work and earned some money. My mom was very generous and self-sacrificing. She would sometimes eat just one meal a day so she could feed people who came by begging for food.

When I completed high school, I wanted to attend college, but my mom could not afford it. My mom's sister, a teacher, gave me Rs. 200, so I registered for college. Apart from my studies, I learned shorthand and typing, and worked as a receptionist in a dance college. I received a scholarship for my second year in college. However, I used that money to help my family and continued to work and study. To save money on books, I would go to the library and copy all I needed by hand.

While in college in Ranchi, I was intrigued by a nearby SDA church. One of my seniors, a church member, invited me there. That was the start of my Adventist journey.

God leads us to His truth through various avenues. How blessed we are!

When God leads us, let us follow Him.

October 18

I Still Say Blessed – Part 3

Kanta Pandit

"The Lord is able to bless you abundantly, so that in all things at all times, having all that you need, you will abound in every good work."

II Corinthians 9:8, NIV

After my dad passed away, being the eldest sibling, I took on the responsibility of providing for my family by working part-time and studying full-time. During the summer vacation after my second year in college, I worked as a receptionist at a dance studio and made Rs. 150 per month – a very good amount! So I decided to stop attending college and work full-time.

The dance professor called me aside and said that if I gave up my education for the sake of my family, I would not be able to take care of myself later in my life. She paid for the next year of college and advised me to concentrate on my studies and not return to work.

That very same month, a forest officer came to our home and offered me a job at his office. I worked there as a clerk during the day and attended evening classes. It was a good-paying job, and I stayed there until I completed college.

My senior, who asked me to attend her church, invited me to her home too. The church and her home were very friendly. I learned truths that I hadn't heard before. I shared this with my mom, who told me to do what I thought best. Two years later, I joined the Adventist church through baptism.

God guided my life and also led me to His church. He will lead us. Let Him.

OCTOBER 19

I STILL SAY BLESSED – PART 4

Kanta Pandit

"Bless the LORD, O my soul, And forget not all His benefits."

Psalm 193:2, KJV

Having lost my father at the age of nine and taking responsibility for my family at a young age, I completed college by working and studying full-time. I came across the Adventist faith and joined the church during this time.

I met my future husband, Bijoy Pandit, at the SDA church in Ranchi. My friends and I coaxed him to join the evening classes, and he became our companion and guard on our way to and from college.

When Bijoy asked for my hand in marriage, my mom informed them that I was the family's primary financial support. The family depended on me. Bijoy and his family agreed that I could continue to support my family even after our marriage. We got married, and they kept their promise. I put my brother through technical school and my sister through nursing school and even helped with her marriage expenses.

We had two sons, Brian and Bennet. My in-laws treated me like their own daughter and cared for our children while I went to work. My day was extremely busy. It began at 4:00 am, and I would go to work at 9:30 am. My husband was an attorney at law and did well until criminals approached him to represent them. It became stressful, so he quit practicing law and started a business. We came to the USA in the mid-1980s.

Through the ups and downs of my life, Jesus has been my constant guide and protection. May you find Him to be yours as well.

OCTOBER 20

I STILL SAY BLESSED – PART 5

Kanta Pandit

"Bless the LORD, O my soul; And all that is within me, bless His holy name."

Psalm 103:1, NKJV

Having gone through financial struggles in childhood after losing my father at a very young age, by the grace of God, I completed my studies and financially supported my family. God led me to the Adventist church, where I met my husband. We then moved to the USA with our two young sons.

Starting life in the USA was difficult. But many friends from the church helped us find jobs and learn the intricacies of life here. I took some classes, and even though English was not my primary language, God helped me achieve A grades on all the tests. Life in the USA has been challenging. We faced many difficulties as a family. God called my husband to rest in 2004. Since then, we have been through various struggles, but God has been our rock.

In 2019, my friends and I started a daily online prayer meeting from 7:00 to 8:00 pm. We have been able to continue this without missing a day. Even when I was admitted to the hospital, or some of my friends were in the hospital, the prayer meetings continued.

Now, I am retired and spend my time serving the church as much as possible. I am thankful for my children, their families, the church family and my friends. Yes, life has been difficult many times, but I can still say that I am blessed by a God who continues to care for me.

May we always find ourselves blessed by our heavenly Father.

OCTOBER 21

HELP IN THE BLIZZARD

Soosan Varghese

"He calms the storm…Then they were glad…He guides them to their desired haven."

Psalm 107:29-30, NKJV

I was at work when an unexpected blizzard arrived early one afternoon in the winter of 2010 and covered the whole DC metro area with about two feet of snow. We had permission to leave early. Co-workers with all-wheel drive vehicles offered rides to others who resided near their neighborhoods.

I did not want to leave my car behind, as my husband was out of town, and without the car, my children and I would be stranded. I asked one of the volunteers who had offered a ride to my area, if I could follow her van, so I would not be alone on the road. She agreed, and we were on Route 29, headed north from Takoma Park. The snow-laden trees and landscape were breathtaking sights, but I would have enjoyed them more if I didn't have to drive in the snow!

Eventually, the van made a right, and I made the next right onto my road. There were no other vehicles in my vicinity on the road, which looked like a sea of snow. The windrift had accumulated so much snow on the road and it was so high that it would pile into the car if I opened the car door. I couldn't see the edges of the road, but had to keep to it for another two miles! There were no tracks to follow and I couldn't afford to make a mistake! I prayed for guidance and continued driving. I got home safely that day!

God is our constant help. May you experience His help daily.

OCTOBER 22

PROTECTION FROM DANGER

Soosan Varghese

"The angel of the Lord encamps around those who fear Him, and delivers them."

Psalm 34:7, NIV

Growing up in a village in my early childhood, I had many memorable encounters with nature and exotic creatures. One of those occurred on the verandah of our house. We used to gather for evening worship and do our homework, sitting around a desk there.

The wall was made of bricks and had a fluorescent tube for light. Small lizards would come around every evening and catch and eat the insects that flew around the light. We named the lizards after each of us kids and considered them our pets.

Watching them, we sometimes observed a weird event. A lizard would suddenly drop its tail and run away. The detached tail would fall to the floor and wiggle for a few minutes and then stop. It was always distressing to witness this. Wouldn't it be painful? But our parents assured us that it was merely a defensive mechanism to distract the predator whenever it feels threatened. The lizard can then escape to safety.

I later discovered that the lizard accomplishes this by contracting the muscles around the unique areas at the base of the tail called the fracture planes. Lizards can drop and regenerate their tails more than once.

Scientists have found that the mechanism that allows the tail to drop off quickly involves nanopores and micropillars. Researchers hope to use a similar technology to develop products useful for humans.

We don't have to detach body parts for our safety. We have a much more effective strategy – calling for God's angels who constantly encamp around us.

OCTOBER 23

THROUGH IT ALL – PART 1

Girly Andrews

"I know the Lord is always with me. I will not be shaken."

Psalm 16:8, NLT

I was in the sixth grade, and my brother was in the seventh, at the Kottarakkara SDA boarding school. My dad, Pastor Gilbert, worked at Kannoor, 280 miles away.

One evening, while on his way to the market, my dad saw a man with two very young girls begging for food on the roadside. They looked pathetic and dirty, with tattered clothes and matted hair. He felt compassion for them and asked the man if he could take the children home and send them to school. He immediately fell at my dad's feet, exclaiming, "You are sent by God!"

My dad took the children home, cleaned them up, and brought them to our boarding school. The girls were enrolled in lower and upper Kindergarten and enjoyed studying there. When it came time for vacation, we planned to take them to our home in Kannoor. It would take a taxi ride, a bus ride, and three train rides to get home. The trip would take several hours, so the cafeteria staff packed dinner for us.

We reached Ernakulam at 4:00 am. The next train would leave at 8:00 am. One of the teachers traveling with us, who lived in Ernakulam, invited us to her home for breakfast. Since we had a four-hour break, we put our luggage in the holding room at the station, and went for breakfast.

Things were going well, and we thanked God for that. When the way is pleasant and enjoyable, let us thank God. He is always with us.

OCTOBER 24

THROUGH IT ALL – PART 2

Girly Andrews

"My presence will go with you. . ."

Exodus 33:14, NKJV

The four-hour break seemed sufficient for breakfast at the teacher's home, but when we returned to the station, the train was already at the platform, ready to leave. My brother told us to board the train while he would fetch the luggage from the storage room and join us. However, the train started before he could get on. I saw him running towards the train, but it was too late. He immediately went out and hired a taxi to get to the next station. However, he was late again. He tried it two more times and finally got on board. When we reached our station, it was night, and the last bus bound for our hometown, two hours away, had already left.

We had no food or money. We helplessly sat at a storefront, with only stray dogs for company! Just then, a police jeep stopped by, and seeing our condition, they took us into the jeep and drove us home. When we arrived home, we saw that the whole congregation from our dad's church had gathered together for fasting and prayer that night and were now praying for our safe return. God answered their prayers, and we were all kept safe.

The girls' father kept in touch with us and soon was happy to join the church. The girls did well in school and completed their higher studies.

Looking back, we can clearly see that God was close to us through good times and challenging times, protecting and guiding us.

We serve an awesome God who is always with us.

(Concluded)

OCTOBER 25

HIT BY LIVE WIRES

Soosan Varghese

"When you pass through the waters, I will be with you…when you walk through the fire, you will not be burned…"

Isaiah 43:2, NIV

In 2003, I was driving alone from Baltimore to Silver Spring when a severe thunderstorm broke out less than 2 miles from my home. Torrents of water poured down from the sky, flooding the road within a few minutes.

Trees swayed in the wind like a category three hurricane. Visibility was barely 15 feet, and the cars crawled along with emergency flashers on. I turned on my windshield wipers to the highest speed, and it vigorously did its job. Suddenly, the wooden electric post on the right side of the road snapped and landed barely a foot away from the bumper of my car. The wires scraped against the car's passenger side, broke the side-view mirror, and left it dangling back and forth. I realized that I was in real danger of being electrocuted. I couldn't move forward or reverse because there were cars behind me. An older gentleman in the car behind me rolled his window down and tried to say something to me. But I couldn't hear him, so I rolled my window down. He yelled above the gust of the wind, "The wires are live. Stay in your car and back away!" and reversed his car.

With an SOS prayer on my lips, I slowly reversed my car. The wires were not entangled, and I was able to pull back safely from the live wires. The danger was real, and so was the protection from God.

May God protect each of us from all dangers.

OCTOBER 26

GOD'S WAY OF MAKING TIME

Soosan Varghese

"For my thoughts are not your thoughts, neither are your ways my ways."

Isaiah 55:8, NIV

My husband called me on his way to the airport to pick up our future son-in-law, who was visiting for the weekend. He said he expected to be home in about an hour as the flight was on schedule.

I was home getting things ready. I had my hands full, as I had to work that day, and then get my 92-year-old dad ready too. I had to help my dad shower, then help him get dressed, then get ready myself. One hour was just not enough time! While putting the final touches to the dishes and setting the table, I prayed and asked God to please help me have everything ready before they arrived. I got my dad ready and brought him to the family room using the stair lift.

The next phone call came – they were on their way and would be home in about 15 minutes. But I still had things to organize. It seemed impossible. I sent up another quick prayer.

Soon, it was time for them to be home; however, they hadn't arrived yet. So, I called my husband, who laughed and said they had taken a scenic route!

He had taken the wrong exit and had to drive an extra 15 minutes. I marveled at this because he has an excellent sense of direction, and the route was very familiar.

Later, I told them about my crunch time and my prayer. They said, "God answered your prayer."

God does find unusual ways to answer our prayers. I am amazed!

OCTOBER 27

THE VALUE OF A TEAR-DROP – PART 1

Biju Thomas

"Hear my prayer, O Lord! Listen to my cries for help! Don't ignore my tears. For I am your guest traveler passing through, as my ancestors were before me."

Psalm 39:12 NLT

My mother's sister migrated from India to the USA in the late 1980s. Ever since that time we were told that we would one day walk the streets of America. As children we cherished this dream in our hearts.

The papers arrived nearly forty years later! But by that time, the circumstances of my life were totally different. I was married and had a family of my own. Then, to our disappointment and dismay, we found that our son, now over 21 years of age, wouldn't be allowed to enter the USA with us. He would have to get his own visa, and there appeared no assurance of that anytime soon.

It was a bitter-sweet experience for us. Do we go ahead and make use of this once-in-a-lifetime opportunity, or do we stay back and lose it altogether?! It was one of the most difficult decisions we had ever faced.

As we struggled through this question, our son told us to go ahead and move to the United States. He would stay back and take things as they came, while we all would keep praying for the visa.

All along, we had highly valued our bond as a family, and believed in our hearts that God could open the way. From that day onwards, as a family, we began to pray earnestly with tears.

There's a song: "God weeps along with man. . ."

Let us never forget that!

OCTOBER 28

THE VALUE OF A TEAR-DROP – PART 2

Biju Thomas

"You keep track of all my sorrows. You have collected all my tears in your bottle. You have recorded each one in your book."

Psalm 56:8, NLT

We had been living together for 26 years, and it was heart-rending to part ways with our son. We tearfully bid farewell at Bangalore's International Airport. When would we see him again? It had taken us decades to get our visas. Would we have to wait that long? The pain was almost unbearable. We wept and prayed earnestly that we would soon be together again.

God heard those tear-filled prayers. After a few months of anxious waiting, our son obtained a visitor's visa valid for ten years! We could hardly believe it! We knew how difficult it was to get visas to the USA. It seemed like a miracle!

When he passed through the immigration checkpoints and came out to us at the Dulles airport, we were utterly joyful! It was a wonderful reunion after months of painful separation and uncertainty.

Sometimes, we are tempted to think that God is too great and too busy, with more important things than the relatively minor details that concern us. But nothing that concerns us is too small for Him to notice! He values each tear-drop that falls. Indeed, He has collected every tear that has wet our lashes and placed them in His bottle. He has recorded every silent groan of our hearts.

The same song says, "Tears are a language God understands." Yes, He does! We experienced that as a family.

How wonderful to know that our God greatly loves each of us.

OCTOBER 29

GOD IS ON TIME

Anonymous

"For I the LORD your God, will hold your right hand, saying to you, "Fear not, I will help you."

Isaiah 41:13, NKJV

My parents were retired and living alone, while we children were living abroad in different countries. We knew they could care for themselves, and we regularly kept in touch with them.

One day, I felt impressed to call them at a very unusual time. I couldn't explain why, because I had just talked to them the day before. It would be 6:00 in the morning for them, and they probably wouldn't even be awake. But since the feeling was so strong, I called.

The phone rang an entire round, but no one answered. That was strange because my mom would always answer, no matter what time we called. I called a second time. Still no answer. I decided to wait 15 minutes and give them time to wake up. When I called the third time, my dad answered the phone and told me what had happened.

When I called the first time, they both were asleep. My dad thought my mom would answer the phone, but when she didn't at my second call, he got up and found mom barely able to respond, because she had gone into a severe hypoglycemic state. Dad immediately called the neighbors to help sit her up and give her glucose drinks. When I called the third time, she was recuperating well.

I thank God that He nudged me to call at that early hour and prevent a dangerous medical emergency and worse!

God steps in on time for us! Let us trust Him!

October 30

God's Provisions

Gloria Moses

"In those days, Hezekiah was sick and near death. And Isaiah the prophet, the son of Amoz, went to him. . .Then Isaiah said, "Take a lump of figs." So they took and laid it on the boil, and he recovered."

II Kings 20:1-7, NKJV

The land where I lived with my mom in Sri Lanka had plenty of wild plants and trees. Some of these plants were poisonous, and so were many insects, like centipedes, scorpions, bees, and spiders.

One day, I was stung on my arm by a bee, and it began to hurt, swell, and itch. My mom immediately brought out a piece of peeled onion and rubbed it in a circle over the site where I was stung. The itching and swelling immediately became less, and after a few more rubs with the onion, all the symptoms had completely vanished.

Years later, when my son was in high school, I told him about this incident. He thought it would be a good project for a science fair, and began to work on it. The Agricultural Department in Beltsville, Maryland, sponsored him to conduct research in their facility, and provided the bee venom and all the necessary equipment for the science fair project. My son discovered that onion fluid contains a very potent antihistamine, an anti-allergy substance, that neutralizes bee venom. He won first prize at the Prince George's County Science Fair and was awarded a full scholarship for a four-year degree at the University of Maryland.

God created fruits and vegetables to be used not only as food but also as medicines. Thank God for His provisions and protection against poisons.

October 31

A Better Decision

Nelson Khajekar

"Daniel purposed in his heart that he would not defile himself with the portion of the king's delicacies, nor with the wine which he drank; therefore he requested of the chief of the eunuchs that he might not defile himself."

Daniel 1:8, NKJV

The story of the three Hebrew youth has intrigued me ever since I was a child. Little did I know that I would apply that same lesson to my life.

Most of us, about 60, begin to think of retiring from the hectic schedules of regular life and take on a more laid back and relaxed attitude. Academic challenges don't invite us, much less studying for a new career and working at the same time. But that is what I ended up doing myself – working and attending nursing school. The demands between work, theory classes, clinical hours, homework, and family were grueling, and I averaged 3 to 4 hours of sleep per night. Besides, my grades were not great.

The NCLEX (the licensing exam for nurses) was just a month away, when a morning devotional reading caught my attention. It was about Daniel in the very first chapter of the book. Using dietary changes, God significantly changed Daniel's physical and mental abilities. Surely, He could do something similar for me. Prayerfully, like Daniel, I decided to make a dietary change – I gave up non-vegetarian food.

Today, I can testify that the God who helped the Hebrew youth, changed my life for the better. At age 60, I felt physically stronger and mentally sharper, and passed the NCLEX at the first attempt. Praise God!

We can take God at His word!

November 1

God Prepares Us – Part 1

Gloria Moses

"And whatever you do whether in word or deed, do it all in the name of the Lord Jesus, giving thanks to God the Father through Him."

Colossians 3:17, NIV

After graduating from my medical technology course, I planned to look for a job in India. But my mom needed help, so she called me back to Sri Lanka to manage her Rojah weaving and brick factories. Naturally, I wondered if going to India and getting a degree was all a big waste! But I loved my mom and happily agreed to help her.

I had never been to the brick factory and was amazed at how beautiful the surroundings were. We had passion fruit, bananas, pineapples, guavas, breadfruit, jackfruit, a variety of abundant vegetables, and a large, clear river flowing by. It felt like Eden!

There, I learned how cloth materials and bricks were made, how to manage people with patience and kindness, how to monitor supply and demand for our products, how to pay salaries, how to keep accounts uptodate, and how to prepare and file income tax reports.

My mom was very compassionate with her workers. When a young female employee lost her eyesight, she immediately took her to an ophthalmologist in the city, who treated her and restored her sight. She encouraged socializing and helped two young female workers find their life partners from among the male employees.

Little did I know that God was preparing me for a future job by giving me this experience with my mom.

Whatever you are going through, trust that God knows the future and is preparing you well!

NOVEMBER 2

GOD PREPARES US – PART 2

Gloria Moses

"Rest in the Lord, and wait patiently for Him; Do not fret. . .because of the man who brings wicked schemes to pass."

Psalm 37:7, NKJV

While working in Sri Lanka, managing my mom's businesses, a local riot broke out, and it was unsafe for me to stay. My mom immediately sent me to India.

I started looking for a job in Chennai, India. Most of my classmates either opened their own labs or had gone abroad. I accepted a job at the K.J. Hospital. The pathologist who worked there was the one instrumental in selecting me for the medical technology course. She made me responsible for the whole lab, including training the medical technology students and residents for their clinical experience. That was a huge responsibility, but I fit right in, using the knowledge and skills I had learned from managing my mom's businesses.

The hospital's owner had trained in a hospital in Pennsylvania, USA, and had set up a very modern lab with uptodate equipment. The patients who came there were famous film stars and high government officials, and I had the chance to talk to these Indian VIPs face-to-face.

I worked there for three years. The pathologist was my mentor and taught me many scientific details used in practical ways in the lab.

The rioters had meant harm, but God had worked things out in advance and guided me, from the time in my mom's business to the work at the K.J. Hospital, and beyond!

God graciously prepares us for our futures. Let us always trust His plans and do our best wherever He places us.

(Concluded)

November 3

Comfort in Sorrow

Soosan Varghese

"Therefore, comfort each other and edify one another, just as you are doing."

I Thessalonians 5:11, NKJV

My parents were getting older and needed help with their daily activities, so we brought them to the USA and had them stay with us. While they were here with us, my dad's younger sister suddenly fell ill and passed away in India. She was his only living sibling, and we were devastated. My dad wanted to attend the funeral very badly; however, we were concerned about his health – whether he would be able to withstand such a long journey at his age. Hence, he did not go.

We held prayer meetings at home, and friends and family visited and shared their condolences. It brought some peace to his sorrowing heart. Being the patriarch of the family and not accustomed to expressing sorrow publicly, we did not see him cry. However, we knew he was hurting inside.

That weekend during the Sabbath School program, a young child walked over to my dad and gave him a bookmark with a picture of serene scenery and a comforting Scripture verse. My dad cherished it very much because it reassured him that God was with him during that painful phase of his life. A few weeks later, during the Sabbath School lesson study at church, he narrated this incident and the peace and strength that little bookmark from the young child brought him.

The little gesture of sharing a bookmark may seem small and inconsequential, but it can lift the spirits of one passing through a dark valley.

Let us continue to show love and care to one another.

NOVEMBER 4

ANGEL IN DISGUISE

Soosan Varghese

"Are they not all ministering spirits sent forth to minister for those who will inherit salvation."

Hebrews 1:14, NKJV

Our elementary school had classes from one to four. So, we felt like "seniors" as we were in the 4th grade. Eight of us, an all-girls club, decided to go on a post-lunch ramble, visiting each other's homes, one house per day.

We brought our lunch to school, ate it quickly, and then went on our expeditions. Most of our mothers were stay-at-home moms, so they entertained us with snacks when we visited.

One day, after one of our visits, we took a shortcut via the side of a paddy field. My foot slipped, and one of my sandals fell into the clear streamlet flowing by. We could see it caught at the bottom between rocks, but none of us could reach it. We stood there distressed as it was getting late. On the other side was land at a high level that had plenty of trees. If only we could reach over and pick a dry branch to help pull up my sandal! But we were too small and just couldn't reach over!

Then, out of nowhere, a very tall young man walked toward us. He saw our situation and, tall as he was, reached over, picked up a dry branch, hooked my sandal with it, and pulled it out. We thanked him and ran off to school.

But I wondered about it because I had never seen anyone that tall in our area. Could it be that God sent an angel to help us? He will send us help, even angels in disguise!

NOVEMBER 5

A FAMINE – PART 1

Anonymous

"The days are coming," declares the LORD, "when I will send a famine through the land. . .not of food. . .or water. . .but of hearing the words of the LORD."

Amos 8:11, NIV

Recently, the Indian news channels reported that export of certain types of rice from India would be banned. This raised fears of a scarcity of rice among the Indian population in the USA. So they rushed to the stores to stock up on rice.

Rice is a staple food in India, especially in the South. We include rice in all our meals, and it is considered an essential and precious food item. I remember stories from my grandparents about how hard they worked for every meal. Hence, we were taught not to waste precious food.

My mother was born into a non-Christian family. My grandfather was staunch in his beliefs, so it was a strict ritual to pay homage to idols and place the "bindi" on the forehead before going to school.

They had been introduced to Christianity by their uncle's family, and there was a Christian church within walking distance. My mother became interested and longed to attend the Sabbath School there, but she knew her father would object to it. So, she begged her mother to help her attend church without letting her father know.

She dared not keep a Bible. So, whenever she heard the words or had the opportunity to read it herself, she memorized portions of it because those words were precious to her.

When things are in abundance, we take them for granted. But let us truly value the words of God and memorize them!

NOVEMBER 6

A FAMINE – PART 2

Anonymous

"And they shall wander from sea to sea. . .they shall run to and fro to seek the word of the LORD, and shall not find it."

Amos 8:12, KJV

My mother was very keen to attend the Christian church near our home. My grandmother supported her and helped her attend church weekly without her father's knowledge. Soon, the whole family got interested and almost everyone accepted Jesus and became Christians.

I moved to Chennai for my college education and became acquainted with a pleasant girl and we became friends. Everyone thought we had become friends because we both had the same name, but the real reason was that she was keen to learn from the Bible. Like my mother, she was from a non-Christian family who were staunch in their beliefs and rituals. She became deeply interested.

I carried a Bible in my bag, and my friend would read from it whenever she could. As soon as the bell rang for lunch, we would rush out, eat our food, and quickly return to the classroom. I would then stand guard at the door while she would kneel on the floor, lift her hands in silent prayer, and then read and memorize portions of the Bible. She was not allowed to own a Bible or pray at home, and these times were very precious to her!

Have we considered our blessings and thanked God for them?! We are free to own and read the Bible. We can pray in our homes, churches, and other places, even in public!

Let us take advantage of these blessings freely available to us by God's mercy and grace.

NOVEMBER 7

OUR STRONGHOLD

Gloria Moses

"The Lord of hosts is with us; the God of Jacob is our stronghold."

Psalm 46:7, NASB

Someone forged my mother's signature and withdrew all her savings from her bank account in Divlapitiya, Sri Lanka. So she opened an account in Colombo, where the security was greater.

When she moved her Roja weaving factory, it was to Godigamuwa, a remote and lonely area, with no neighbors nearby. She hired some female workers, and for their security, she constructed a dorm for them.

The land had good clay to make bricks, and some men worked on that part of the business. Soon, the businesses prospered, and cloth from the weaving factory and bricks from our kiln were regularly transported to the stores and companies in Colombo. Once again, the thought of security crossed her mind, and she hired a security guard and gave him a place to stay on the campus.

One night, some masked robbers came and tied up the security guard, and proceeded toward my mom's place. In the meantime, the security guard was able to free himself, run over to the next property, enlist the help of a few others, who armed themselves and came running back. Seeing so many of them, the robbers ran away and never returned.

I am sure God helped the security guard free himself and have the presence of mind to get more people. The robbers went away empty-handed, and my mom and the female employees who were in the dorm, were kept safe from those wicked men.

Let us always remember that "The Lord of hosts is with us; the God of Jacob is our stronghold!"

November 8

God Honors Those Who Honor Him – Part 1

Biju Thomas

"But now the Lord says: 'Far be it from me; for those who honor Me I will honor, and those who despise Me shall be lightly esteemed.'"

I Samuel 2:30, NKJV

My beloved mother-in-law, currently 93, is a God-fearing gentlewoman who worked tirelessly to bring up her children after her husband passed away quite early in her life. She had to cater to nine children, including six girls.

Despite doing her utmost, she often found it difficult to make ends meet. So, how did she manage month after month for all those years? She once told me her secret. Every month, as soon as she received her salary, which appeared insufficient to meet the requirements of her family, she would place the money on the table, kneel and place herself at the feet of Jesus. She would plead, with tears, for God to help her utilize every bit wisely and thus meet her family's needs.

It is amazing to consider how she, as a single mom, managed to educate all her children and see them well-settled with good marriage partners! She prayed for each one, and treated her children and their spouses with respect and dignity. Her gracious words were: "I have nothing material to give you, but I will pray for you with tears, so that God will provide all your needs from His bounty!"

This prayerful life and her complete surrender at the feet of Jesus was a wonderful testimony to say that God provides for those who honor Him through a fully surrendered life.

Let us honor God with all we have, and He will honor us.

November 9

God Honors Those Who Honor Him – Part 2

Biju Thomas

"May the LORD bless you from Zion. . .may you live to see your children's children. . ."

Psalm 128:5,6, NIV

My mother-in-law set us a great example of faithfulness to God, surrender to His guidance and leading, and love for her children and family. Every time we visited her, she made it a point to tell us inspiring stories of God's love and His marvelous dealings, with which He had led her throughout her life. Her happiest moments were when she had all her children sitting around her at the meal table enjoying a meal, or having family prayers together in the evenings.

She was especially grateful and immensely proud that God had graciously granted her the privilege of seeing the third generation after her – children, grandchildren, and great-grandchildren!

She frequently pointed to the fact that all her faculties were clear and intact at her age, and attributed all these unique blessings to the mercy and goodness of God. God had shielded her from the many ailments that could have afflicted her and protected her throughout her life. Her beautiful and long life is a powerful witness to how wonderfully God deals with those who trust their all to Him.

Our verse for today points out the source of all our blessings – the Lord from Zion! Seeing grandchildren and great-grandchildren is a very special blessing indeed, and it is promised to those who humbly rely on God and choose to surrender their lives to Him and walk in His ways.

As we witness such a bright and beautiful testimony, may we choose to honor God in all our ways.

November 10

Only A Prayer Away

Vidhya Melvin

"Call upon me in the day of trouble, I will deliver you, and you shall glorify me."

Psalm 50:10, NKJV

When I was working in Maharashtra, India, some days, my work shift would start early in the morning instead of at noon. One morning, I was on a bus, rushing to get to work on time. The bus fare was five rupees, and I didn't have the exact change. That made the bus conductor irate and upset. He shouted at me to get off the bus immediately. The entire tirade was in the Marathi language, which I could understand, but could not speak well. I felt insulted and utterly humiliated. On top of that, I had no other way to get to work, because it was during peak hours, and no other mode of transportation would get me to work on time! For a moment, I stood there, not knowing what to say. So, I sent up a silent prayer for help.

A woman nearby, a complete stranger to me, quickly approached me and handed me the five rupees for the ticket. I gratefully accepted it and thanked her with the few Marathi words I knew. Everything was settled, and I got to work on time.

It's been about ten years now, and I don't remember her face anymore. To some, this may appear as a minor incident, but I was in distress, in an unfamiliar situation, and I believe that God appointed a human to help me in my despair.

May we be ready today to be that God-appointed helper to those in need, as an answer to their prayers for help.

November 11

Discerning God's Voice

Anish Joseph

"The LORD makes firm the steps of the one who delights in Him."

Psalm 37:23, NIV

I was content with my career, and after the birth of my second daughter, in 2015, my life appeared settled in Pune, India. So, when my sister-in-law made a passing remark that my destiny lay in America, I dismissed it as a joke. However, over the ensuing months, two friends unexpectedly mentioned my future in the United States. It did pique my interest, but they seemed only coincidences.

When I was not chosen as a sponsored candidate for a PhD program in the Philippines, my wife suggested that God had better plans, and amazingly, mentioned America – again!

During a summer intensive at Andrews University, Michigan, USA, I met a retired professor, who treated me like a son, and became a spiritual mentor to me. He mentioned that scholarships for PhD studies were available in American seminaries. Little did I realize that this encounter, among others, was God's way of reaching out to me.

The story of Samuel's calling made me realize how easy it is to miss God's voice amidst the flurry of our own perceptions. Like Samuel, who did not recognize God's call initially, I had overlooked the various ways God was speaking. However, the pieces fell into place when I brought all the encounters together in prayer. God then opened the door to a scholarship for a PhD. in Intercultural Studies at Fuller Theological Seminary, Pasadena, California.

It was a reminder that God's voice is not always thunderous, but more often soft and gentle, guiding us through the lives and words of others around us.

NOVEMBER 12

RELIANCE ON GOD

Anonymous

"When my spirit was overwhelmed within me, then thou knewest my path."

Psalm 142:3, KJV

I had submitted a written project as part of my certification process at work, for the third time. And now, I was asked to re-submit it because of specific deficiencies and data errors. Then, I fell ill and had to be admitted for treatment. After I had recovered, I started working on the project again, but felt very weak and tired. I couldn't focus on it and had to take frequent breaks, because I was so exhausted. I knew I needed help, and so I prayed that God would carry me through.

I submitted it, expecting the response to be even worse, because I hadn't been in good health when I had done it this time. Three days later, my boss called me to her office. I expected the feedback to be very embarrassing, but to my surprise, she said that I had done such an excellent job that her superiors were very impressed and wanted me to present it at the headquarters!

I was blown away! As I walked away, something dawned on me. Each time I had earlier submitted it, I had relied on my abilities and wisdom. It was only at the fourth time that I had felt helpless and weak, and had leaned on God to take me through. The difference in how I had approached it was clear, and so was the difference in the results!

It is tempting to be self-reliant and do things independently, but let us acknowledge our weaknesses and depend on His grace and strength. We can safely trust Him!

NOVEMBER 13

COMPANY OF FOOLS – PART 1

Bimal Nowrangi

"The mind of a person who has understanding searches for knowledge, but the mouth of fools feed on stupidity."

Proverbs 15:14, GW

Like most normal growing teenagers, I also had a few close friends with whom I hung around. We had fun and looked out for each other. But I have to admit that all we did then as teenagers could not be considered prudent or wise. While each had a unique personality, I was often the more gullible one who could be persuaded to do things that were foolhardy.

Once, we went to a school camp and pitched our tents beside a huge water reservoir. During our spare time, we watched the dam's spillway with other visitors. We stood on a bridge overlooking the stream and watched the foaming and frothing, gushing torrents below us. We were enjoying this breathtaking sight when one of my friends suggested that someone jump from the bridge right into that rushing stream. It sounded like a real thrilling challenge to me. So, without thinking much, I jumped in and was swept along by the tons of cascading cold water that went through a metal tunnel and on downstream!

Only later did I realize how foolish it was to jump into rushing water that I knew nothing about! I came out with only a few minor bruises, but it could have been a lot worse! I thanked God later for letting me survive the ordeal.

But I had learned my lesson that, "Whoever walks with wise people will be wise, but whoever associates with fools will suffer." Proverbs 13:20 GW. Let us choose with wisdom.

November 14

Company of Fools – Part 2

Bimal Nowrangi

"Although they claimed to be wise, they became fools"

Romans 1:22, NIV

In my youth, I engaged in many activities with my siblings and friends, and although we thought of ourselves as great planners, some of our activities were not planned or executed wisely.

We spent many of our summer vacations with our grandparents in the wild country areas of Jharkhand, India. Our parents would send us out there into nature rather than into the cities. We spent our days scouting around, climbing trees, catching fish in the streams, and exploring mountain caves. While roaming the jungle, we had several close encounters with jackals, bears, deer, and even leopards.

One day, some of us explored the hillside caves where leopards supposedly lived. We had nearly reached the top of the hill, when our guide suddenly told us to stop moving, and motioned toward a huge rock. Sitting under it was a leopard staring directly at us! But we could see only parts of the body and its twitching ears.

We decided to turn back immediately but were somewhat disappointed because we had not seen the whole body of the leopard. So, on our hurried descent, one of us picked up a stone and flung it hard towards the leopard to bring it out!

Thinking back later - what if it had come charging out at us! I am glad that the leopard ignored the stone and stayed right there. God had kept us safe despite our foolishness.

It is better to be prudent and "Stay away from a fool, because you will not receive knowledge from his lips." Proverbs 14:7 GW

November 15

Miracle Chevy Baby

Nilima Nowrangi

"You are the God who does miracles. You show the nations that you are very powerful."

Psalm 77:14, EASY

A few decades ago, when my husband was the Dean of Men at Spicer Memorial College (Spicer Adventist University,) we lived in an apartment that was attached to one of the two dormitories. We were expecting our third child very soon – any day, any time!

One morning, when my husband returned home after completing the Dean's regular duties, I began to feel the signs of the baby's imminent arrival. I immediately asked my husband to rush me to the designated city hospital.

We made arrangements to care for our two small children, and called a faculty member to help us. He arrived in minutes and loaded the two of us into the back seat of his car and sped off toward the hospital about six miles away. But our precious baby was not going to wait until we reached the hospital. She came enroute, in the back seat of the vintage Chevy car!

The situation appeared grave, and the driver pulled into the nearest hospital on the side of the road, but was curtly told that such complicated cases were not accepted there. We (now three of us in the back seat!!) had no option but to drive on. We reached the hospital where our miracle "Chevy baby" was gently handed over to the medical staff for evaluation and care. She grew to be a beautiful daughter!

It is in dire situations that we recognize God. We rejoice and thank God for His constant watchcare.

Our God is caring and performs miracles even today.

November 16

God's Providence

Gloria Moses

"For I know the plans that I have for you," says the Lord, "plans for your welfare, and not for calamity, to give you hope and a future."

Jeremiah 29:11, NHEB

My sister, Deborah, finished high school in Sri Lanka, in the late 1950s, and then tried different jobs, including teaching and being an office secretary. She was not satisfied with either and decided to become a medical doctor. She went to India and gained admission into the Chennai Medical College.

She felt very homesick during one of her college breaks, and planned to visit home. The airfare was quite expensive, so she decided to travel by train to Rameswaram, the southern tip of India, from where she would take a boat to Talaimannar, in Sri Lanka. The final leg was a bus ride to our hometown.

The train journey required a change of trains at Madurai, where there was a long layover. She was tired, and when she found a comfortable spot in the women's waiting room, she fell fast asleep, and missed the train to Rameswaram. It seemed like a bad mistake!

However, the next morning, the newspapers reported that a railway bridge had collapsed and the train that she had missed, had plunged into the water leaving no survivors.

We received word three weeks later from my sister that she was safe in Chennai. We thanked God for His providence that kept my sister from danger and death.

His plan for our lives is far better than we think, and His hand is always over us. Let us trust the plans that He makes for us. They are always the safest!

NOVEMBER 17

FATHER'S LOVE

Gladwin Mathews

"As a father shows compassion to his children, so the Lord shows compassion to those who fear him."

Psalm 103:13, ESV

During my final semester of college, I would stay awake late at night to study and finish my project assignments. It had become my daily routine and I thought all was going well until a few weeks into that routine. I began to have abdominal discomfort and pain which would start around 2 am every night. I became alarmed and went to the hospital for a checkup. The doctors diagnosed an ulcer in the duodenum, and advised surgery.

I didn't want surgery. It would upset my schedule of preparations for the Comprehensive exams, which would decide whether I would graduate that semester. So I kept right on with my schedule despite the symptoms, and by God's grace, did well in the exams.

When I got home, I told my dad about the diagnosis of the ulcer and the doctors' advice for surgery. It affected him greatly. That was the first time I had seen him look so concerned. He immediately began to think of alternate treatments for me that wouldn't require surgery. His entire focus was on finding the best way forward for me. The next morning we consulted a doctor whom he had known for quite some time, and in a few weeks, I was well again.

This reminded me of the care and concern that our heavenly Father has over each of His children. He always looks out for the best remedy for those who come to Him in faith.

How reassuring it is to have such a loving heavenly Father!

November 18

God's Healing Touch

Biju Thomas

But Jesus looked at them and said, "'With men this is impossible, but with God all things are possible."

Matthew 19:26, KJV

One of my colleagues who worked at the Amazon office in Bangalore, was involved in a horrific car accident. He was returning home from work on the high-speed airport road, when an SUV traveling at about 100 miles an hour, hit his small car head-on. It was thrown violently 15 feet into the air, then came crashing down, and rolled over multiple times, before coming to a stop. The rescue workers had to break open the doors to pull out the passengers, and he was rushed to the hospital in a critical condition.

When we visited him, he was groaning and writhing in pain. He had been cleaned and bandaged multiple times, but was still soaked in blood. He had sustained multiple fractures all over his limbs, chest and backbone, and was semi-comatose and restless. He could barely mumble out our names, and the doctors could not guarantee his survival.

We decided that the best we could do was to pray for him and leave the outcome with God. I was chosen to lead in the prayer. Amid that secular environment, I pleaded with God to intervene in that life-and-death situation and provide life and recovery.

About six months later, we all rose to our feet at our office and applauded as he entered on crutches, alive and strong! We all knew that it had been a remarkable recovery!

I breathed a silent prayer of gratitude to God for answering our prayers. Yes, with God, all things are possible! Trust Him!

NOVEMBER 19

GOD'S IMMEDIATE ANSWER

Pansy Chintha

"For I know the plans I have for you," declares the Lord, "plans to prosper you and not to harm you, plans to give you hope and a future."

Jeremiah 29:11, NIV

As a child in India, my dad loved to attend fairs. He was six when his grandma said she was going to a fair. He asked his mom if he could go with grandma. She responded, "No! What if you get lost in the crowd?" He promised not to leave grandma's hand, and persisted asking until his mom gave in.

The fair was big and very crowded. The sights and sounds, the aroma from the food stalls, and the toys and clothes in the stores, gripped his attention. He was distracted and soon left his grandma's hand and wandered away. When he couldn't find her, he began to cry.

A farmer saw him lost and crying, and probably thinking he was an orphan, he promised to take him to his own home. He didn't know what to do, and began to meekly follow him, but kept crying out for his grandma.

His mom had taught him to pray, so he closed his eyes and prayed that God would help him find his grandma. He opened his eyes, and there was his grandma in the distance! He left the farmer's hand immediately and ran to his grandma.

He grew up to become a minister, and served God for many decades both in Maharashtra, India, and in the USA before he was called to rest. God supervised his life right from the start.

God has plans for us, and will guide us until the end.

NOVEMBER 20

NUDGES OF AN ANGEL

Bessy Thangavelu

"Casting all your care upon him, for he careth for you."

I Peter 5:7, KJV

Life was busy. I was working full-time, taking care of four little children, my elderly parents, as well as my 82-year-old grandmother. I returned home at 10 pm on September 21, 2012, and had to leave at 6 am the next morning. I set the alarm and went to sleep.

At 3 am, I felt someone tapping my shoulders. I awoke from deep sleep, and assuming it to be my imagination, I went back to sleep. A few minutes later, I felt a stronger tap. I jumped out of bed fearing a burglar was in. I walked out of the bedroom and noticed that the alarm was still on. Once again, I thought it was my imagination, and so, slipped into bed again. Soon I felt an even harder tap on my right shoulder. I knew I had to get up and respond. Was this a nudge to check Mom's blood sugar?!

I looked at the blood sugar reading in near disbelief! It was dangerously low, and her breathing was shallow. I had to act quickly. My medical background helped, and I knew exactly how to avert a medical emergency.

What might have happened if I had not been nudged? What if I had ignored the taps, especially the third one?! I would have never forgiven myself.

The Lord's mercy woke me that night. He had sent His angel to nudge me repeatedly until I helped my mother in that critical situation!

He always cares for His children! When He nudges us, let's pay attention and respond.

NOVEMBER 21

HANG IN THERE WITH GOD

Neena Eapen

"So do not fear, for I am with you; do not be dismayed, for I am your God. I will strengthen you and help you, I will uphold you with my righteous right hand."

Isaiah 41:10, NIV

1996 was a very difficult year for me. I was hit hard back-to-back with unexpected life situations. I was worried about the future and couldn't find answers. To add to my misfortunes, my dearest mom, the strong support of my life, was snatched away from us by cancer. She was too young to go, and I was too young to have lost her. I couldn't attend her funeral, and desperately struggled to find closure.

Hurt and disappointed, I began to question: "God, why me? Why my mother? Couldn't He pull me out or save my mother?" I asked many to pray for me, but simultaneously, I fought with God. It was like an intense battle!

One night, as I was talking with my dad, who was still mourning the loss of his dear wife, he told me something I will never forget. "Hang in there!" he said, and repeated the promise in Isaiah 41:10. I had heard this verse before. Mom used to make us memorize Bible verses with promises, and I knew it by heart. But this time, it spoke to me. I started to tell myself, "Hang in there, Neena!"

Now, whenever I start to feel anxious or stressed, I remind myself that God is with me. He is holding me with His hand saying, "Hang in there!"

God is with us, so do not be dismayed, no matter the situation.

NOVEMBER 22

I AM WITH YOU

Jency Suresh

"When you pass through the waters, I will be with you."

Isaiah 43:2, NKJV

One summer in India, when my children were young, our family along with two other families decided to go out to a nearby canal for some fun in the water. The canal is usually full to the brim with fast-flowing water, but that day, the water was only waist deep. The men and children got in and played around near the bank, but then got bored and decided to go across to the opposite side. We ladies stayed out and watched them.

They started out holding each other's hands. Halfway across they stopped, and their faces were filled with fear. The strong undercurrent was threatening to sweep them off their feet. We didn't know that, and two of us ladies got into the water intending to help them. They shouted out to warn us, but we thought they were joking! So, we continued until we also could feel the strong current, and suddenly realized that we were in grave danger. We dared not move forward or backward! All we could do was stand right there clinging onto the children for dear life, wondering what would happen next!

There seemed no way out, when suddenly a young local boy, who was probably watching us, jumped in, pushed us to safety, and then confidently swam out of the current.

We had been close to danger, but God had kept us safe, and we were grateful that God's eyes were over us. His hands are always ready to help even before we call!

God's protection is real. May we always trust Him.

NOVEMBER 23

IN THE SKIES AND THE CLOUDS

Bimal Nowrangi

"Your loving kindness and graciousness, O Lord, extend to the skies, Your faithfulness [reaches] to the clouds."

Psalm 36:5, AMP

While studying at the Raymond Memorial Higher Secondary School in Falakata, West Bengal, India, I participated in several extra-curricular activities. "Ingathering" was one such activity. It was a fundraising program designed to collect donations from the public to assist the social, educational, and medical services of the church.

A group of students along with our teachers went to a beautiful, small town in the foothills of the Himalayas. After we had collected donations from various people – those at home, shopkeepers, and workers of an orange juice factory – we went for a hike. A few of us climbed the nearest hills, which were part of the 1,500-mile-long Himalayan Mountain range.

Our enthusiasm and curiosity kept us climbing higher and higher until we found ourselves among the clouds! We could feel the brushing of the wisps of cloud on our faces. When we climbed to the top of one of the peaks, we could see the clouds floating below us and a beautiful horizon spread out before us! We were way up there, away from the crowds, the noise, the pollution, and the usual disturbances in the cities down below. It was exciting and exhilarating!

We are going to have a much bigger thrill soon: "...then we which are alive and remain shall be caught up together with them in the clouds, to meet the Lord in the air: and so shall we ever be with the Lord. Wherefore comfort one another with these words." I Thessalonians 4:17,18, KJV

November 24

JESUS LOVES HIS CHILDREN

Anonymous

"Let the little children come to me, and do not hinder them, for the kingdom of God belongs to such as these."

Mark 10:14, NIV

It was late in the afternoon on a Sabbath day, and it was raining continuously. My children were playing together on the sofa, hiding, with pillows over them. A few moments later, one of them popped up and said, "Mommy, Jesus is not listening to our prayers. We prayed to Jesus to stop the rain, the thunder and lightning." I was taken aback. I didn't expect this, and it took a few seconds to process the information and prepare myself to convince the children that rain is a blessing. We needed water for drinking, cooking, etc., so we should pray for rain, and for people to be kept safe from thunder and lightning. But before I could say anything more, the other child said, "Come on, let's pray silently for a long time." So, they hid themselves again under the pillows and knelt on the sofa.

I checked the weather prediction for the day and prepared my speech about why the rain was necessary. The children walked over to me with their eyes on the sky. I had just started my explanation when suddenly, their faces began glowing, and they said, "Mommy, look! Jesus answered our prayer. The rain has stopped!" They stepped onto the deck and kept saying, "Jesus answered our prayer."

Seeing the little ones happy because Jesus had answered their prayer was heartwarming. It was a lesson for me. Jesus loves His children dearly and is ready to answer their prayers in so many ways.

GOD'S MARVELOUS PROTECTION

Gloria Moses

"He shall give his angels charge over thee, to keep thee in all thy ways."

Psalm 91:22, KJV

In 1975, I attended Columbia Union College (now Washington Adventist University) in Maryland. We had a babysitter who watched over my son while I was at school.

One day, after classes, I picked up my son and headed to the bus stand, when a severe thunderstorm broke out. I opened my umbrella, but it flipped backward, leaving us open to the drenching rain. Just then, a taxi came by, and we got in. But the roads were flooded, and we soon reached a spot where the road was totally submerged. How would we get across? The taxi driver assessed the risks and, without a word, drove through the floodwater, landing us safe on the other side.

I took out my wallet to pay him, and was shocked to find I had only two dollars. He had taken quite a risk to drive us home, and now might ask for more. What would I do!? When we stopped at our apartment, I gave him the two dollars and said, "That's all I have. Please take it." He said we didn't have to pay him anything!

I felt a surge of gratitude in my heart. It was as if God had sent a guardian angel to provide help for us when we needed it. At that moment, I made a promise that when I got my own car, I would help others. God helped me keep that promise many times, and I have felt blessed.

God promised His protection over us, and He always keeps His word.

November 26

A Shield of Feathers and Faithfulness

Bimal Nowrangi

"He will cover you with his feathers, and under his wings you will find refuge; his faithfulness will be your shield and rampart."

Psalm 91:4, NIV

The day had started well, but sometimes, days don't end that way! After a full day's work, I arrived home around 6:30 in the evening. I parked the car in the street in front of our house. With the car keys in my hand, I got out to open the trunk to take the groceries home. Suddenly, three hooded young men stood in front of me, ready to rob me.

One pointed his gun at me and asked if I had any cash. I told him I did. The second began searching my pockets and took everything I had, including my wallet. The third demanded the car key. I handed him the bunch, which also contained my house and office keys. He quickly searched the car.

That done, the gunman ordered me to the ground. And that's when I felt I was walking "through the valley of the shadow of death." Was he planning to shoot!? I readily complied, and as I went down on my knees, I asked the Lord to save my life.

Suddenly, they turned and ran. Dazed and blurry-eyed, I saw them head toward their nearby getaway car. My wife was barely twenty feet away in the house when this terrifying incident occurred! She was waiting for my return, which might never have happened!

I thank God that his shield of feathers and faithfulness is far stronger than anything known to man! May God's shield be over us always.

JOURNEY ACROSS THE OCEAN

Josiah Aiden Samuel

"And when he was entered into a ship, his disciples followed him."

Matthew 8:23, KJV

I am seven years old as I write this story. My parents, my two older brothers, and I decided that we would like a new adventure. So, we immigrated to America in 2019. I packed all my toys, clothes, games, and iPad.

I prayed when I left home in England, and was excited as I was going to live closer to my cousins in America. I crossed the Atlantic Ocean on an airplane. As I peeped out of the window, I saw the big, mighty, blue ocean, and there was no end to it! I then started playing games and Sudoku and watched movies until I eventually fell asleep.

I remember how Jesus and His disciples traveled in Biblical times. They rode donkeys and horses on land and used boats to travel across the seas. On one such boat ride, Jesus was so tired and fell asleep. I recalled how Jesus calmed the roaring waves, and I prayed that Jesus would bring me safely to America. I thank Him for bringing me safely across.

I learned that boats were the only method of transport across seas in Biblical times, and the journey took a long time. Whereas airplanes that exist now fly above the ocean, and take a shorter time.

One day, when Jesus comes as the King of Kings, I will not use an airplane but will fly and meet Him in the sky and use golden chariots like Elijah.

Do you want to come with me in the golden chariot with Jesus and all His angels?

NOVEMBER 28

MY FAVORITE TEACHER

Biju Thomas

"And you will be blessed, because they cannot repay you; for you shall be repaid at the resurrection of the just."

Luke 14:14, NKJV

I had been battered, bruised, and broken by COVID-19. I had a cataract in my right eye and was so disabled that I had to use a walker to move around for the previous six months. It was in this condition that I went for a job interview. Even though I could hardly see anything in my favor, I found the courage to try anyway.

You see, my favorite English teacher at school, now headed the institution, and I hoped that he would know my capabilities enough, to grant me the job I so desperately needed. When I walked in, he greeted me with a warm smile, but said, "You know, you were part of the most notorious batch that I ever taught!" My heart sank! What were the chances of getting the job in such circumstances? I thought I was certainly going to pay the price for my notoriety in school!

However, he was gracious. He saw past my youthful behavior, appreciated my other qualities and gave me the job that day. I shall always be grateful to my favorite teacher for his fairness and his role in allowing me to work and find my way, when I was in deep distress.

I may never be able to repay him. But he did it without expecting anything in return, and God says that such people will be abundantly blessed in the end.

May we also learn to give without expecting anything in return. It spreads blessings all around!

NOVEMBER 29

POOR YET RICH

Gloria Moses

"Sorrowful, yet always rejoicing; poor, yet making many rich; having nothing, and yet possessing everything."

II Corinthians 6:10, NIV

After my older sister Deborah began to teach at the Adventist school in Sri Lanka, she moved out of our house to live closer to the school. That left my mom, my younger sister, and me at home.

Mom was running a business, and often went to Colombo to keep it going. Sometimes, she would return much after dark. She was afraid to leave us alone after dusk, so she arranged for us to go to her friend's house. She had three children and lived in a very small house. It had just two rooms: one small front room and another small room, which served as the kitchen as well as the sleeping area. When we felt sleepy, we would go there and fall asleep. She treated us well and was always kind to us. When her children were bored during the day, they would come over and play at our place.

Mom's friend had to face many problems and found support from my mom. In turn, she also supported my mom. They shared their good times as well as their difficulties and supported each other. I thank God for providing such a good friend for my mom, who was also a reliable and caring babysitter. Yes, her place was very small, but she shared it willingly, and it was a great blessing for my mom and us.

Let us remember to do good and share whatever God has given us. Even if it is small, it can be a great blessing to others.

NOVEMBER 30

WIDOW OF ZAREPHATH

Gloria Moses

"The jar of flour was not used up, and the jug of oil did not run dry."

I Kings 17:16, NIV

My mom became a widow at the age of 28, and was left to care for three very young daughters. My father had been a very successful businessman in Sri Lanka, with a rice mill, a saw mill, and a fiber manufacturing company. But after his death, we lost the business and all the equipment, and my mom was left poverty-stricken.

However, she knew that God was by her side, and she slowly built up her own businesses. One of them was to make and sell bricks to building contractors. The land our mom owned had good clay for making bricks. It was dug up and used for making good quality bricks. The more the clay was dug, the bigger the hole in the ground was supposed to get.

However, something amazing and wonderful happened. Just like in the story of the widow in the Bible, our ground filled up with clay over and over again! Every time it rained, water from the streams and rivers brought soil and clay to fill up the big hole caused by our digging process. There was always enough clay to dig up to make bricks!

When my sisters and I went for higher education, the college fees climbed up steeply. But God blessed my mom's efforts and supplied all our needs.

We completed higher education, married, had children, and enjoy stable careers today. God wonderfully helped my mom and us! God's faithfulness of old still sustains His children who trust Him. Blessed be His name!

December 1

Divine Intervention

Vinciya Pandian

"For I know the plans I have for you, declares the Lord, plans for welfare and not for evil, to give you a future and a hope."

Jeremiah 29:11, ESV

My whirlwind itinerary included a trip to India, then Portugal, followed by Rhode Island, and then Tennessee, where I was to preside over an international conference of a specialized society of nurses as its President.

With the conference fast approaching, I found myself running out of time to prepare, and the final preparations were done on the flight to Tennessee. I had nearly finished when it was time to land, and all laptops were to be stowed away. I slid it into the seat pocket, and disembarked without it at about 8:30 am.

I was preparing for a crucial board meeting at 12:30 pm, when I realized that my laptop was not with me! Panic seized me as I recalled where I had left it.

As I was wondering what to do, the airlines called and said they had located my laptop and it was waiting for me at the arrivals area of the airport. But my board meeting was to commence in 30 minutes! It was hopeless; I would never get it in time!

The airlines suggested that someone else pick it up. One of the Board Directors, whose flight had been delayed, was contacted while in the air, and he offered to help.

I began the meeting, speaking from memory, and within a few minutes he walked in with my laptop!

Amidst life's rounds of activities, a Divine plan is at work. Let us place our confidence in God's grace.

DECEMBER 2

JOURNEY OF LIFE – PART 1

REJECTED

Anonymous

"Thou hast laid me in the lowest pit, in darkness, in the deeps."

Psalm 88:6, KJV

Like everyone else who has dreams and aspirations, I had a dream to become a doctor. My parents were supportive, and provided the right environment to help me achieve my dream. When I entered the 11th grade, I began to focus keenly on my studies. I knew that my grades would be a major deciding factor, and I spent so much time studying that I hardly slept for two hours each night. Other parents encouraged their children to stay awake and study! My parents requested that I get more sleep! I had only one goal – to get into medical college. There was no other path in my mind.

I had the top grades in many subjects in school and went through two years of preparations. I moved to different places to take additional coaching for the entrance exams. Despite all these preparations, I fell short by less than one percent and failed to get in.

I was shattered and felt utterly dejected. I could not imagine a future outside this career, and I felt like it was the end of life! I questioned the value of hard work and of trusting in God, because I felt rejected by Him. I did not want to pray anymore.

My mom saw it all and got into the battle on my side – upon her knees. She fasted, wept, and prayed for me, early mornings, late at nights, and throughout the day. It made all the difference.

Please pray for anyone you see dejected in life.

(To be continued)

DECEMBER 3

JOURNEY OF LIFE – PART 2

HIS WILL

Anonymous

"As the heavens are higher than the earth, so are my. . .thoughts than your thoughts."

Isaiah 55:8,9, NKJV

I was devastated that I did not get into a public medical college, and although private institutions were a possibility, they were out of our reach, because we simply couldn't afford the exorbitant fees.

My mom prayed for me. My aunt brought a priest from her church to our home for a prayer meeting. Everybody was worried about how I was reacting to this failure. After the prayer meeting, the priest approached me and said that God had a different plan for me, and that I would be an engineer and end up in the USA. I did not trust this prediction of the priest. I thought he was using God's word just to divert my mind. I even laughed about it – I was a girl from a village in India! I had no relatives in the US to help me get there!

I moved to Chennai and reluctantly joined an engineering college. But I did so well that the professor was impressed in the very first year and assured me that I was in the right place.

Gradually, I began coming out of my spiritual slump and dejected attitude. I thought back and realized that I had never asked God for His plans for my life. My prayer was, "God, I want to be a doctor. Please help me become one." Now, I began to ask for His will to happen in my life.

Yes, God has better plans for us. Let us submit to His will.

(To be continued)

DECEMBER 4

JOURNEY OF LIFE – PART 3

HIS PRESENCE

Anonymous

"For God speaketh once, yea twice, yet man perceiveth it not. In a dream, in a vision of the night. . ."

Job 33:14.15, KJV

I had gone through a period of deep dejection after not getting into medical school. A Christian priest predicted that I would become an engineer and end up in the USA. I didn't believe him, but I did join an engineering college in Chennai.

During my second year in college, I had a strange dream. I saw myself in the USA, crossing the Niagara River using a bridge made of rope. It appeared a precarious life-and-death walk. I struggled at every step, but every time I won, a green leaf fell into the river.

I had no clue what Niagara or the USA was really like. When I shared my dream with my friends, one of them said, "Stop dreaming and get back to reality!" and we all had a good laugh. I did not think that this dream was connected to my life in any way!

I am very thankful that God provided me with good friends in college. We started a youth ministry and met every evening for worship. Students of other faiths joined us; some eventually accepted Jesus as their God. We felt fulfilled and blessed. Challenges arose, as well as opposition. But God always brought us favor in the eyes of the right people, and we were able to continue having an enjoyable time during those years because God's blessings were over us at all times.

God's presence is constantly with us, even when we do not perceive it.

(To be continued)

DECEMBER 5

JOURNEY OF LIFE – PART 4

HE IS IN CONTROL

Anonymous

"It is the Lord who goes before you…do not fear or be dismayed."

Deuteronomy 31:8, ESV

In my final year in college, one part of the course was an in-house training period after which we were tested on our ability to handle things in the corporate world. For one whole month, all the 2000 final year students stayed on the campus, going through a rigorous schedule of training with only eight hours of break in 24 hours!

One session was on social skills. We were given topics and asked to participate in group discussions. I was not given to talking much, and people in the entire final year class, many of whom I didn't know at all, were involved! It was truly nerve-wracking! By the time I had thought of a point, somebody else would beat me to it. So, I said nothing during that session, and did the worst in the entire school. I became the subject of everyone's jokes. I was certified: "Not fit for the corporate world!"

Memories of my earlier failure and the dejected feelings I had experienced, flooded my mind. I was severely tempted to think that I was not fit for anything in life! However, this time, I went straight to God in prayer, and did not let this failure take control.

A few weeks later, the giant tech companies of India came for in-campus placements. It was a tough selection process, and in the end, I was thrilled to hear that the top IT company had selected me!

Let us always trust in God. He is in control.

(To be continued)

DECEMBER 6

JOURNEY OF LIFE – PART 5

MIRACLES

Anonymous

"For I know the thoughts that I think toward you, saith the LORD. . .thoughts of peace. . .to give you an expected end."

Jeremiah 29:11, KJV

This was the first time I was stepping into the corporate world. I was sent to Ahmedabad for a six-month training period with people from different colleges around India. I was from an engineering background, and this was an IT company, so I struggled to cope.

We were doing robotic evaluation for coding, and it was difficult to understand the programming concepts, and I could see that I was not doing well enough. I knew that doing well in the first phase was crucial, and so I clung to God with many tears through anxious nights.

Many, including me, didn't pass the robotic evaluation phase. However, the program's leadership reviewed the process and gave us all another chance. I noticed another girl from West Bengal who was in tears, and although I also had failed, God prompted me to pray for her. That helped because He, not I, became the one in focus.

I would keep an empty chair beside me, keep my hands on the monitors, and ask God to sit next to me and teach me. Then, everything fell into place – everything that seemed complex, I now understood well! I started teaching the others who were preparing for the re-evaluation.

I performed so well in the next phase of the training, that even before I had completed the training, General Electric Company selected me to provide consulting services for them in Mumbai!

We serve a miracle-working God! Let us trust Him!

DECEMBER 7

JOURNEY OF LIFE– PART 6

GOD GUIDES THE FUTURE

Anonymous

"Therefore I say to you, Do not worry about your life, what you will eat or drink."

Matthew 6:25, NKJV

Working for GE in Mumbai, I was in a team with more than 50 others from North India, everyone of whom was more experienced than I was. But I believed God was in control of my life, and I did my best.

I had spent one and half years there, when one day, a top executive asked to have a private meeting. I thought something had gone wrong, but he said, "I've been observing you during my rounds, and I have always found you to be diligent and faithful. We have considered sending you to Mexico." However, a few days later, he said, they would send me to the USA instead.

Others in the team were more experienced and deserving, and wanted the opportunity to go to the USA. One of them was very upset and said, "Do you think you are more fit and worthy to go to the USA, when there are more knowledgeable and experienced personnel in the team? We will make sure to give you a tough time and see that you return to India!"

Life in the USA was not easy, but since it was God's plan, He always made a way for me. He sent people who supported me in my career, even though I had not known them or met them before. He guided me throughout and I completed the long assignment.

God has a plan for our lives. Let us allow Him to bring it to fruition.

(To be continued)

DECEMBER 8

JOURNEY OF LIFE – PART 7

GOD'S PLANS NEVER FAIL

Anonymous

"I have planted, Apollos watered; but God gave the increase. So then neither is he that planteth anything, neither he that watereth; but God giveth the increase."

I Corinthians 3:6,7, KJV

In the story of Caleb in the Bible, God fulfilled all His promises to Moses long after he was gone. I was meditating on this passage when I was reminded of my own life story. I was dejected after not making it into medical school, when a priest brought God's promise of a life in the USA after becoming an engineer. I have never seen him after that day, but his prediction came true. God was faithful to His word, although I have let Him down more than once.

I remembered the dream I had in college, of walking across Niagara River. I counted the number of obstacles, and it was equal to the number of years until I came to the USA. The very first place my colleagues took me to see in the USA, was Niagara Falls! I felt the reassuring presence of God as I saw these places, in reality, with my own two eyes!

I am thankful that I have survived and done well. But I can clearly see that this was possible because of so many people in my life – my praying mother, other members of the family, my coworkers, my bosses at various jobs, and even strangers whom I had not known before. It appears like a series of well-planned events supervised by God.

All glory be to Him, for He plans our life, and His plans never fail!

(Concluded)

DECEMBER 9

THE HEAVIEST LOAD – PART 1

Anonymous

"For whoever shall keep the whole law, and yet stumble in one point, he is guilty of all."

James 2:10, NKJV

When I arrived at the Shimla railway station in Himachal Pradesh, I looked for a porter to help carry my luggage – 4 suitcases, a large bedding roll, a huge bulging shoulder bag, and a briefcase. When he came, I told him he would need another porter, but he said he could carry the whole load himself. With his ropes and scarf, he skillfully lifted the full load onto his back. He was bent with the load, but he carried it hundreds of yards, all uphill, to my destination.

I thought back to another load I had experienced years earlier. I was walking over a grassy plain towards the hostel where I stayed. I walked slowly, deep in thought. I recalled the verse above, and suddenly, I realized that my guilt was too heavy to bear; my case was hopeless before God. I had stumbled, not on just one, but on countless points. So, what would be the extent of my guilt?!! I stopped in the middle of the path, unable to move. I felt weak, and had to sit down right there on the ground. Everything, including my final destiny, seemed too dark for me to handle.

I remembered this, while climbing up the hill in Shimla. The porter was bent over double with the load he was carrying. But the load I had experienced years before was far heavier.

Guilt is the heaviest load humans carry. But God planned an amazing solution. Let's always be thankful to Him!

(To be continued)

December 10

THE HEAVIEST LOAD – PART 2

Anonymous

"Come to Me, all you who labor and are heavy laden. . ."

Matthew 11:28, NKJV

I picked myself up from the ground and slowly walked to the hostel. Everything seemed drained of joy or even of interest. But there was just that tiniest spark of hope in my mind, and I didn't slide into depression. However, the load remained, and I didn't know how to get rid of it.

Words like, "God is a loving Father," didn't make sense. I had no grounds to go to Him, for I had broken His rules! The motto of the Dutch football team that won the World Cup said: "When the going gets tough, the tough get going!" But that didn't help - I was not feeling tough at all!

I continued to go to church as a ritual. One day, in church, the preacher said that Jesus had come only for sinners. The word, "only," got my attention. I felt fully qualified, and should have been happy, but I still had questions. Then another word gripped me: "whosoever" in John 3:16. He said that the word was stronger in meaning than even if my own name was in that verse! I realized it was true, for if my name was there, it might have possibly meant someone else who had the same name – not me. But the word, "whosoever," absolutely included me!!

He also pointed to the verse above. I put all three ideas together – "only," "whosoever," and "heavy laden," and the prison doors began to open.

Have you felt the load of guilt? Don't buckle under it. There is a remedy!

(To be continued)

DECEMBER 11

THE HEAVIEST LOAD – PART 3

Anonymous

"...I will give you rest."

Matthew 11:28, NKJV

I pondered the three points for a long time: 1. Jesus came "only" for sinners. 2. "Whosoever" definitely included me! 3. The call was to those who were "heavy laden," and that was my condition.

I had always thought that I had to earn God's favor and acceptance by producing acceptable behavior in my life. Since my actions had broken God's rules, I felt my behavior was unacceptable, and I could not find favor with God. No, not in a million years! So, I had continued to bear my load of guilt, and it was an awful killjoy!

O, I knew all the rules and regulations, and I had made sure they were from the Bible. However, that didn't help either! There was a disconnect somewhere.

When the preacher asked if I had identified the source of my problem, I confessed that I could not identify it. I knew my duties, and also knew that I had not done them. Now what?!

He asked if I was willing to do some detective work, like Sherlock Holmes. He said, "Read John 5:39, 40 very carefully, and place the word 'You' at the start." I did that and this is what I found: I should read the Scriptures carefully and through it come to Jesus, who is the actual solution to my problem. Merely knowing what is written in the Scriptures is not the real solution!

I found that the block was not my bad behavior; rather, it was not going to Jesus, who alone can deal with bad behavior!

Let us always go to Jesus!

DECEMBER 12

GOD REWARDS US

Anish Joseph

"And everyone who has left houses or…father or mother or wife or children…for My name's sake, shall receive a hundredfold, and inherit eternal life."

Mark 10:29,30, NKJV

I can witness that God has fulfilled many promises in my life.

In the summer of 2023, my dear brethren from Kenya, Nigeria and Ghana, living in California, embarked on mission trips, leaving behind their spouses and children. The spouses couldn't drive, and so they requested me to help them get to church every Sabbath day.

The fact was, I did not possess a car, and so, I would drive the children to church in their own car! That way, the children were happy because they were taken to church, where they enjoyed participating in the Sabbath School program. And I was happy too, because I got a complimentary ride, and was blessed to join the congregation in worshiping God!

This went on for one month, and at the end of that time, to my astonishment, the church treasurer and an elder came up to me and handed me a check with a generous amount, far surpassing what would be the usual payment for such a service. I was most pleasantly surprised!

I can clearly see how God fulfills His promise that those who render service in His name will be blessed to a greater extent than usual. God had impressed these fellow believers, who came like angels to repay me for helping the children.

It is true – the Lord always notices all our work and repays us more than we deserve. God keeps on giving. Let us serve Him with joy!

December 13

Jesus-Our Ever-Present Help

Seth Isaac

"God is our refuge and strength, an ever-present help in trouble."

Psalm 46:1, KJV

I was 13, and my brother was 8, when my family attended the Adventure Club camp that summer. We had to set up our tent and put everything in place, including the two air mattresses for us and our parents.

The first few days and nights went as planned, and we had a great time. Then, in the middle of one night, I woke up because I was uncomfortable. I realized that the mattress on which my brother and I were sleeping had deflated, and so had tilted. Being a heavy sleeper, I just shrugged it off and went back to sleep.

The next thing I knew was my mom pushing me to the other side of the bed and my dad trying to wake me up. I had to stand up and move away from it eventually. My dad quickly grabbed the mattress pump and filled air into our mattress. I don't remember hearing anything after that as I went right back to sleep.

In the morning, my parents told me what had happened. When the mattress slowly deflated, I rolled onto my brother's side. That tilted the surface even further, and my brother slid in between the mattresses and got stuck there. My mom heard him struggling to breathe and noticed his hand sticking out of the crevice between the mattresses. She woke up my dad immediately, and they pulled him out. Thank God, He woke my mom on time and saved my brother.

God is always our help in times of trouble. Let us stay ever close to him.

December 14

Lifting the Load – Part 1

Anonymous

"Casting all your care upon Him, for He cares for you."

I Peter 5:7, NKJV

I had been on the road for some time taking a heavy load of luggage in my little car. The car struggled with that load. Now, I like to drive fast, and don't like others overtaking me on the freeway! But with this load, I couldn't accelerate freely and, much to my chagrin, watched others go by, especially on the upward slopes. Moving out of the way for the faster vehicles was a humiliating experience!

At one of the stops, I met a friend who was also headed in the same direction in his powerful pickup truck. He saw the load in my car and offered to help. In fact, he took all the luggage into his truck. After that, the drive was an absolute pleasure! Nobody overtook me, and we reached our destination before time!

Attempting to gain favor and acceptance with God by our behavior is like carrying a very heavy load in a very tiny car. It cannot function in a normal manner. You will not even reach your destination! However, if there is a pickup truck into which you can unload the whole baggage, that truck can bear the entire burden, and you can drive freely and well. In such circumstances, reaching the destination is all but guaranteed.

Jesus is the fire truck, ambulance, and pickup truck, all in one! If we come close to Him and allow Him, He will take the entire load of guilt off our shoulders and bear it Himself! He saves us from our load. That's why He is called a Savior!

DECEMBER 15

LIFTING THE LOAD – PART 2

Anonymous

"...I am the Lord, And beside Me, there is no Savior." Isaiah 43:11. "Thus says the Lord your Redeemer..."

Isaiah 43:14, NKJV

I grew up in Salisbury Park, Pune, India, among many friends. One of my childhood friends had gotten into trouble with the law. He was arrested and locked up pending trial, because he had no way to post a bond for bail. His father heard of it and immediately went and paid the amount and posted a bond to get him out. He then paid the full restitution amount charged against his name, and saved him from even going to trial. My friend was smiling as he came out of police custody. He was free again, and I was happy for him.

Later, as I reflected on the events and thought of my own load of guilt, I wondered if God would be this kind to me on the Great Judgment Day.

One day, some time later, my eyes fell on Isaiah 43. I was startled because it seemed like an answer to my question. Just like my friend's father who had saved his son from deep trouble, the Lord is our Savior. He is the fire truck, the ambulance, and the pickup truck all in one.

We are in deep trouble with the Law of God, but in great mercy, He becomes our Savior.

The only way He could free us from the sentence that would rightfully be passed on us, was to pay the full price required by the Law.

He did it willingly and gladly, out of His deep love for us. Let us forever be grateful for such an undeserved gift!

December 16

Lifting the Load – Part 3

Anonymous

"Our Redeemer from Everlasting is your name"

Isaiah 63:16, NKJV

I had been quite frustrated that a certain trial was being delayed, and vented my feelings. A lawyer took me aside and explained that the delay was because a few factors had to be proved authentic before they could be admitted into the court proceedings. He explained that the plaintiff had to prove his standing to move the court. The jurors had to be screened for bias. The lawyers had to prove that they were licensed to practice law. Even the court had to establish jurisdiction over the case. Without meeting these criteria, the proceedings would not be counted as real justice. I nodded as I began to understand a little of how the wheels of justice turned.

In ancient times, the word "redeemer" was not necessarily a religious term, but more a legal term. It pointed to the person who would buy back land that had been mortgaged and return it to the original owner. In those days also, legal processes had to meet certain criteria to be considered authentic. The redeemer had to meet three criteria: 1. He should be able to pay. 2. He should be willing to pay. 3. He should be a blood-relative.

Would Jesus have to meet the third criteria in order for Him to be an authentic redeemer to pay for my load of guilt? The beautiful meaning of Christmas then dawned on me. He came to earth to be born into the human family, to remain forever as a blood relative to the human race. Christmas established Him as an authentic Redeemer!

Let us joyfully and gratefully celebrate Christmas!

December 17

Lifting the Load – Part 4

Anonymous

"I have blotted out, like a thick cloud, your transgressions. . .Sing O heavens, for the Lord has done it!"

Isaiah 44:22,23, NKJV

He tipped the scales at 550 pounds! And had registered with the NEWSTART program at the Weimar Institute in California to reduce his weight. I too was registered as an observer. He had a good sense of humor and we soon became friends.

One evening, he told me of his past life. He had been a member of the ruthless Hell's Angels motorbike gang, and had robbed and beaten up many people. But now, the guilt weighed heavily on his mind. "I'm 550 pounds, but my guilt weighs far heavier!" he said.

He also spoke of his son whom he loved very dearly. I asked if he could ever bring harm to his son on purpose. "Never!" was his reply. I told him of a Father-Son duo who had agreed to let the Son come to harm so that He could pay for all the guilt of the human race, and that included his guilt too. His eyes grew big. "Really? And you're not kidding!? What was the basis?" "God's love for you is the same as for His Son. That's the bottom line! If He did that much, you can trust Him to keep his promise." I read Isaiah 44:22,23.

"Confess your wrongs, ask for His mercy and grace, and believe that God keeps His promise for His Son's sake!"

He responded, "My head is spinning. I need to think. It sounds too good to be true!"

Early the next morning, "Friend," he shouted across the hallway, "my guilt is gone! Hallelujah forever! What a merciful Redeemer!!"

God stands ready to remove all our guilt. Let us trust Him.

December 18

Death Sentence or Test

Anonymous

"Do not fear; for God has come to test you."

Exodus 20:20, NKJV

I was sitting in the cancer specialist's office. I already knew the diagnosis; what I wanted to know was the stage. The doctor put up the PET Scan, and there before me were all the features of an advanced stage. The usual questions of "Why God? Why me?" flashed through my mind, but I dismissed them as utterly useless to help in any way! Instead, I slowly bowed my head and accepted my condition and the inevitable outcome.

Six months later after the requisite rounds of treatment, I was once again in the specialist's office to assess the outcome. He put the PET Scan up, and we reviewed it in detail. There were no signs of abnormal activity at all. I had reached the stage of remission! But it wasn't over yet, for this type of cancer could still return. We would have to monitor it for five years.

At the end of five years, I was still in remission. Praise God!

And the same questions ("Why God? Why me?") came back, but in a very different setting. I could not deny that I had been granted a tremendous blessing! I was now a " survivor!"

"Why God? Why did you bless me with added life?"

Aristotle stated that any explanation of an object or event is not complete unless its purpose is also described. We often ask, "Why God?" when tragedy strikes. We should learn to ask those same questions in the same intense manner, when we receive huge undeserved blessings.

Sometimes, God blesses us to clarify our calling.

December 19

Abundance

Subodh K Pandit

"I have come that they may have life, and that they may have it more abundantly."

John 10:10, NKJV

We were in the process of building a house in South India when the building contractor said that the suppliers had sent more sand, cement, and bricks than was needed. Returning the extra stuff would cause hassles, so we decided to keep them and build a water tank for the garden. It became a symbol of abundance.

One day, as I was watering the garden, I looked at it and then at the house, and asked whether I would count the tank as abundance if I did not have the house. I then realized that the idea of abundance is dependent on the presence of that which is absolutely necessary. Once that was obtained, anything else, however insignificant, would be considered extra – an abundance.

In God's plan of salvation, the absolutely basic commodity is eternal life. Only if that has been obtained, will other things be considered extra. And it is at this very point that we understand the beautiful, benevolent, and self-sacrificing character of God. He willingly went through indescribable torture to provide eternal life as a free gift to anyone on earth who believes in Him.

If we trust Him, it is ours; and once we have that, everything else becomes extra – an abundance. Food, friends, jobs, homes, etc., all, no matter how minuscule or insignificant, are now expressions of the abundance of God's blessings. Without the basics – eternal life – these could never count as abundance!

Let us thank God for the basics that make all that we have on earth a super-abundance!

DECEMBER 20

TRUE REST

Subodh K Pandit

"Come to Me . . . and I will give you rest. . . rest for your souls"

Matthew 11:28, 29, NKJV

It was going to be a long, 3-day train journey from the south of India to the North East, and so I made sure I had reservations on a sleeper coach. I also took along my sleeping bag, so I could rest at night.

After the first night, I felt somewhat rested and spent the rest of the day in relative comfort. After the second night, although things were tolerable, I began to long for my bed at home. After the third night, I wanted to get home as soon as possible! It was a wonderful feeling when I reached home.

When I had started out, I was willing to forego certain comforts. But later, even though I had a place to sleep and a sleeping bag, the sleep was not fully refreshing. I had even lost some of my appetite, and the journey was no longer exciting and enjoyable. I knew that the rest I longed for would be found only on reaching home.

What if our journey has no destination? Well then, we will try every method to find satisfaction with the things afforded during the journey. So also, if our eternal destiny has not been settled, we cannot artificially produce rest – peace of mind.

God, in His mercy, invites us, "Come to Me." If we heed this invitation, He will settle our eternal destiny and bring us to the point of true rest – rest for our souls.

It is a priceless gift. Let's accept it and live in peace and confidence!

DECEMBER 21

GRANDMA AND PSALM 91

Cinthya Daniel

"Give thanks unto the Lord. . ..sing psalms unto him, talk ye of all his wondrous works."

I Chronicles 16:8,9, KJV

Growing up in a small town called Nagercoil in South India, summer holidays were all about going to my grandma's home in another small town called Nazareth.

Every year, as soon as school was over, our family would go to my grandparent's place to spend time with them, before heading back to start another school year. Those were some of the best days of my life – playing outside the whole day with cousins and friends.

While going back and forth, in and out of the house, I would notice grandma reading the Bible and praying on her knees. One day, I decided to sit beside her as she read the Bible. She surprised me by reciting the whole of Psalm 91! Then she explained to me why it was of such significance – how it is filled with beautiful promises and assurances from God based on His goodness and power. She encouraged me to memorize it so I could use it to find support in times of need or despair. I was inspired to memorize it.

Today, whenever I am in distress, pain, or anguish, I turn to Psalm 91 and recite it. It makes me look to the Lord for help. He has never failed me. He has always answered me and delivered me, and made my confidence in Him grow strong.

May this beautiful Psalm that the LORD has given us, and which my grandma and I memorized and often recite, be of comfort to us all in times of need.

December 22

Superior Customer Service

Anita Jeffrey Samuel

"...Inasmuch as ye have done it to the least of these my brethren, ye have done it unto me."

Matthew 25:40, KJV

On February 26, 2020, during the daily meeting at our workplace, the Nurse Manager announced that I had been granted the Superior Customer Service Award. I was surprised and super-excited! With the certificate, came the trophy and two huge gift baskets. One of the factors evaluated was providing care with love and excellence. Actually, all I had done was reflect the values I had learned as a child during family worship and Sabbath School classes – be kind, be loving, be patient, and work with all your heart!

God gave me a chance to practice these values at home when He blessed us with an autistic son. I learned that looking after the vulnerable in our society, church, and family is an important responsibility. The care and love shown to those who are helpless and needy make a big difference in their lives. Our own lives become purposeful and beautiful when we deal with them as precious persons, and not focus on their handicap.

Jesus was constantly at work among those who were weak and disabled – the blind, the lame, the paralyzed, the leper, etc. God has a purpose in allowing disability among us. Let us seek to fulfill that purpose, and serve with compassion even when no one notices. This is a true reflection of God's character.

The blind hymn writer Fanny Crosby wrote about the time when God will give His children eternal awards: "My blessed Lord will say 'Well done!'"

May we hear those words from Jesus when He returns.

DECEMBER 23

PRAY FOR OTHERS – PART 1

Anonymous

"I urge, then, first of all, that petitions, prayers, intercession and thanksgiving be made for all people."

I Timothy 2:1, NIV

When my husband and I were expecting our first child, we often met with many of our best and long-standing friends. One day, we were with a non-Christian couple who had been married for more than five years but were still childless. They were hoping and longing for a child.

Toward the end of the visit, the wife unexpectedly touched my abdomen and asked for me to pray that they have a child. According to their belief, if a pregnant woman prays for a childless person, God hears those prayers and answers immediately. She too, wanted to get pregnant so that our children would be born around the same time and grow together, and be friends like we were! Her earnest request as she put her hand on my abdomen and her intense longing for a baby, deeply touched my heart.

This experience inspired me to pray for families who were waiting for a baby. I wrote down their names and added them to my prayer list. I became more diligent and earnest after we had our baby, and had realized the joys of motherhood. I wanted my friends to enjoy the same blessing. I wrote down the names of four families I knew who wanted to have a baby.

I decided to pray for them in confidence. I never told them about my prayers, and they had no clue regarding what I was doing.

Let us remember that many around us need our prayers, and let us pray for their needs.

December 24

Pray for Others – Part 2

Anonymous

"Therefore, I tell you, whatever you ask in prayer, believe that you have received it, and it will be yours."

Mark 11:24, ESV

After my encounter with my family friend, I was inspired to pray for others, especially for married couples who were longing to have a baby. The wife of one such couple was a high school classmate. We had lost contact for about ten years, and even after connecting through social media, we hardly spoke to each other during the next five years. And when we did, it was about ordinary topics like politics.

One day, recently, I had the urge to call and check on her. Imagine my surprise when she told me that she was expecting a baby soon – after 15 years of marriage! Only her immediate family knew of the good news, and she felt she should share it with me. She hadn't known of my prayers. Of course, I knew that others also had been praying for them, but it gave me great assurance and encouraged me to continue praying for others.

Sometime later, I was talking with a Christian couple who had been married for more than ten years and was hoping against hope to have a baby. I shared the story of my classmate, and that testimony encouraged this family not to lose hope.

God hears every prayer, whether big or small. It doesn't matter who we are or what role we play in their lives. The real source of power lies in the One who hears the prayer; not in the one who prays!

Let us continue to pray with trust and confidence.

DECEMBER 25

RAPID RESPONSE

Bessy Thangavelu

"In my distress I called upon the Lord, and cried unto my God: he heard my voice out of his temple, and my cry came before him. . ."

Psalm 18:6, KJV

I was driving to work a little after 6:00 AM, in August, 2013. The day was beautiful, but my heart was heavy. I thought of all the cares of life and the "to-do" list I had for the day. Tears fell on the steering wheel and seat, for I felt I had no one to help, and the burden seemed more than I could carry.

Mom had just undergone a below-knee amputation. She could fall and hurt herself, if she attempted to get out of bed without realizing that her leg was missing! That was a scary thought! Dad had medical needs too. Our elderly grandma lived with us. Our four children were in pre-K through middle school.

My husband suggested placing Mom in a nursing home, but I couldn't think of that. And now, life's load seemed simply too heavy!

I lifted my eyes to the skies and cried out, "Lord, where are you now? I'm helpless! Please come down to help me. I am your child. Don't hide your face from this hurting daughter of yours."

While I was pleading with God, the phone rang. It was my cousin. She called to inquire about Mom and assured me of her plan to bring her mom to keep company with my mom until she was discharged!

I did not expect an answer this quickly. But it had come, and my load was immediately lightened.

Praise God, for He knows exactly when to answer.

DECEMBER 26

PRAYER CHANGES THINGS

Juanita Kemp

"And whatever things you ask in prayer, believing, you will receive."

Matthew 21:22, NKJV

I was praying for guidance at a very low point in my life, when it seemed like God's voice was telling me to "get back to school." At that stage in my life, I knew I would have to go for a Master's Degree. But how would I be able to pay the tuition fees?

I had worked earlier as a volunteer, counseling teenage girls in juvenile detention. So I enrolled in the Master's Degree program in Clinical Social Work at Wayne State University. I had heard of the Graduate Professional Scholarship, and then learned that the Social Work Department had its own financial aid program. I was interviewed for the financial aid package by a very gracious lady. I was a bit hesitant when she asked me how much I wanted. But she advised me to include the cost of books and parking fees, and then approved the entire amount! The first year was taken care of.

When I went to receive my assignment for the second year, the lady in the office saw that I had a 4.0 GPA for the first year! She handed me my assignment paper with a note on it, "This student could benefit from a State Stipend." She then encouraged me to apply for the Graduate Professional Scholarship, which was granted. It paid for my tuition, books, and everything I needed to complete the Master's Degree Program!

I had prayed, and the way had been opened step by step by a gracious God! Praise God! Prayer changes things! Let us pray about everything.

December 27

Prayer for a Helpmate

Juanita Kemp

"My help comes from the LORD, who made heaven and earth."

Psalm 121:2, NKJV

A friend of mine had made a suggestion to write down, on a 3x5 card, all the qualities I would like to have in a husband. Sometime later, sitting in a church, before the service was to begin, I prayerfully began thinking of that suggestion. I slowly wrote out a list, numbered them from 1 to 10, and slipped the card into the Bible, in the Book of James.

Number one on the list was "a man who loves the Lord as his personal Savior."

Two years later, attending my nephew's wedding in Maryland, I saw my sister and brother-in-law's neighbor and golf partner at the reception. His name was Kester. I had met this handsome widower several times during my visits, but that day it seemed like we both could feel the "sparks" flying between us. We talked extensively during that weekend. Kester appeared to fulfill all the items on my list.

Three weeks later, Kester invited me to go to Michigan to meet his brother Pr. Kemp, who invited me to join the group going to the Holy Land. That experience was the highpoint of my life. I walked where Jesus walked, and visited many of the locations noted in the Bible. Kester sang in the Church of the Holy Sepulcher. I read from the Scriptures in the tomb. I cried in the Garden of Gethsemane and was baptized in the River of Jordan.

God bonded us in the Holy Land, and we were married the next Easter Sunday.

Let us bring our desires to God!

DECEMBER 28

MULTIPLE TROUBLES

Gloria Moses

"Behold, God is my helper, the Lord is the upholder of my life."

Psalm 54:4, ESV

My mom, my younger sister and I were living together in Sri Lanka. One day, my mom had to go to Colombo, the city, leaving us at home. I was doing my homework when I heard an unusual flurry of sounds from the chicken coop. I went to see what was happening.

As I was inspecting the chicken coop, I suddenly saw a huge snake dangling right above me from the roof of the house. I ran for my life in panic. I didn't see where I was going, and stepped on a large nail, which stayed stuck in my foot. Hopping on one leg, I reached the porch and called my sister for help. My foot was bleeding, and the pain was excruciating. The nail looked rusted, so we pulled it out.

We did not know what to do next, so we prayed. Soon our truck arrived and we asked the driver to take us to the hospital. There, a nurse cleaned the wound and bandaged it. The doctor then gave me penicillin by injection and I immediately passed out! It took some time for me to regain consciousness and get home.

Twenty years later, I learned that I am allergic to molds. Penicillin is made from a specific mold, and I had had an allergic reaction which might have caused a much more serious reaction.

Jesus kept me safe through all those multiple troubles that day. God had sent the right people in the time of our need.

Thank God that He helps us and upholds our lives.

December 29

The Right Direction

Juanita Kemp

"Holding fast to the word of life, so that in the day of Christ, I may be proud that I did not run or labor in vain."

Philippians 2:16, ESV

When I arrived at my husband's church, I looked over the audience in the sanctuary and noticed that hardly any of them were young. No children were in the sanctuary, and only a few family groups were on the balcony. I said to my husband, "This is a dying church!"

A little later, I started a "Greeters Ministry" and invited the young adults who sat on the balcony to join in. They responded very well, and that ministry became a tremendous success. However, due to some reasons, including the spiritual atmosphere there, I decided to leave that church. I was asked where I was going. I responded, "Only God knows, and He hasn't told me yet!"

A few weeks later, I heard about a seminar being held at the Southern Asian SDA Church, and attended the six-week series. The Bible was explained in such detail, with pictures, charts, and timelines, that it became exciting to learn. My husband also got caught up in that excitement and joined me. I was amazed to see the number of family groups attending the service on Sabbath. At the end of the seminar, I chose to join the Seventh-day Adventist church.

God had chosen the right direction for me. I have found open arms, the spoken Word, and the experience of the in-dwelling Holy Spirit at SASDAC.

May we allow God to lead us in the right direction and help others prepare for the day of Christ.

DECEMBER 30

STRONG FAITH

Josy Thomas

"Now faith is the substance of things hoped for, the evidence of things not seen."

Hebrews 11:1, KJV

We met Mr. S., an apple grower, at the Shimla Sanitarium and Hospital, when we were working there in the early 1990s. He was a friend of the staff and had been coming to the hospital for many years. At times, he came just to chat with us. Although he was not a Christian, he believed in the God who was worshiped in the hospital. In gratitude to that God, he would give each staff family a crate of the best of his golden delicious apples every year.

I once asked him why he did that year after year. He said that he believed God blessed his orchards every year. During one particular apple season, untimely frost and snow had destroyed the crops in all the other orchards in that vicinity. His orchard alone was spared, and it produced a bountiful crop that year. He believed it was because of his trust in the God who was worshiped by the people in the hospital, and his association with them! He seemed very sure of that!

I was prompted to examine my own faith. Did I believe in my God with a faith as strong as his? His experience also taught me that God cares, for not only those of us who profess His name, but also for all who trust Him and associate with His people.

May God teach us how to grow in faith and recognize our responsibilities in the communities in which we live. May we see that our faith also helps those who associate with us.

December 31

BEYOND OUR IMAGINATION

Helina Somervell

"Now to Him who is able to do more than all we ask or imagine. . .be glory. . .forever. . .Amen."

Ephesians 3:20,21, NIV

I arrived in Orlando, Florida, in 1991 with high hopes and plans of further education and progress in my career. But they were all quickly dashed because the Florida Hospital where I was to work was on a hiring freeze. I did not expect my plans to get derailed this badly, and was now faced with unemployment and uncertainty. My cherished dreams seemed distant and ready to vanish away.

It was not until the following year that I was able to be employed. I got a job as a travel nurse, and my first assignment was on the beautiful Island of St. Thomas, in the US Virgin Islands. There, I met another travel nurse who was an Adventist. When our assignment was done, she wanted to go to Maryland to be with her brother, and invited me to join her and apply to Johns Hopkins Hospital. I had never heard of this hospital before, but when I got there and applied for a job, the doors flew open. God paved the way for me to fulfill my dream of graduate and doctorate degrees, with all the fees paid by the institution's tuition assistance program!! I could never have imagined this. It was much more than I had hoped for!

Nearly thirty years later, I can attest to God's wonderful ways. He may not remove your problem, but He will provide a way through it. God is truly able to do more than we ask or imagine. Trust Him. He will never let you down!

Contributors

Abraham, George: February 5

Alfred, Veena: July 7, July 8

Andrews, Girly: October 23, October 24

Bekkam, Govardhan: March 7

Benjamin, Samuel: February 21

Biju, Jaya: August 31

Borge, Milind Lazarus: January 21

Charles, Vijayan: March 17

Cherukuri, Suhasini: August 23, August 24

Chintha, Pansy: July 15, July 17, July 19, November 19

Christian, Richard T: March 28

Daniel, Cinthya: February 3, February 19, February 20, March 3, May 1, June 9, December 21

Daniel, Kevin: February 15

David, Duraiswamy Paulson: January 1, February 24

David, Esther Pauline: January 4, January 12

David, Joel: August 17, August 18, October 15

David, Mark: March 18

D'Souza-David, Pamela: January 2

Eapen, Joseph: April 29

Eapen, Neena: January 20, January 29, November 21

Edison, Rajam: April 15, April 27

Fernando, Lovella: January 17, February 8

Fernando, Merlyn: April 6

Foster, Maya: July 12

Garland, Makeda: July 1

George, Kurian: January 9

Guria, Abigail: September 28, September 29

Hansdak, Amod: April 4

Hembrom, Achsha: February 16

Injety, Sherlyn (Sweety): February 11

Isaac, Saharsh: June 19

Isaac, Seth: December 13

James, Energy: March 23

Joel, Jeremiah: March 4

Joel-Morse, Elsie: January 27

John, Steve: February 9

Joseph, Anish: November 11, December 12

Joseph, Kavitha E: April 3

Joseph, Lillykutty: June 21, August 6, August 22, September 4, September 12, September 14, October 12, October 13

Kemp, Juanita: December 26, December 27, December 29

Khajekar, Nelson: October 31

Khandagle, Sarah: January 25

Kolluri, Francina: January 22

Massey, Julinda: March 2

Matthews, Gladwin: February 28, May 12, May 20, May 24, May 30, June 1, June 3, June 5, June 8, June 10, June 13, June 15, June 18, June 27, June 28, June 29, July 9, July 10, July 11, July 16, July 21, August 4, August 7, August 10, August 11, August 14, August 16, August 19, August 20, August 26, August 30, September 3, September 5, September 7, September 13, September 25, October 3, October 14, November 17

Mathew, Susy: July 18

Mathews, Shifali: March 29

Mathews, Shikha: March 30

Melvin, Vidhya: February 25, March 14, August 13, August 15, September 8, September 9, September 10, November 10

Mesipam, Subhashini: February 14

Mohan, Anita B.R: June 14, June 22, June 24, June 30, July 2

Mora, Naveena: May 21, May 25, June 16

Morgan, Ellen G: March 5

Morse, Jasmine: February 18

Morse, Reina: March 27

Moses, Gloria: February 29, June 23, July 20, July 22, July 23, July 24, August 8, August 29, September 23, October 2, October 7, October 9, October 10, October 30, November 1, November 2, November 7, November 8, November 16, November 25, November 29, November 30, December 28

Moses, Saroja: March 6

Muppiri, Jeanette: March 11

Murmu, Jercilla: September 17, September 21

Navarose, J S : January 5, January 10, January 13, January 14, June 2

Nowrangi, Atul: March 15

Nowrangi, Bimal: March 9, March 19, April 7, April 10, April 12, April 17, April 19, April 21, April 23, April 26, April 30, May 6, May 8, June 25, July 6, July 13, July 25, July 26, July 27, July 28, July 29, July 30, July 31, September 16, September 18, September 20, September 22, November 13, November 14, November 23, November 26

Nowrangi, Nilima: June 26, November 15

Nowrangi, Sheetal: March 20, March 21, April 1

Palivela, Nina: March 13

Pandian, Vinciya: December 1

Pandit, Kanta: October 16, October 17, October 18, October 19, October 20

Pandit, Subodh K: May 9, May 10, May 15, May 18, May 19, May 23, May 27, May 29, December 19, December 20

Paul, Sybil: March 26

Pedapudi, Joseph Kelly: February 17

Pedapudi, Nischitha: March 31

Pedapudi, Praveen: May 2

Ponraj, Merlin: March 24

Prabhakar, Sahasramsu: March 25

Prates, Sonali Gupta: February 6

Rozario, Hallie: April 2

Ruiz, Vivian: July 3, July 4

Samuel, Anita: April 13, December 22

Samuel, Bernice: January 8

Samuel, Josiah Aiden: November 27

Samuel, Rathna Pushparaj: February 27

Samuel, Richard: January 3

SEC: February 10, February 22, February 23, February 26

Selvadurai, Beula: February 1

Sharlin, Daisy: January 6, January 23, January 24, January 30, February 2, February 13, March 10, April 11, May 4, June 4, June 11, June 12, June 20

Solomon, Susy: September 24

Solomonraj, Amber: April 22

Somervell, Helina: April 18, December 31

Suresh, Jency: November 22

Suresh, Paul: March 16

Thangavelu, Bessy: November 20, December 25

Thapa, Carol: January 18, January 26, January 31

Thomas, Biju: March 1, March 8, April 8, April 24, April 28, May 13, May 14, May 17, May 22, May 26, May 28, August 12, August 21, August 27, August 28, September 2, September 6, September 26, September 27, September 30, October 1, October 4, October 5, October 8, October 27, October 28, November 9, November 18, November 28, May 31, August 1, August 2

Thomas, Josy: December 30

Thomas, Selena Kelly: May 5

Thomas, Usha: January 16, April 20, May 3, May 7

Thummalapalli, Serena K: April 5

Thummalapalli, Shantha: April 14

Varghese, Johny: February 4

Varghese, Soosan: January 28, February 7, April 16, April 25, May 11, May 16, August 3, October 21, October 22, October 25, October 26, November 3, November 4

Venkatraj, Edna: January 19

Made in the USA
Columbia, SC
24 June 2025

c281c281-e667-4ca6-b3bd-ad80e755d3a7R01